T0320861

Changes by Competition

Changes by Competition

The Evolution of the South Korean Developmental State

HYEONG-KI KWON

OXFORD
UNIVERSITY PRESS

OXFORD
UNIVERSITY PRESS

Great Clarendon Street, Oxford, OX2 6DP,
United Kingdom

Oxford University Press is a department of the University of Oxford.
It furthers the University's objective of excellence in research, scholarship,
and education by publishing worldwide. Oxford is a registered trade mark of
Oxford University Press in the UK and in certain other countries

© Hyeong-ki Kwon 2021

The moral rights of the author have been asserted

First Edition published in 2021

Impression: 3

Published in the United States of America by Oxford University Press
198 Madison Avenue, New York, NY 10016, United States of America

British Library Cataloguing in Publication Data
Data available

Library of Congress Control Number: 2020952299

ISBN 978–0–19–886606–0

DOI: 10.1093/oso/9780198866060.001.0001

Printed and bound by
CPI Group (UK) Ltd, Croydon, CR0 4YY

Preface

As I remember, it was in 2009 when I visited the International Center for Business and Politics (ICBP) in Copenhagen, Denmark that I began to take a look at Korea as my research subject, although Korea is my home country. Until then I had explored advanced democracies, including Germany, the United States, Ireland, and Nordic countries, doing field research for my dissertation and subsequent studies. I never forget the ICBP's sincere hospitality during my two visits. But most impressive was Professor Peer Hull Kristensen's gentle smile and his thought-provoking question: "Why are you wandering around these European countries, far away from your home country Korea?" At that time, I could not reply immediately and avoided giving him an answer. However, what I avoided was not just an answer to Professor Kristensen, but more importantly, to myself. I wanted to avoid studying deeply the politics of my home country because Korea was divided into different political and ideological opinions. People I felt deeply attached to fought each other, forcing me to take one side or the other. I refused to take a side in such conflicts after studying abroad. However, I changed my mind about studying Korea, not only because my foreign acquaintances had continuously asked me about my home country—for academics and policy-makers, Korea is an important test case for theoretical debates on economic development and democratization; but also, I knew that avoidance is not the best way to deal with the conflicts.

Conflicts in Korea are not tapering. On the contrary, they continue to amplify to the current day. People who lean toward democracy tend to disregard Korea's successful economic development which almost all emerging nations try to emulate, whereas people who emphasize Korea's successful economic growth tend to underestimate democracy, sometimes admitting authoritarianism for economic growth at the expense of democracy. While studying the prevalent theories on political economy, I discovered that the exclusive ideas of democracy versus economic development are not ordinary Koreans' responsibility, but are based on academic theories. In particular, developmental state (DS) theories, which gained significant ascendancy in accounting for East Asian economic developments, hold that for successful economic development, the state should be unitary, cohesive, and unaffected by social forces—authoritarianism strong enough to direct private actors with their unitary rationality.

However, through exploring the stories of successful economic development, I observed that in contrast to the DS theories, successful developmental states, including Korea, Japan, Taiwan, and China, are neither unitary nor cohesive, but fragmented and full of rivalry and conflicts, particularly among policy-making elites. Even the Park Chung Hee regime, regarded as an archetype of the DS cohesive state, was full of rivalry and conflicts among economic ministries, including the Economic Planning Board (EPB), the Ministry of Finance (MoF), and the Ministry of Commerce and Industry (MCI). Furthermore, I found that competition and conflicts among elites are not always bad for economic development, as shall be examined in this book. On the contrary, collective deliberation and pragmatic experiments through rivalry and competition among elites can significantly contribute to economic development through flexible institutional adaptability in response to new challenges resulting from ever-changing contexts of domestic and international political economy. Elite competition in the fragmented and decentralized structure can elicit diverse local knowledges and enable innovation in policy and institutions. Innovation and creative ideas come into being not in unitary and conflict-free minds, but in minds full of conflict with diverse perspectives. However, competition and conflicts should be properly resolved and coordinated, whether through vertical hierarchy or by horizontal adjustments and building common norms; otherwise they result in disarray or stalemate. I found that democracy or collective deliberation is not contradictory to economic development; on the contrary, more democracy may be needed for sustainable development; but, more democracy for sustainable development needs more coordination.

Pursuing this study has been a long but thankfully not lonely journey. Without the help of numerous people, I could not have finished this book. First and foremost, I would like to express my deepest appreciation to my academic mentors, Professor Gary Herrigel at University of Chicago, who guided me though the murky process of this project, and Professor Su-Ik Hwang and Professor Myung Chey at Seoul National University (SNU), who taught me how to study and provided tremendous encouragement and soul-caring advice. I also thank Professor Gerald Berk and Professor Tuong Vu at University of Oregon, who gave me insightful advice as well as heart-warming hospitality and office space during my stay (2018–19) in Eugene, Oregon, where I wrote the draft of this book. I also thank Professor Glenn Morgan who gave me helpful advice. I am grateful for my academic mentors and gifted colleagues in the Department of Political Science and International Relations, SNU, who provided priceless encouragement.

In making this study, I visited numerous people for interviews, including government officials, managers in large and small firms, and trade association and union leaders, from early 2010 to 2018. Though they were complete strangers to me, they graciously provided time for my interviews. My deepest appreciation goes to all of them. In the course of preparing this book, I also have many debts of thanks to my graduate students, including Kyung Mi Kim, Hyun Lee, Yunsoo Lee, Hee-Jung Sohn, Seungmi Kim, Jiyeong Jeon, and Sun-min Jeon, who helped me tremendously to transcribe interviews and find newspaper sources and data. I also thank Adam Swallow at Oxford University Press, who gave me the opportunity to publish this book, as well as anonymous reviewers who helped improve the manuscript.

For this study, I relied on the financial support from two institutes, the National Research Foundation of Korea (NRF) and College of Social Sciences at SNU. This work was supported by the Ministry of Education of the Republic of Korea and the National Research Foundation of Korea (NRF-2016S1A5A2A01023345). Thanks to this support I conducted field and literature research in 2016–19. In addition, this work was supported by "Overseas Training Expenses for Humanities and Social Sciences" through Seoul National University (SNU). With this funding, I could focus on writing the manuscript during my sabbatical (2018–19) in Eugene, Oregon. This financial support was invaluable to my research.

Last but not least, I would like to thank my family members for their endless sacrifice, love, and encouragement. My brothers Oh-Sung and Oh-Soo, and my lovely sister Jung-Hee deserve my deepest appreciation. My mother-in-law Woojo Park also deserves my deepest appreciation from the bottom of my heart. I owe special thanks to my wife Jung-Hee Choi, who always stands by me with wordless love and sacrifice, without which I could not finish this project. I cannot forget to give special thanks to my son Woohyeok, who has made the most important contribution—bringing happiness to this project, as well as to my life. In particular, his time with me in Eugene gave me great joy. I dedicate this book to my parents, Taek-Yong Kwon and Youngja Ko, who taught me how to live a meaningful life by their own example.

Table of Contents

List of Figures

List of Tables

1

Introduction to the Evolution of the South Korean Developmental State

South Korea (hereafter Korea) has successfully changed its economy, from very poor and agricultural to highly advanced and industrialized, over the last half century. As its per-capita gross national income grew dramatically from only $79 in 1960 to $31,000 in 2018, it has attracted the attention of policymakers as well as political economists. However, scholars differ in accounting for why Korea was able to achieve such sustained economic success from the 1960s to the 2010s. Neoliberals and neoclassical economists emphasize the advantages of the free market, while developmental statists underline the state's interventionist role and its institutional conditions, such as a unitary and cohesive bureaucracy, which enable the state to direct private firms with its developmental policy. Focusing on the role of the state, the statists and neoliberals differ in whether the Korean model of economic development is market-conforming or market-distorting.[1] In the first round of debate of the 1990s, developmental state theory gained ascendancy, but after the Asian financial crisis of 1997 the neoliberal account became more prevalent. Actually, Korea has significantly changed its economic system by liberalizing its finance and globalizing its industries, allowing its successful change to a highly innovative and knowledge-based economy.

What is the Korean model of economic development that accounts for its sustained and high economic growth over approximately 50 years? Is such long-term sustained growth due to the neoliberal free market or the state's institutional conditions, such as bureaucrats' competency and cohesiveness of the state? The significant changes in Korean capitalism over the last 50 years raise questions concerning the relevancy of existing development theories, whether neoliberals' universal relevancy of the free market or the statist accounts based on institutional conditions. Rather than offering neoliberal celebrations of free market and the statist emphasis on the stringent Weberian state, this book focuses on the flexible adaptability of Korean state-led capitalism, with which it has adjusted its

---

[1] For example, Amsden (1989; Chapter 6) emphasizes the state's intentional distortion of market price for Korea's economic success. For the debate between government-led or market-following, see Wade (1990) p. 28, and Chapter 10.

Changes by Competition: The Evolution of the South Korean Developmental State. Hyeong-ki Kwon, Oxford University Press (2021). © Hyeong-ki Kwon. DOI: 10.1093/oso/9780198866060.003.0001

methods and strategies of development through competition among elites inside and outside the state, as new challenges, never met with an apparent solution, have continuously emerged.

Meanwhile, in order to corroborate their theories, neoliberals and the statists examine competitively and contest the extent to which the Korean economic system has changed. Can we say that it has transformed into a neoliberal free market system? Not only neoliberals and Marxist globalists, but even long-time developmental theorists including Chang and Shin hold that Korea has changed to a neoliberal free market since the late 1990s.[2] However, recent empirical studies, including my own, reveal that unlike the liberal and neutral state, the Korean state still plays an active role in coordinating its economy for industrial competitiveness, although it gave up its traditional interventionist methods and policy instruments of the 1970s.[3] In addition, the state and large corporations called *chaebols* continue to form the dominant coalition, excluding labor, in the institutional changes of labor markets and corporate governance as well as in development strategies (Jo 2016; Morgan and Kubo 2016: 68, 85; Whitley 2016: 36).

How can we understand Korea's continuance of state-led capitalism despite significant changes in methods and policy instruments? Many institutionalists and developmental theorists emphasize resistance to changes in path dependence, such as institutional stickiness (Stubbs 2009; Fields 2014) or institutional adherence to historical legacy (Dent 2003; Hundt 2009) or continuance of a taken-for-granted "developmental mindset" (Moon 2016; Thurbon 2016). In order to criticize market-driven convergence and emphasize the continuity of the existing pattern, they tend to underestimate or disregard the significant changes. However, Korea has significantly changed its traditional developmental state policy by liberalizing its finance and giving up control of market entry and direct subsidy in the course of liberalization and globalization in the 1990s and 2000s.

In order to understand continuity in the course of change, this book emphasizes that the continuity of state-led capitalism could be possible, not by resistance to change nor self-reinforcement of existing practices, but by innovative changes and adaptation to external challenges, such as global competition and foreign pressure of liberal trade and finance, as we shall explore in detail. Continuity does not exclude changes; rather, it can happen by changes.

In order to better account for these dynamic changes and continuity, this book brings back politics among key actors. Unlike the institutionalist scenario, actors

---

[2] For such long-time developmental theorists, see Chang and Shin (2004); Chang and Chung (2005); Chang and Evans (2005); Chang et al. (2012).

[3] For the argument that the Korean state has reconstituted its core institutional capabilities for a new version of developmentalism, see Chu (2009); Kim, Kyung Mi. (2020); Kim and Kwon (2017); Kim, S.-Y. (2012, 2019; 2020); Larson and Park (2014); Lee and Kim (2018); Thurbon and Weiss (2019), and Weiss and Thurbon (2020).

are not unilaterally constrained by institutions. Instead, facing new challenges, including economic crisis and competitors' challenges, key actors reinterpret the meaning of institutions and their existing practices in the course of political interaction. The meaning of challenges is not always apparent, but problems and solutions are always contested among actors' interpretations.

Additionally, to better understand the continuity of state-led capitalism in the course of dynamic politics, this book emphasizes economic elites' competition for legitimate authority or influence. The Korean state is not a unitary actor, but consists of economic elites—for example, the Economic Planning Board (EPB), the Ministry of Finance (MoF), the Ministry of Industry (MoI), and the Ministry of Information and Communications (MIC)[4]—each with different perspectives. This situation sharply contrasts with the existing developmental state (DS) theory, which emphasizes state cohesiveness and a single rationality as institutional conditions of the developmental state (Evans et al. 1985; Wade 1990; Evans 1995; Chibber 2002, 2003; Haggard 2018: 3; 1990: 43–45). The DS literature holds that the reason for East-Asian states' economic success, in contrast to the failure of India and Latin American states, is due to the stringent Weberian state, cohesive and strong enough to discipline and direct private businesses with a single rationality. However, even at the height of the classical developmental state in the Park Chung Hee era, the Korean state was divided into rival ministries competing for legitimate authority with different strategies. We will explore how EPB emphasized large capital investment, whereas MoI focused on industrial linkages and backward integration to build national industries in the Park Chung Hee era.

In addition, this book emphasizes the institutional adaptability through elite competition for such sustained economic growth, not only in Korea, but also in other East Asian states as shall be examined in the final chapter of this book. The reason for Korea's sustained economic success over a long period of time is due not to the institutional elements of a stringent Weberian state, but to the Korean state's flexible and effective adaptation to newly emerging challenges over a long span of time. Korea is deeply immersed in developmental logic, but its strategies and methods have continuously changed in response to new challenges. Korean

---

[4] The Korean governments changed the names of key ministries frequently. For example, Korea's Ministry of Commerce and Industry (MCI) changed its names several times, from the Ministry of Commerce and Industry (MCI) in 1948–93, to the Ministry of Trade, Industry and Energy (MoTIE) in 1993–4, to the Ministry of Trade and Industry (MoTI) in 1994–8, to the Ministry of Commerce, Industry and Energy (MoCIE) in 1998–2008, to the Ministry of Knowledge Economy (MKE) in 2008–13, and to the Ministry of Trade, Industry and Energy (MoTIE) in 2013–present. This book will use the Ministry of Industry (MoI) to refer to the changed names after the MCI. In addition, the Ministry of Communication (MoC) changed its name to the Ministry of Information and Communication (MIC) in 1994–2008, and later, to the Ministry of Science, ICT, and Future Planning (Ministry of Future Planning) in 2013–17 and then the Ministry of Science and ICT in the present.

developmentalism is not given as an apparent single rationality, but has been rearticulated and rearranged through competition among elites.

In order to better account for the endogenous changes, this book also focuses on the competition among elites. Competition among economic elites for legitimate authority incurs innovations in institutions and policies, whose effectiveness enabled the continuity of state-led capitalism. For example, as shall be examined later, the Korean developmental state of the 1960s changed to an extreme version of its developmentalism in the 1970s through competition between EPB and MoI. To preserve their existing influence, key actors should be innovative in response to competitors and external challenges. Similarly, the Korean state could continue its developmentalism, not by resisting changes nor by sticking to the existing pattern, but by changing its developmental strategies and methods through competition among elite organizations.

In order to trace the dynamic evolution of Korean state-led capitalism, this book relies on intensive and extensive personal interviews with Korean government officials, as well as key people in lead firms, suppliers, and trade associations in the Korean automobile and electronics industries. Interviews for the preliminary study were conducted from May 2010 to March 2011, and from April 2013 to June 2018 for the main field research. The 81 personal interviews include 34 respondents in government and government-affiliated research organizations, 27 in private companies, and 20 in trade and labor associations. To trace the processes of competition among key actors, I also examined not only memoirs of bureaucrats and economic leaders but also Korean monthly journals and newspapers. I also use extensive quantitative Korea Exim Bank data and various data collected by international organizations, including OECD.

We begin now with a critical review of the existing debate on Korean capitalism, and elaborate the theoretical alternative. In the empirical Chapters 2 and 3, I explore to what extent Korean capitalism has evolved to date, and how we can locate current Korean capitalism from a comparative perspective as well as historically. In Chapters 4 through 8, I trace the historical evolution of the Korean developmental state, focusing on competition among elites inside and outside the state. Chapter 4 examines the classical version of developmental state in the Park Chung Hee era; Chapter 5 explores the transformation in Korean capitalism in the late 1970s and 1980s. Chapter 6 addresses the transition period of the Roh Tae-woo (1988–92) and Kim Young-sam (1993–7) administrations. Chapter 7 examines the Kim Dae-jung (1998–2002) government's developmentalism in the aftereffects of the Asian financial crisis. And Chapter 8 explores the Roh Moo-hyun (2003–07) government, and the Lee Myung-bak (2008–12), Park Geun-hye (2013–17), and Moon Jae-In (2017–present) governments. Chapter 9 extends the theoretical implications of the Korean experience into other East Asian DS and emerging countries.

Critical Review on Literature and Theoretical Alternative

Due to its long period of successful economic growth, Korea has offered an attractive case for competing developmental theories, including neoclassical economics and the developmental state theory. The tide of theoretical competition has seen ups and downs through the 1980s to 2000s. In accounting for why Korea achieved economic success, neoclassical economic approaches gained ascendancy initially in the 1970s and 1980s.[5] However, in the late 1980s and first half of the 1990s, developmental state (DS) theories proved more persuasive, mostly based on their empirical studies of the heyday 1970s. But since the late 1990s, particularly with the Asian financial crisis of 1997, the neoliberal view has prevailed, based on the universal relevancy of the free market. Not only Korea but also many countries reform under the pressure of globalization, particularly with the neoliberal reforms as a condition of the IMF bailout. In recent debates on Korean capitalism, even many developmental state theorists, including Ha-Joon Chang and Peter Evans (2005), have admitted that the Korean developmental state met its demise and turned to neoliberalism. This section explores recent prevalent theories regarding whether Korea has changed to a neoliberal free market system or continues its state-led capitalism.

When evaluating whether a state remains a developmental state (DS) or comes to its demise, most scholars tend to focus on the institutional elements of DS capability which DS theorists emphasize differentiates DS from the liberal state. In contrast to neoclassical economists who emphasize free market policies as the cause of East Asian economic success, including open trade and limited state intervention, DS theorists emphasize the strong state's institutional capabilities, such as meritocracy and the cohesiveness and rationality of bureaucracy, which enable the state not only to extract, mobilize, and target resources to a particular purpose, but also to sanction private firms for not making productive use of state resources.[6] For example, in accounting for why Japan, Korea, and Taiwan could succeed in economic development while Latin American countries and India failed, the DS theorists emphasize the state's institutional capability to impose its development policy on business (Evans 1995; Kohli 2005). Amsden (1989, 2001) suggests reciprocity as a control mechanism to impose discipline on economic

---

[5] For neoclassical economic approaches regarding the East Asian economic success, see Little et al. (1970); Cole and Lyman (1971); Chen (1979); Hughes (1980); Krueger (1980); Balassa (1981); Balassa and Williams (1987); and World Bank (1993). They emphasize free market policies for the causes of East Asian economic success, including open trade, comparative advantage, and limited state intervention.

[6] For an overview of developmental state theory, see; Woo-Cumings (1999); Stubbs (2009); Routley (2012); Fine (2013); and Haggard (2018, 2015). For classical developmental theory, see Johnson (1982); Amsden (1989, 2001); Haggard (1990); Wade (1990); Chang (1994); and Evans (1995).

behavior: "In Korea, Japan, and Taiwan...the state has exercised discipline over subsidy recipients. In exchange for subsidies, the state imposed performance standards on private firms. Subsidies have not been giveaways, but instead have been dispensed on the principle of reciprocity" (1989: 8). For DS institutional capacities to impose a control mechanism, DS theorists emphasize bureaucrats' competency, relative autonomy from social groups, and cohesiveness of the state.

In particular, many DS theorists emphasize the internal cohesiveness of the developmental state to promote developmental policy. Chibber (2002, 2003) succinctly notes: "In order to promote development, states need to be able to act as corporate entities with broadly collective goals, rather than the sum of the individual strategies of their functionaries. So one way to make states 'developmental' is to enhance their capacity, and the means to do that is through securing their internal cohesiveness" (2002: 952). Haggard (1990, 2015, 2018) also points out "the cohesiveness and centralization of decision making" as a key element of the DS. For internal cohesion or coherence of bureaucracy, many DS theorists emphasize the Weberian bureaucracy features, including clearly specified rules and career promotion (Wade 1990; Evans 1995: 12–14; Evans and Rauch 1999), whereas Chibber suggests a powerful nodal agency, like the EPB in Korea, and its hierarchical power (Chibber 2002: 952, 957–959).

Thus for DS theorists, intrabureaucratic conflicts are a sign of the DS demise (Haggard 1990: 45; Lim 2009: 91; Wade 2010: 158; Yeung 2017: 88–89). For example, Yeung (2017) points to the abolishment of the Korean pilot agency Economic Planning Board (EPB) and fragmentation as evidence of the Korean DS demise, saying that "[this] decentralization and fragmentation of the key pilot agency in turn made it even harder for the state to coordinate industrial policy in the face of mammoth chaebol in the domestic market" (Yeung 2017: 88). Wade (2010: 158) also emphasizes that "Democratization in Korea had the effect of fragmenting the state" and thus the Korean state lost its effectiveness in developmentalism.

Both the DS theorists and DS demise theorists now focus on the existence, or disappearance, of the institutional elements of state capability to extract and strategically distribute resources and impose its developmental will on subsidy recipients, such as state control over finance and the disappearance of the nodal agency like the Korean EPB, and intrabureaucratic conflicts. Initially, the DS demise theorists emphasized democratization in the developmental states which removed authoritarian state power. By assuming that the developmental state is an authoritarian strong state which extracts and distributes national resources strategically, autonomous from social pressure, the DS demise theorists hold that democratization dissolves authoritarianism, enfeebling the state's institutional capability, and thus, engenders the demise of the DS.[7] In addition, DS demise theorists

---

[7] See Moon (1994); Moon and Kim (1996); Kim, Eun Mee (1997); Hart-Landsberg and Burkett (2001: 412); Hundt (2005); Lim (2009: 91); Wade (2010: 158); Yeoung (2017: 88–89).

emphasize that domestic changes toward democratization and liberalization contribute to the "greater fragmentation of the developmental state and its elite bureaucracy" (Yeung 2016: 189). However, state-led capitalism is not necessarily authoritarianism, as seen in Japan and France. Similarly, democratization, the rise of social demands, and intrabureaucratic conflicts in Korea have raised some challenges, but not decisively prevented the state from pursuing industrial development.

More importantly, intrabureaucratic rivalry has encouraged industry-related ministries to pursue new industrial policies competitively, as we will examine later. In a stark contrast to the prevalent belief that intrabureaucratic competition or rivalry is the demise of DS, this book emphasizes the effectiveness of elite competition for economic developmentalism. This book holds that intrabureaucratic or elite competition within and outside the state can significantly contribute to the sustained economic development through its effective adaptability in response to newly emerging challenges, rather than causing the demise of state-led developmentalism. Without innovative changes in institutions and policies, Korea's classical state-led developmentalism might have failed in achieving such sustained economic success in the contexts of the complexity of domestic economy and the changed global economy. Korea could succeed in economic development through effective changes in institutions and policies, which have resulted from elite competition. As shall be examined in the final chapter, the effectiveness of the institutional adaptability for sustained economic development can be extended to other East Asian countries, including Japan, Taiwan, and China.

On the other hand, most DS demise theorists emphasize neoliberal globalization as the cause for the DS demise. First, as the Japanese economy, an archetype of the developmental state, fell into crisis in the late 1980s, the developmental state's effectiveness fell into question (Dornbush 1998; Lindsey and Lukas 1998; Katz 2003). In addition, as Korea and neighboring developing countries fell into the Asian financial crisis of 1997, the demise thesis of the developmental state gained a clear ascendancy. Most DS demise theorists believe that following the Asian financial crisis, Korea changed from a developmental state to a neoliberal free market system.[8] Not only was the financial crisis of 1997 believed to clearly signify the effects of globalization and financialization, but also that the *state failure*, due to overregulation, state-controlled finance, crony capitalism, and moral hazard, was a key cause for the crisis (Krugman 1994, 1998). Not only Korea but relatively crisis-free countries including Japan and Taiwan began to reform their economic systems. Korea eased regulation and opened its financial market. In order to remove state control over finance, Korea revised its laws concerning its

---

[8] For the argument that Korea has transformed to neoliberalism since the 1997 crisis and subsequent reforms, see Kirk (2000); Kong (2000); Kim, Y.T. (2005); Lim and Jang (2006); Kwon (2010); Lim (2010a); Ji, Joohyung (2011); and Kim, Eun Mee (2014). For the debate on the developmental state 10 years after the 1997 crisis, see articles in *Asian Survey* vol. 47, no. 6 (2007).

central bank and financial supervisory system (Jayasuriya 2005). Corporate governance and labor markets were also reformed by market principles.

Neoliberals, theorists of global production networks (GPNs), and Marxist-oriented scholars now hold that developmental states in general, along with Korean state-led developmentalism, are no longer relevant under globalization. For example, scholars of global production networks (GPNs) such as Yeung (2016) hold that as GPNs grow and national corporations nurtured by the developmental state become disembedded from the state, even the most cohesive and most powerful state "could not wield sufficient power in charting new directions for economic development" (Yeung 2016: 189, 205). Neoliberals hold that developmental policies should be limited under globalization in order to optimize comparative advantages.[9] Howard Pack and Kamal Saggi hold the neoliberal view that industrial policies, whether new or old, are irrelevant in the course of globalization because they hinder optimal use of the advantages of "international supply chains" by the free market (Pack and Saggie 2006: 276). They suggest adhering to the Washington Consensus on the free market.

Marxist-oriented scholars of the Global Capitalism School agree with neoliberals and GPN theorists on the point that developmental states, as well as nation-states' intervention in the market, are now irrelevant under globalization, although they disagree on the moral effects of a global free market. The global capitalism school, anchored around a Marxist political economy and particularly the writings of William Robinson (2004, 2014) and Jerry Harris (2009), holds that globalization marks a new epoch, as nationally-based elites are no longer the central locus of power in the world order with the rise of a transnational capitalist class. They argue that as production has globalized, so have class relations, with the rise of a transnational capitalist class whose interests are no longer tied to a single nation-state. They maintain that the nation-state itself is becoming, or already is, anachronistic.

In addition to the rise of global production networks, financial globalization and liberalization provide evidence of the developmental state's dismantling (Pang 2000; Jayasuriya 2005; Pirie 2005, 2008, 2016; Ji, Joohyung 2011). With Korea, financial liberalization measures adopted since the 1990s undermined key elements of the traditional developmental state's policy instruments, such as control over finance. Due to financial liberalization measures in Korea, including independence of the central bank and openness to foreign financial institutions, the Korean state could not pursue traditional developmental methods such as the highly leveraged, debt-based national champion strategy. Thus, even some developmental state theorists agree with neoliberals on the point that under globalization, Korea changed to neoliberalism during the 10-year span of the Kim

---

[9] For neoliberal globalism, see McKinsey and Company (2003); Friedman (2007); Bhagwati (2010); Sirkin et al. (2011).

Dae-jung (1998–2002) and Roh Moo-hyun (2003–07) administrations following the 1997 Asian financial crisis.[10] They hold that the Korean state gave up its traditional developmental policies such as economic planning, state coordination of capital investment, and protection of domestic industries, and sold out Korean incorporations to transnational capital.

With the rise of GPNs and financial liberalization, trade liberalization is also mentioned as a cause for the demise of the developmental state. Due to world trade rules, such as the WTO's rules to constrain subsidies, the existing developmental states' industrial policies became irrelevant. Many scholars including Jayasuriya (2005) and Pirie (2008) hold that the Korean developmental state became dismantled because its key instruments for developmentalism were hamstrung, turning the Korean state into a neoliberal regulatory state, rather than toward interventionist developmentalism (Jayasuriya 2005; Pirie 2005, 2008).

However, we will examine how the Korean state did not simply retreat in facing the Asian financial crisis of 1997, but revised its existing developmental policy while disciplining large corporations and creating a new version of industrial policies, shifting from an input-oriented to a knowledge-based economy, creating venture companies and an innovative industrial ecosystem. Korea no longer uses old-style subsidies directly given to large corporations, in order to avoid violating the WTO rules. However, it uses more R&D support as a developmental policy to strategically target industrial development. As many empirical studies show, the Korean government has maintained its initiatives in technology development through agenda setting and industrial targeting.[11] For example, Korea has been much more involved in setting strategic priorities and coordinating R&D programs in the ICT sector than even France (Lee and Yoo 2007: 466). Korea does not use old developmental methods, such as mobilizing massive capital and funneling it to a few large corporations exclusively, to realize economy of scale. Instead, it focuses on improving innovative capability through collaborative relations among large and small firms. Unlike the GPN theorist expectation, the Korean state focuses on building industrial commons and an industrial ecosystem at home to avoid the hollowing-out of national industries, and it upgrades its innovative capabilities, as described in Chapter 2.

In contrast to DS demise theorists, institutionalists and developmental state theorists emphasize the path dependent persistence of the developmental state. They maintain that existing developmental states including Japan, Taiwan, France, and Korea do not converge toward a neoliberal free market system, but extend their long-established national economic models, based on the timing of industrialization, trajectories of economic development, and patterns of state

---

[10] For the demise thesis by the developmental state theorists, see Chang and Shin (2004); Chang and Chung (2005); Chang and Evans (2005); Mo (2009); and Chang et al. (2012).

[11] For the literature of the recomposition of Korean state-led developmentalism, see footnote 3.

intervention.[12] In order to criticize the neoliberal convergence theory, they emphasize institutional constraints for continuity of different models. For example, Whitley (2016) holds that due to domestic institutional arrangements, even East Asian developmental states including Japan, Taiwan, and Korea differ in their business systems, such as ownership and control of major companies, the extent of their vertical and horizontal integration, and interfirm relations. These different national models, which arose from domestic institutions including state organizations and financial systems, continue their basic patterns despite minor changes following the dismantling of the Bretton Woods system in the 1970s (Whitley 2016: 36). The institutionalists emphasize the persistence of these different models even throughout the Asian financial crisis of 1997 and subsequent globalization. However, as Walter and Zhang (2014a: 9) observe, this literature tends to disregard or underestimate significant changes in the Asian states in order to emphasize the persistence of national patterns.

Many institutionalists and developmental theorists underestimate or disregard significant changes in order to point out the continuity of different models, and find difficulty in accounting for dynamic politics. Most institutionalists emphasize the unilateral constraints of institutions, such as institutional stickiness toward changes, institutional inertia, and a taken-for-granted mindset, overlooking key actors' active interpretation of the meaning of institutions in the political contest.[13] For example, Fields (2014) emphasizes institutional stickiness toward change in accounting for why Japan, Taiwan, and Korea continue their models of developmentalism, rather than converge toward Anglo-Saxon-style neoliberalism, as follows:

> In accounting for the evolution and variations between and within these three national economies [Japan, Taiwan, and Korea], the final section argues that emerging change coalitions, declining state autonomy and capacity, and a policy

[12] For the account of continuity in the developmental state even under globalization, see Schmidt (2003); Weiss (2003); Wong (2004); Mo and Okimoto (2006); Fields (2014); Thurbon (2016); and Whitley (2016).

[13] For institutionalist accounts for continuity in general, see Tseblis (1990), Hall and Soskce (2001), and Levi (2009) in the rational choice institutionalism which emphasizes the stable equilibrium outcome of the actors' strategies; Ertman (1997), Esping-Andersen (1990), Katznelson (2003), Krasner (1984; 1988), and Pierson and Skocpol (2002) in historical institutionalism which emphasizes choices in the critical juncture and the stable reproduction of the path; March and Olsen (1989) and DiMaggio and Powell (1991) for sociological institutionalism which emphasizes an unreflexive culture and mindset. Recently many historical institutionalists, including Thelen (2004, 2006), Streeck and Thelen (2005), and Mahoney and Thelen (2010), emphasize gradual and endogenous changes as an alternative to the existing institutionalist account of "punctuated equilibrium" in which the institution fell into breakdown and sudden replacement in a critical juncture by external shocks. However, the recent institutionalist accounts for the incremental and cumulative changes are a quasi-functionalist explanation because their changes are explained by objective necessity. They have difficulty in accounting for why and by whom the changes occur through political and idea contests, rather than so-called objective necessity that cannot always engender the outcome. For criticism of the recent historical institutionalist accounts, see Kwon (2013).

discourse of neo-liberalism have attenuated the DS in all three cases. But in each instance, *'sticky' institutional arrangements* constituting the respective DS have proven difficult to dislodge, even in the face of unprecedented economic crises, recessions, long-term structural changes, and prevailing global norms.... Although the collapse of Japan's asset bubbles in the early 1990s dealt a substantial blow to the legitimacy of this DS system, the unfolding of the next two decades would demonstrate that increasing institutional dysfunction does not necessarily yield dismantling. *Path dependency, institutional inertia, vested interests,* and no small degree of rational retention have kept Japan's DS relatively coherent in spite of increasing calls for change and significant remodeling. Likewise...both parties [Korea and Taiwan] continued to benefit from their collaborative ties and the institutional networks binding them together.

(Fields 2014: 48–49; emphasis added)

Institutionalists account for the continuity of state-led capitalism by institutional resistance to changes, not by creating a new version of divergence through key actors' proactive political choices. They tend to explain the current continuity of developmental states by historical legacy or prolonging its life by repetition of the same institutions.[14]

Recently, DS theorists have emphasized the taken-for-granted mindset or informal norms for continuity of the developmental state.[15] For example, Moon (2016) points out Confucian ethics for Korean developmental success, while Chang (2005: 27) emphasizes informal norms and policy mindset, evidenced in presidents' policy priorities for economic success and continuity of Korean developmentalism. In particular, Thurbon's (2016) recent study on continuity of the Korean developmental state emphasizes the persistence of a developmental mindset, despite significant changes in Korean capitalism. She argues as follows:

My explanation for this revival [of financial activism in Korea] has centered on the *enduring presence of a developmental mindset* among key segments of the Korean political and policy elite. I have shown how this mindset involves a set of shared beliefs and understandings about the state's primary goals (national strength via manufacturing capacity, technological autonomy, export competitiveness) and the appropriate role of the state in achieving them (strategic interventionism, including financial activism).

(Thurbon 2016: 143; emphasis added)

[14] For the arguments of historical legacy for the continuity of DS, see Noland (2002: 8); Mo and Moon (2003: 137–139); Kalinowski (2008); Hundt (2009); Stubbs (2009: 9, 12); and Lim, H. (2010a).
[15] For the arguments of taken-for-granted norms and mindset as cause for DS continuity, see Chang (2005); Moon (2016); and Thurbon (2016).

Thurbon argues that the persistence of developmentalism in Korea reflects an enduring developmental mindset shared by key economic elites, which has been more or less galvanized either by external challenges such as the rise of the Chinese economy, or by developmentally-minded presidents (Thurbon 2016: 90–91).

Although Thurbon's and other ideational approaches rightly note the importance of correcting the approach of simple adherence to formal institutions and policy instruments such as state financial control as criteria of developmental state, they have difficulty in addressing how the mindset or informal norms have been (re)constituted through political contest among elites. They emphasize instead the consensus and cohesiveness among top economic policymakers, in the vein of the DS tradition (Thurbon 2016: 34, 59). However, Korean developmentalism is not a contest-free idea commonly shared by economic elites, as we shall explore later. The Korean state's strategic interventionism has been continuously contested by economic organizations both within and outside the state. Even at the height of classical developmentalism of the Park Chung Hee era, Korean developmentalism is not the repetition of the same mindset, but contested, particularly by ministries inside the state, such as EPB, MoF, and MCI.

Meanwhile, a recent version of historical institutionalism accounts for path dependence or institutional continuity by power politics, rather than unilateral determination of institutions.[16] For example, Thelen and Mahoney (2015) and Pierson (2015) rightly bring the power conception back, criticizing its underestimation or disappearance in American political science. For example, Pierson (2015) identifies three dimensions of power: open contestation, mobilization of bias, and ideational elements of power. Power-oriented institutionalists explain path dependence by a self-reinforcement process of power politics in which actors gain power to achieve authority and institutionalize it to stabilize their authority. Pierson (2015: 130) holds that "political contestation is both a battle to gain control over political authority and a struggle to use political authority to institutionalize advantage—that is, to lay the groundwork for future victories." By utilizing current power distributions gained at a critical juncture, and further consolidating power by institutionalization, winners expand their power over losers and reinforce their development path. Pierson names five mechanisms at work as "power begets power": transfer of resource stocks, alteration of resource flows, sending powerful signals about the relative capabilities of the contestants, altering discourse, and inducing new investments (2015: 134–141).

The power approach of historical institutionalism rightly brings back the concept of political contest and power, criticizing behavioralists' and institutionalists' lack of a concept of politics. However, they too easily assume consolidation of

---

[16] For a power approach to historical institutionalism, see Mahoney (2000); Pierson (2015); Thelen and Mahoney (2015).

winners' power in a predeterministic way. Although winners gain power at a critical juncture and institutionalize it, winners must renew justification for their authority in contest with losers or new groups. Sometimes winners' successful practices incur new challenges which threaten to undermine institutional stability. For example, the Korean developmental state nurtured large corporations' capability by the success of its own developmentalism, which in turn undermined the state's traditional disciplinary power. The winners' self-reinforcing practices can undermine the stabilization of their power. And in the debate on whether to drive the development of heavy chemical industry (HCI) or not, the Blue House secretary and MCI won in Korea of the 1970s, while the EPB lost its influence. However, the winners' self-reinforcing practices caused them to lose power due to their overinvestment in HCI in the late 1970s. By contrast, the loser EPB regained its influence because it lost in the process of the HCI drive, and thus it was free of responsibility for the HCI crisis. However, Korea did not pursue the neoliberal free market in the DS crisis of the late 1970s because MCI created new industrial policy in reaction to EPB's liberalization. The process of political contest is not an apparent single direction of self-reinforcement, but a more complex and uncertain process by political interaction.

Theoretical Alternative

To better understand the dynamic evolution of Korean state-led capitalism, we emphatically revive the politics among diverse actors. Unlike the institutionalist emphasis of institutions' unilateral constraints on agency, we first focus on the embedded actors' creative interpretation and strategic choices. Actors are not isolated, but embedded by social, political, and cultural institutions. Yet they are reflexive, empowered, and purposive in their strategic use of the advantages of institutional resources. Embeddedness is neither quasi-natural nor taken-for-granted. Rather, actors proactively reinterpret the meaning of institutions and reconstitute the institutional embeddedness.[17]

In particular, we emphasize the political interaction in which actors reinterpret their preferences, strategies, available resources, and feasible options, while they acknowledge the significant uncertainty that key actors face. Even the most experienced bureaucrats rarely know precisely what their developmental policy will produce. They may lack information, but more importantly, they have difficulty in fully knowing what options are available, as the Knightian uncertainty

---

[17] This book's embeddedness is closer to that of Granovetter (1985) than of Polanyi (1944) in that Granovetter focuses on a relational understanding of embeddedness while Polanyi's conception is based on structures. However, in contrast to Granovetter, this book highlights the actors' constitutive role in recombining purposively the elements of the embedded institutions through political interaction. For social embeddedness and purposive actors, see Heidenreich (2012).

shows.[18] Key actors face significant uncertainty particularly when they are forward looking rather than backward looking. Not only are actors' interests and the problems they face unclear, but they need interpreting. An idea as a cognitive lens matters. However, the idea that this book focuses on refers not to a complete set of ideas independent of practices, but actors' ideas in their practical context. For example, in Korea of the late 1950s, the Ministry of Commerce and Industry (MCI) might know export theory, but lacked confidence in the feasibility of the export of manufacturing products. Through practices in 1962–63, MCI came to have confidence in export-led industrialization.

More importantly, we emphasize that ideas are contested. Ideas about an economic crisis and solutions are not the same, but are very much contested among key actors with different perspectives. Key actors in Korea have faced economic crises periodically, such as in the late 1960s, the late 1970s, the late 1980s, and in the Asian financial crisis of 1997. However, the nature of each crisis was not apparent and needed interpretation. One key cause for these crises was the state's developmental policies themselves. However, large corporations' neoliberal free market solutions or labor's social democratic solutions failed to create a credible alternative. By contrast, state elites could continue their developmentalism by bringing new solutions to improve national industries' competitiveness.

In the sense that the problems and solutions are not apparent and the various interpretations are contested, this book differs from the prevalent state-centered approaches, including the DS theory, which emphasize the state as a unitary actor while criticizing the functionalism, pluralism, and Marxist social class approach (Nordinger 1981; Evans et al. 1985). In particular, the DS theorists emphasize the cohesiveness of state elites as an institutional condition for the developmental state. The DS literature holds that late-developing countries tend to have an interventionist state, but not all of them are developmental states. They argue that some states such as India and Latin American countries failed, while East Asian states succeeded in developmentalism. For the successful DS, they need Weberian state institutions to impose its will on business in a coherent fashion. They assume that intrabureaucratic conflicts are evidence of DS failure or demise, as with many Latin American countries and India, in contrast to East Asian developmental states (Haggard 1990; Wade 1990; Evans 1995; Chibber 2002, 2003; Thurbon 2016).

Unlike many DS theorists' assumptions, the state is not a unitary actor, but a fragmented locus in which state elites compete for power with different solutions and strategies. Incoherence and competition among key actors, particularly state elites, are more the norm than the exception because they interpret the same crisis differently, with different perspectives and priorities. At the height of Korean

---

[18] Knightian uncertainty does not mean the simple failure of calculation on the probability and actors' preferences given an option, but it refers to the uncertainty in which actors do not know what solutions and options are available. For Knightian uncertainty, see Blyth (2002: 31–33).

developmentalism in the Park Chung Hee era, state elites including EPB, MoF, and MCI, were divided into rival groups and competed for authority with different solutions and strategies for development, as shall be examined later on. Competition and conflicts among state elites are not unique in Korea, but prevalent even in the successful DS states, including Japan, Taiwan, and China, as shall be examined in Chapter 9. For example, as many neo-pluralist studies in the 1980s reveal, Japan has not been ruled by a cohesive bureaucracy. On the contrary, Japanese policy-making can be identified as "patterned pluralism" or "compartmentalized competition" where economic policies are constituted through contest and negotiation among diverse elites, including politicians and interest groups, as well as bureaucrats. Furthermore, unlike the DS thesis of cohesive bureaucracy, Japanese bureaucracy was not a monolith, but fragmented and internally competitive, even in the Japanese DS heyday of the 1960s.[19]

In Taiwan, elite competition inside the state also prevails, in contrast to the DS thesis of the cohesive state.[20] As Arnold (1989) and Wu (2004) show, Taiwanese policy-making even in its DS heyday was not monolithic but fragmented between "technocrats" in the Council for Economic Planning and Development (CEPD) and "administrative bureaucrats" in the Ministry of Economic Affairs (MOEA). In addition, even post-Mao China, which succeeded in rapid economic development through active state interventionism, is not monolithic, but "fragmented authoritarianism," where policy-making is contested among functionally differentiated clusters.[21] Faction elites in the Chinese Communist Party competed against each other in pursuit of supremacy by being deeply involved in local officials' experiments to demonstrate the effectiveness of their policy across the chessboard of China's territorial administration. Competition, rather than cohesiveness and coherence, among elites within the state, as well as between state and non-state actors, is our central approach.

Further, unlike the statist DS thesis of cohesiveness, competition and contest among elites does not necessarily produce negative effects on economic development. On the contrary, as seen in the successful DS of the East Asian countries, elite competition contributes to the economic development by improving the institutional adaptability in the continuously changing contexts of domestic and international political economy. The reason for Korea's success in economic development over a span of 50 years is neither because of the free market, nor some institutional elements of stringent Weberian state, but institutional adaptability

---

[19] For studies on the fragmented structure of the Japanese state, see Fukui (1987); and Muramastsu and Krauss (1984, 1987); and Muramatsu (1987, 1993). For conflicts among Japanese ministries in the 1960s, see McKean (1977); Campbell (1984); and Muramatsu (1993).

[20] For elite competition inside the Taiwanese state, see Noble (1987); Arnold (1989); and Wu (2004).

[21] For studies which regard Chinese polity as a fragmented structure, see Lieberthal and Oksenberg (1986, 1988); Lampton (1987); Lieberthal (1992); and Heilmann (2008a, 2008b).

through elite competition. Korean elites could achieve long-term economic success by arranging and rearranging their mode of intervention and innovation of policy, through competitively and pragmatically constituting an innovative strategy with a whole array of perspectives on how to approach new challenges, which they have never met with an apparent solution.

Many scholars of Chinese politics also point out the benefits which resulted from decentralized experimentation through elite competition (Heilmann 2008a: 1). Due to this decentralized experimentation, the single party state of China could make institutional and policy innovation for economic reform to flexibly adapt to rapidly changing environments. Competition among rival factions at the center enabled local officials to competitively initiate local experimentation, and the factional competition at the center helped to identify the diverse local experiments and speed the expansion of useful discoveries, and thus overcome resistance to reform.

Indeed, modern economic theories on development emphasize the organizational adaptability, rather than a single formula like capital accumulation, in the context of ever-changing challenges. Hoff and Stiglitz (2001) emphasize the importance of flexible institutional adaptability rather than fixed and apparent formulas for economic development, as follows:

> The past 50 years have seen marked changes in our understanding of development.... There are clearly no sure-fire formulas for success.... Some strategies seem to work for a while and then stall; some strategies seem to work in some countries and not in others.... A view shared by all the perspectives on development...is that industrial and developing countries are on different production functions and are organized in different ways. Development is no longer seen primarily as a process of capital accumulation but rather a process of *organizational change*.   (Hoff and Stiglitz 2001: 389; emphasis added)

Elite competition can produce benefits to economic development though organizational adaptability in response to ever-changing challenges if the competition and conflicts are properly coordinated. The Korean economy, as well as the East Asian DS economies, could have sustainable development over a long period, not because of apparent and standardized growth formula, nor because of some institutional elements of a stringent Weberian state, but because elites have been capable of change, adaptation and adjustments over a long period through their competition regarding what a better policy should be for the entire national economy. Competition among elites can elicit various local knowledges with diverse perspectives, and thereby help to create innovation in policy and institutions. Through collective deliberation for development, elites can not only adequately reformulate their developmental strategy, but also improve their adaptability in changing environments.

In order for collective deliberation to be workable over time, key actors should have vested interests for which they are willing to invest their time and energy in policy decision-making. In this sense, competition among elites can sustain the collective deliberation over time, because conflicts of ideas among key actors, such as different bureaucratic ministries, are not a matter of simple puzzle-solving, but involve vested interests in power. Competition among state elites appears as competition among ideas, but it is actually politics for power, in which elites attempt to increase their organization's legitimate authority. The competition for legitimate authority provides motivations for policy innovation. As Genieys and Smyrl (2008) point out, "[in] any given situation, there will always be actors who have an incentive for change" (2008: 44). Even the winners should be innovative in finding new solutions in the new context which their successful practices produce, as well as creatively finding new justifications in reaction to the new ideas that the losers suggest in order to change the current situation.

For collective deliberation to be self-sustaining, conflicts among elites should be properly resolved and coordinated for a developmental goal. If conflicts among elites are not coordinated for a developmental goal and fall into disarray or stalemate, even East Asian DS states like Taiwan cannot succeed in their industrial policy, as seen in the failure of Taiwan's industry policy to promote its auto industry (Arnold 1989; Chu 1994). In addition, the deliberative process through elite competition should be effective in the economic performance in order to be sustainable. Otherwise, collective deliberation would be abandoned for a unilateral dictate or fall into disarray.

On the other hand, politics or competition among key actors can better account for the endogenous changes in institutions and developmental strategies—*changes by competition*. Continuity of a development pattern, say state-led developmentalism in Korea, is neither by institutional stickiness to change or repetition of a taken-for-granted mindset, but by *continuity by changes*, changing the existing practices and finding new policy or strategy. For example, MCI in Korea could regain its influence and continue its developmental policy in the context of early 1980s liberalization, not by its traditional industrial policies based on control of market entry and direct subsidy under protectionism, but by adopting open trade and creating new industrial policies, such as R&D-based policy. A senior official of the R&D strategic team in the Ministry of Industry reports in a personal interview: "If we continued the traditional permission rights of market entry as industrial promotional policy, we would fail, and now how could Korean firms succeed?"[22] In order to preserve their existing influence, actors must be innovative. We firmly argue that continuity is not exclusive to changes; rather, continuity is possible only by changes.

---

[22] Personal interview with a senior official of R&D Strategy and Planning Bureau in the MoI on June 18, 2018.

Unlike the DS literature's assumption of fragmentation inside the state as evidence of DS demise, we emphasize that competition among elites inside the state contributed to the continuity of developmentalism by changes of developmental policies and strategies. In the Roh Moo-hyun administration (2003–07), Korea's industry-related ministries inside the state, including MoI, the Ministry of Information and Communication (MIC), and the Ministry of Science and Technology (MoST), agreed that Korea needed to build hi-tech next-generation industries and improve industrial competitiveness. However, they disagreed about how and what to do. They competed against one another to take the lead in industrial policies. In competing for the initiative in national development, they elaborated their rationales of industrial policy by establishing new targets and methods, while also expanding their affiliate organizations, including research institutes and subcontracting organizations. Despite some problems, such as overlapping R&D policies, competition among ministries inside the state both complemented and contributed to the continuity of Korean developmentalism. Intrabureaucratic competition may not engender the demise of the DS, as many DS and DS demise theorists expect. Rather, elite competition can complement and continue the state's active role through ongoing changes in industrial policy. As shall be extended to the East Asian DS countries in the final chapter, endogenous changes and flexible adaptability by elite competition could sustain state-led developmentalism, through effective innovation in policies and institutions, and also because their innovative alternatives are confirmed by successful performance. Thus, this book claims that in order to better account for continuity and changes in an economic system, politics among elites inside and outside the state should be considered.

2

Locating Korea from a Comparative Perspective

This chapter and the next locate Korean capitalism in a comparative and histor-ical sense, tracing the evolution of Korean capitalism by examining why the clas-sical developmental state of Korea was formed in the early 1960s, and how it has evolved. To explore the extent of change in Korean state-led capitalism and whether the developmental state remains effective under globalization, this chapter first examines what a developmental state is, compared with the Anglo-Saxon free market system and social corporatism, and then locates the Korean develop-mental pattern in globalization from a comparative perspective.

Developmental State as an Ideal Type

This section begins by briefly reviewing what the developmental state (DS) is. Recently, the DS demise theorists have tended to conflate "context-specific" elem-ents of Korean authoritarian developmentalism of the 1970s with state-led devel-opmentalism in general. In contrast, defenders of DS continuity, like Thurbon (2016), emphasize a too broad conception of state-led developmentalism. Thurbon identifies the developmental state with the ambitions of economic nationalism, disregarding different modes of improving national competitiveness. What is the developmental state in general, different from the neoliberal, free market system and social corporatist systems? By criticizing a too narrow con-ception of context-specific developmentalism or a too broad conception of devel-opmental ambition, we focus on how developmental goals are implemented, compared with the neoliberal state based on a free market, as seen in the United States and recent Mexico, and with a corporatist deliberation system, as in Germany.

In response to the traditional DS theorists' focus on the state's institutional capabilities to discipline private corporations (Haggard 2015: 40–51), the DS demise theorists emphasize the dissolution of traditional policy instruments and institutional elements, such as liberalization of finance, dissolution of pilot

Changes by Competition: The Evolution of the South Korean Developmental State. Hyeong-ki Kwon,
Oxford University Press (2021). © Hyeong-ki Kwon. DOI: 10.1093/oso/9780198866060.003.0002

agencies like the EPB in Korea, and intrabureaucratic conflicts.[1] In particular, as Thurbon rightly points out, the DS demise theorists rely heavily on "the context-specific, highly centralized, and coercive Korean state of the 1970s" and "the specific set of industrial polices it pursued in that period" (Thurbon 2016: 11). They conflate context-specific elements with the developmental state in general.

For example, assuming that the developmental state is the authoritarian strong state, like the Korean state of the 1970s, many theorists hold that democracy and pluralism weaken DS to that extent (Moon 1994; Moon and Kim 1996; Kim, Eun Mee 2014). In particular, most DS demise theorists focus on the embrace of financial liberalization as evidence of developmental state dismantling in Korea (Jayasuriya 2005; Pirie 2008; Ji 2011). Pirie (2008) identifies the developmental state with a policy of promoting large champions through the state's top-down control of bank-based finance. Thus, he argues that financial liberalization in Korea is evidence of the demise of the Korean developmental state.

However, the demise of specific instruments like state-directed lending or the independence of a central bank must not be conflated with the demise of the developmental state itself. For example, Taiwanese central banks were already independent, and Taiwan used more tax breaks as investment incentives than Korea's state-directed lending instrument in the 1970s.[2] In fact, Korea has significantly liberalized its financial market since the 1990s. The Korean central bank now became independent of the administration, while private banks adopted global lending standards. Foreign financial institutes encroached widely upon Korean financial markets. Today the Korean state has difficulty in directly controlling private banks' loans. The current Korean state cannot leverage private banks to lend massive capital exclusively to a few large corporations, as the traditional DS in the Park Chung Hee era did. As chaebols rely on their internal capital and direct financial market, the initiatives in investment decisions are not in the hands of the Korean state.

However, despite financial liberalization, the Korean state still plays an active role in improving national competitiveness by using other measures, including developing an industrial ecosystem within strategic industries, rather than simply retreating or becoming a nonstrategic neutral state. Unlike the DS demise theorist accounts, private initiatives in investment decisions are not evidence of the DS demise. The Korean state has shifted from direct coordination of investment decisions to private investment initiatives since the early 1980s as the Korean economy became bigger and more complicated. Even the smartest bureaucrats cannot know all the economic opportunities. As the Korean economy grew, the state's

---

[1] For DS demise theorists, see Kirk (2000); Hundt (2005); Jayasuriya (2005); Pirie (2005, 2008); Lim and Jang (2006); Kwon, O (2010); Ji, J. (2011); Kim, E.M. (2014); and Yeung (2016). For more detailed accounts, see Chapter 1 of this book.

[2] For state developmentalism in Taiwan, see Fields (1995) and Thurbon (2001, 2003, and 2007).

direct control became an obstacle to developmental goals such as building an innovative economy. Nevertheless, the Korean state's release of old-style direct control of finance and investments does not mean the demise of the DS. To achieve its developmental goals, the Korean state still plays an active role by addressing the market failure from the abstract perspective of national economy, rather than involving itself in detailed decisions, using indirect methods such as tax breaks, R&D support, easing regulations, and planning programs.

Yet rightly criticizing the DS demise theorist conflation of the context specific elements of the coercive state and its policy instruments with the developmental state in general, Thurbon (2016) emphasizes developmental ambition and goals as evidence of the DS. As distinguishing features of state-led developmentalism, Thurbon suggests policymaking elites' developmental mindset, "their priorization and unwavering commitment to the goal of economic growth" (2016: 15). However, it is difficult to differentiate diverse modes of development only by referring to policymakers' ambition and economic nationalism as criteria for a developmental state. For example, both French and German policymakers pursued the similar goal of national economic development in the postwar era, but they developed different modes of economic development. French policymakers pursued state-led developmentalism, based on the state's centralized control over finance and creation of large enterprises, as Korean policymakers did. By contrast, German policymakers tried to avoid state interventionism as the neoliberal laissez-faire state normally does. However, unlike the neoliberal free market system, postwar German policymakers developed a decentralized but corporatist coordination system based on the *formierte Gesellschaft* and parapublic organizations in order to avoid the detrimental social consequences of the unfettered free markets (Shonfield 1965; Zysman 1983; Hall 1986; Katzenstein 1987; Fioretos 2011: 105–107, 138–144).

To differentiate state-led developmentalism from other types of economic development, including neoliberalism and social corporatism, in the sense of ideal-type governance systems, we emphasize the different modes of economic operation and governance, rather than focusing on simply some institutional elements, including state cohesiveness and state control of finance, or on too broad worldviews like economic nationalism or a developmental mindset. In particular, we focus on the state's economic role—whether the state is liberal laissez-faire or interventionist in economic development.

The liberal states in the sense of ideal type are neutral to the competition of economic players in the market. Even the neoliberal states may use industrial policy, but they normally use horizontal policy in which they tend to provide general services and infrastructure available to all citizens. By contrast, in the ideal sense, the developmental state is "plan-rational," giving first priority to economic development or improvement of economic competitiveness. Although the developmental state recognizes the initiatives of private actors, the developmental state intervenes in the market more strategically and selectively from the perspective of entire national development rather than individual firms' goals of profit maximization. The developmental state builds the developmental priority, selects strategic industries or firms, and provides favorable conditions to the selected (Johnson 1982; Amsden 1989; Wade 1990). For example, neoliberal and developmental states differ in implementing their policy, although they both focus on R&D policy or industrial policy for small and medium-sized enterprises (SMEs). As seen recently in Korea, developmental states are more strategically selective in nurturing knowledge-intensive industrial linkages among some strategic industries, rather than providing general services to all SMEs based on firm size.

State-led developmentalism differs from social corporatism in the sense of economic governance systems. In social corporatism, as seen in Germany, the state is more neutral to market competitors than the developmental state. Social partners in the corporatist coordination system have a parapublic status and negotiate with the state regarding social and economic problems. In state-led developmentalism social partners, such as the labor and business groups, lack a formal parapublic status. They may have some voice but they lack formal rights to decide and lead economic policies. For example, in Korea labor organizations failed to establish themselves as state-level partners, or equal partners within corporations even after the democratization of 1987 (Jo, H.J. 2016; Morgan and Kubo 2016: 85). Although both state-led capitalism and social corporatism try to solve market failure through strategic coordination, they differ in how to solve the problem. The developmental state strategically leads the solution through centralized coordination, whereas social corporatism develops a decentralized and socially horizontal negotiation system.

In the next section we locate Korea more clearly from the comparative perspective of economic operation and governance in the course of globalization.

Locating Korea in Globalization

By exploring how Korea overcomes the challenges of globalization from a comparative view, this section examines whether state-led developmentalism is still relevant in an era of globalization, and importantly, whether Korean capitalism of the 2010s has changed into a neoliberal free market system or how, as state developmentalism, it differs from neoliberal and corporatist capitalism in globalization.[3] Neoliberals and globalists, based on global production networks (GPNs),

---

[3] The rest of this chapter heavily relies on my published articles, including Kwon (2012, 2017) in *Politics & Society*, although I significantly revised and expanded them. The latter article was written with Kyung Mi Kim. I appreciate her permission to use them.

hold that state developmentalism or strategic industrial policies are no longer effective under globalization. In the same vein, the DS demise theorists argue that the Korean developmental state dismantled and changed to neoliberalism. However, as we will see in this section, the Korean state plays an active role in globalization, different from the role of neoliberal states, including the United States and Mexico, and the role of corporatist coordination systems, like Germany.

Diverse Patterns of National Economy in Globalization

As competition has increased worldwide, corporations in national core industries have disintegrated their value chains and reorganized fragmented value chains across national borders in order to utilize various advantages of local production, including low wages, hi-tech parts, and various specialties of parts suppliers. As corporations recompose their value chains across national borders for competitive advantage, their global reorganization of production effects changes in the national economy, including the hollowing-out of domestic jobs and dissolution of current interfirm relations.

However, neoliberal globalists remain optimistic, holding that offshoring of national corporations is not a cause for worry.[4] Neoliberals, based on comparative advantage theory, hold that globalization of national corporations is good for both home economies as well as host countries, free of state intervention and open to free-flowing capital. According to neoliberals, for developing countries like Mexico and India, offshoring is not worker exploitation but provides workers with jobs and a chance to develop their human capability; for developed countries, offshoring reduces input prices and increases profits which will be invested in new competitive areas and create more jobs. Neoliberals dismiss worries about job losses through offshoring because the loss of industrial jobs and closing of factories in the course of globalization are a process of creative destruction: low-skilled jobs at home are offshored to developing nations; and offshoring then saves input prices and frees up the domestic economy to upgrade to higher value-added production. Neoliberals hold that in order to optimize dynamic advantage, the allocation of resources should be driven only by the free market, and state intervention should be reduced to the minimum. Neoliberals like Howard Pack and Kamal Saggi hold that industrial policies, whether new or old, are irrelevant in the course of globalization (Pack and Saggi 2006: 276).

However, unlike the neoliberal prediction, not all nations fare well in the course of national corporations' globalization. Some countries upgrade their current industrial competitiveness, while others do not. For example, Korean,

---

[4] For neoliberal globalism, see Ramaswamy and Rowthorn (2000); McKinsey & Company (2003); Friedman (2007); Bhagwati (2010); and Sirkin et al. (2011).

Table 2.1. Automobile Corporations' Overseas Production in 2012

	United States	Germany	Japan	Korea
Domestic production (cars)	5,467,642	4,480,655	6,597,736	3,491,000
Overseas production (cars)	11,784,693	9,754,716	12,506,924	3,635,000
Domestic production (%)	31.7	31.5	34.5	49.0
Overseas production (%)	68.3	68.5	65.5	51.0

* Note: US automakers include GM, Ford, Chrysler; German automakers: Volkswagen, Daimler, BMW; Japanese automakers: Toyota, Nissan, Honda; Korean automakers: Hyundai, Kia.
Source: OICA (Organisation International des Constructeurs d'Automobiles) Statistics

German, and US corporations in the automobile and electronics industries have increased their overseas production, but their outcomes at home are significantly different. As seen in Table 2.1, the United States, German, and Japanese automakers as early movers have significantly increased their overseas production by 65 to over 68% until 2012. Korean automakers, relatively late in globalization, also significantly increased overseas production in order to survive global competition. Since 2012, Korean automakers' overseas production began to surpass their domestic production up to 58.9% in 2016.

However, unlike the neoliberal optimistic view, the effects of national corporations' globalization on domestic economies vary widely. Despite similar globalization trends, Germany and Japan did not lose domestic production. Japanese domestic production of cars holds the level of 1993 production despite ups and downs. Japanese domestic employment in the automobile industry slightly increased from 755,000 in 1998 to 865,000 in 2008. Germany also achieved more success than Japan in sustaining domestic production. Domestic production of German passenger cars increased from 4.36 million in 1995 to 5.55 million in 2010 (Japanese industrial census; Kwon 2012: 586–587).

The most contrasting cases are the United States and Korea. Domestic employment and production in the US automobile industry have significantly declined, but in Korea have apparently grown. For example, in the US automobile industry, overseas production increased from 7.4 million cars in 2000 to 10.0 million cars in 2010, while domestic production significantly declined from 8.0 million cars in 2000 to just 3.4 million cars in 2010 (OICA statistics). By contrast, despite the rapid growth of overseas production, the domestic production of cars in Korea increased from 3.5 million cars in 1995 to 4.3 million in 2010.

Figure 2.1 shows changes in employment and productivity in the US and Korean automobile industries, assuming that the level of 1999 is 100. US employment declined from 100 in 1999 to 67 in 2008, while Korean employment grew from 100 to 135 in the same period. Despite similar growth of productivity (36% in Korea and 35% in the United States between 1999 and 2008), changes in employment and production of both Korea and the United States are significantly

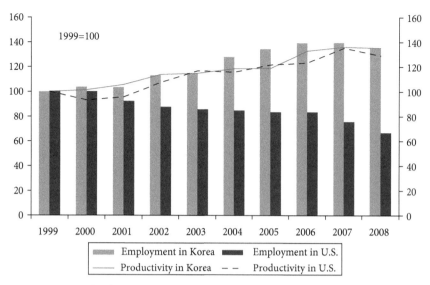

Figure 2.1. Trends of Productivity and Employment in US and Korea Automobile Industry

Source: US Bureau of Labor Statistics; Korean Statistical Information Service for Korea employment; Korea Productivity Center for Korea productivity.

different. This means that changes in domestic employment are more related to the ways of globalization than growth of productivity.

However, unlike the neoliberal optimism of win-win, in which advanced countries save costs by offshoring, and upgrade their economies by reinvesting the saved money at home, not all nations have automatically upgraded their industrial capabilities. Figure 2.2 compares changes in trade balance in hi-tech industries, including Aerospace, Electronics-Telecommunications, Pharmacy, Scientific Instruments and Non-electrical machinery, defined by OECD and Eurostat. Korea, along with Germany, shows relatively stable growth of trade balance in the hi-tech industries, whereas competitiveness of US hi-tech industries significantly declined. Korea achieved a steady growth of trade surplus in the hi-tech industries, by 374%, from approximately $11 billion trade surplus in 2000 to $52 billion in 2010. By contrast, since the early 2000s, trade in the United States plummeted into a $180 billion trade deficit in 2015.

What makes the difference? In regard to the varying effects of corporations' globalization on their national economies, this book focuses on the "industrial commons" as collective capabilities in the industrial ecosystem.[5] The industrial commons refers to shared capabilities in the industrial ecosystem in which suppliers, customers, partners, skilled workers, and local institutions such as

---

[5] For industrial commons and ecosystem, see Pisano and Shih (2012); and Berger (2013).

Trade Balance (USD in Billons)

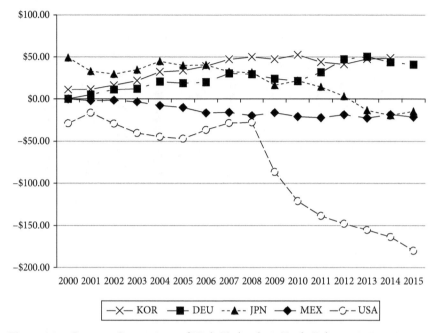

Figure 2.2. Country Comparison of High-Technology Trade Balance, 2000–15
Source: UN, Comtrade database, 2016.

universities and research institutes share complementary capabilities. Many firms depend on the commons when they create new ideas and transform their ideas to new products in the market. The industrial commons are a key source of competitiveness for national industries. The challenge is how to organize or upgrade the industrial commons in the course of globalization in which private corporations reorganize their inputs across national borders to pursue their own interests, rather than preserving the industrial commons at home. This section shows the diverse ways to build the industrial commons in the course of globalization. In particular, we hold that unlike the neoliberal argument, a developmental state can play a critical role in upgrading the industrial commons in the course of corporations' globalization. Unrestrained free markets, in which corporations go abroad for their individual short-term profits without considering collective innovative capabilities at home, can lead to the loss of the industrial commons, as seen in the United States. Now, let us examine briefly how the diverse modes of economic governance have different effects in the course of globalization.

Unlike the neoliberal argument, uncoordinated free market economies, including the United States and Mexico, do not generate the improvement of national industrial capabilities. On the contrary, in the absence of state and social coordination, neoliberal free market economies are more likely to lose their industrial commons in globalization, as seen in the United States which lost its industrial capabilities in the course of globalization. As the MIT research team and Harvard business team reveal, many holes in the US industrial ecosystem occurred as US corporations went abroad individually, pursuing their own interests in the free market (Pisano and Shih 2012; Berger 2013; many articles in *Harvard Business Review*, special report in March 2012). Most innovative ideas in hi-tech products, including semiconductors, flat-panel displays, light-emitting diodes (LEDs), optical coating, advanced batteries, precision bearings, optoelectronics, wind turbines, ultra-heavy forgings, and so on, originated in the United States but now have vanished or are rapidly vanishing in the United States because the industrial commons are disappearing in the course of corporations' globalization.[6]

In this situation, according to the MIT and Harvard research teams, brilliant young Americans might have difficulty in commercializing their idea in the United States, such as a creative development for a digital camera, because complementary capabilities such as testing and making prototypes are missing in the country. According to MIT research, start-ups in areas such as Silicon Valley, Austin, Texas, and Cambridge, Massachusetts, may excel in new ideas for product development, but often falter in scaling up their products for commercialization because they lack production technology, multiple parts suppliers, and long-term capital. Due to the lack of complementary capabilities outside the firm, America's most innovative start-ups result in an M&A exit, not an IPO, and go abroad. Similarly, most firms outside innovation hubs such as Silicon Valley and Cambridge struggle to improve their innovative capabilities because "they do not find any complementary capabilities they can draw on in the industrial ecosystem as they try to develop new components: little outside funding, few connections with community colleges, weak trade associations, no research consortia" (Berger 2013: 13). Due to the disappearance of many valuable complementary capabilities in the United States, including multiple suppliers and training and test centers, US industrial capabilities for innovation are increasingly enfeebled.

Unlike the neoliberal optimism in globalization, a national economy is not automatically upgraded to a higher innovation-oriented economy by free markets. In the United States, corporations' increased profits, resulting from saved input prices in the course of globalization, were not necessarily reinvested at home to upgrade the domestic industrial system. The US trade deficit in advanced technology products expanded as seen in Figure 2.2, because, as Gregory Tassey

---

[6] For the disappearing or "endangered species" of the US hi-tech industries which had their roots in the United States, see Pisano and Shih (2012: 8–13); see also articles in the *Harvard Business Review* special report in March 2012, including Kochan (2012); Pisano and Shih (2012b); and Porter and Rivkin (2012).

(2010) observes, domestic research and development in American corporations declined due to the rapid growth of US corporations' offshore R&D (Tassey 2010: 283–333). Although US corporations might earn more profits by using foreign intermediaries, many industrial commons, such as parts suppliers and skilled workers, disappeared (Berger 2013: 20, 204–205).

In addition, unlike the neoliberals' argument, developing countries like Mexico, which receive foreign direct investment, are not automatically upgraded to a higher-innovation economy, due to the lack of collective coordination to build the industrial commons in their national economies. For example, Latin American countries including Mexico and Brazil, which rely for their industrialization on foreign direct investment (FDI), failed to improve their economies to hi-tech or knowledge-intensive economies in the 2000s, because foreign MNCs were not interested in improving knowledge-intensive capabilities in these countries (Amsden 2001: 252, 271). For example, the duty-free maquila and disguised maquila firms in Mexico, which are mainly built by foreign MNCs for export, lead Mexico's economic growth. However, they failed to upgrade Mexican industrial competitiveness. Many empirical studies show the problem of the maquila and parallel maquila firms in Mexico, "as tied to a largely unregulated production process driven by and for transnational capital—overwhelmingly from the United States—[which] has resulted in the marginalization of Mexico's dwindling industrial base. Unable, except in the rarest of instances, to participate in this production process, Mexico's endogenous technological capabilities have atrophied" (Toledo 2007; Canas and Gilmer 2009: 10; Cypher and Wise 2010: 107).

Contrary to neoliberal optimism, the maquila and parallel maquila corporations in Mexico could not improve their innovation capabilities. For example, according to Toledo's (2007) empirical study, productivity in the Mexican maquila firms paradoxically declined to 95% in 2002, from the 100% level of 1993 (Toledo 2007: table 2). In addition, the value-added portion of the Mexican maquila firms in the global production networks dropped from 18.2% in 1988 to only 8.2% in 2003, a decline of 55% (Cypher and Wise 2010: 82). Particularly, it is noted that the foreign MNCs' production in Mexico lacks backward industrial linkage with endogenous firms. In Mexican manufacturing in general, national inputs cover approximately 30%. But only 3% of total production value in the maquila arises from national inputs (Cypher and Wise 2010: 82, 94). Contrary to the neoliberal prediction, with such lack of industrial linkages, the foreign MNCs do not have effects of technology diffusion and learning effects in Mexico.

Learning and innovation take place as individuals or companies move ideas beyond design and prototype. Upgrades in industrial capabilities take place as researchers at research institutes, and designers, engineers, and technicians at various test centers and parts companies interact throughout the production process. The current problem for neoliberal market economies, including in the

United States and Mexico, is that in the absence of collective coordination at the system level, they fail to build the industrial commons in the course of corporations' footloose moves across national borders. The free market system is less likely to solve the collective action problems in building the industrial commons, such as sharing commonly available resources and capabilities including training, local banking, and multiple suppliers.

By contrast to the United States and Mexico, as seen in Figure 2.2, Germany and Korea have had more positive outcomes in improving their competitiveness in hi-tech industries in globalization, because their economic coordination systems were more likely to solve collective problems in globalization. However, their modes of economic governance are different, with Korea's state-led developmentalism and Germany's corporatist coordination. For example, in contrast to the US free market, as well as to the Korean developmental state, Germany has developed more social corporatist coordination in globalization. In most US corporations, employers, who are more concerned with shareholders' value, unilaterally decide how to globalize, excluding their employees' voices. By contrast, in Germany, the main actors—including employers, works councils, and trade unions—bring to the globalization process varying degrees of influence in developing collective agreements. In German metalworking industries, employers and labor representatives have created constructive solutions while contesting where to invest and how to globalize, as seen in Volkswagen's Auto 5000 project. Based on VW's successful experiment, German labor negotiated with employers over how to improve domestic production in the course of globalization.[7]

In the course of globalization, German labor attempted to find an alternative to the global strategy through collective negotiation, from the company outward to national levels. Works councils (*Betriebsräte*) as shop-floor organizations representing workers, which have access to the company's key decisions due to Germany's codetermination law, in fact agreed with the concept of globalization to enhance the company's competitiveness. For example, around 1999, when Volkswagen was about to decide where to produce its SUV Touareg, globalization became an increasing threat to works councils. In the selection of production sites for high-quality SUVs, severe conflicts between the company and labor lasted several months. Until that time, a rough consensus at VW was that high value-added cars would be produced in Germany and low-priced cars would be produced in Central and Eastern Europe. Labor at VW expected that the production of SUVs would go to Hanover. However, the Hanover plant could not meet the production cost requirements that VW management suggested. From the employer's point of view, the production of SUVs should be more cost competitive in order to compete effectively in the crucial US market.

---

[7] The German story of 5000 GmbH in Volkswagen in this section is based on my article Kwon (2012).

VW labor representatives worried whether they would ever get another chance at a new model if they lost such hi-tech car production. When management would not budge, the labor representatives in Germany conceded Touareg production to the Bratislava plant in Slovakia; but in exchange, they began new negotiations for development of a specific car production project to employ more workers in Germany. That agreement is the "Benchmark Production 5000X5000." Few cases have attracted as much public attention as VW's project organized as Auto 5000 GmbH. From its initial creation all the way through to its successful integration of Auto 5000 employees into Volkswagen AG in January 2009, the project has been closely watched. Against the background of debate over Germany as a production site, in which neoliberals doubted the existing German model of production based on "rigid" collective bargaining and high labor costs, the Auto 5000 project was a test case of whether Germany could hold its place in manufacturing.

From initial planning for production of the minivan Touran, German social actors, including VW management, IG Metall, and VW works councils, negotiated the Auto 5000 project. Due to the economic success of the Touareg, bonuses and wages were raised every year to make up the difference. Based on its economic success, Auto 5000 was completely integrated with Volkswagen in January 2009 with the same wage level as the rest of Volkswagen. Auto 5000 achieved economic success due to its highly innovative production organization. According to a midterm evaluation by the Sociological Research Institute (SOFI) at Georg-August University in Göttingen in 2004, Auto 5000 had already made large profits as well as significant improvements in quality and production.

A key feature of Auto 5000 production is the continuous improvement of production processes by collective deliberation, which utilizes the unused potential of all relevant employees. Workloads and personnel deployment are collectively decided by management, works councils, and work teams. Production processes are continuously optimized through horizontal and vertical communication. Another key feature of Auto 5000 is an emphasis on "learning plants" (Lernfabriken). First, Auto 5000 developed a high level of initial and ongoing training. Based on collective agreements between company and union, workers engage in further training three hours per week—a uniquely high level in the automobile industry. Furthermore, Auto 5000 systematically integrates work and learning. Auto 5000 has built large conference rooms near the production lines, in which the relevant managers, engineers, and specialists from various trade vocations meet to discuss continuous improvement in production. This collective deliberation directly affects continuous improvement in workers' competence as well as finds new efficiencies in the production process. Due to its economic success and significant improvement on productivity and quality, VW management decided to give the production of a new SUV Tiguan to Auto 5000, which began production in August 2007.

VW's 5000 project has been used as an effective alternative model when German unions negotiate with employer organizations over where and how to globalize. The German metalworking union IG Metall allowed unions to be actively involved in company-level bargaining and suggesting an alternative to employers' production relocation. For example, in the 2008 economic crisis, IG Metall attempted to expand VW-style codetermination and cooperative solutions to the suffering Opel and small and medium-sized companies like Schaeffler.

Korean State-led Developmentalism in Globalization

German social coordination is not the single, viable solution to building innovation capabilities at home in the course of corporations' globalization. Korea has upgraded its industrial learning and innovative capabilities, neither through the neoliberal free market nor through social corporatism, but through the state's efforts to upgrade the industrial ecosystem. As seen in Figure 2.2, Korea is one of the most successful countries in continuously upgrading hi-tech industries in the course of national corporations' globalization from 2000 to 2015. Particularly, Korea has successfully transformed from the traditional input-oriented economy to a technology-intensive and knowledge-based innovation system. According to a study of the Korea Institute for Industrial, Economics and Trade (KIET), a government industrial research institute, traditionally the main cause for Korean economic growth was capital inputs. However, in the 2000s, total factor productivity, which spurred economic growth from 8.5% in the 1970s to 61.7% in the 2000s, mainly due to innovation in the production process, became a major driving force of economic growth (KIET 2008: 2–3).

Recognizing the limitation of input-oriented growth strategy in the 1990s, particularly in the financial crisis of 1997, the Korean government shifted its policy priority from traditional capital concentration on a few mass producers to realize scale economy to building the industrial ecosystem for innovation. To do this, the Korean government in the 2000s increased its support for R&D activities of private companies, and put important focus on building an effective ecosystem (Kim, Kiwan 2007: 267). As shall be examined later, Korean government R&D funds mainly aimed at building consortia, where public research institutes, including Korean Automotive Technology Institute (KATECH), Electronics and Telecommunications Research Institute (ETRI), and Korea Institute of Industrial Technology (KITECH), in most cases coordinate collaborative research of large OEMs and parts suppliers. In contrast to simple R&D tax credits and cash support directly awarded to individual corporations in the United States, the Korean government focuses on expanding and reinforcing the existing industrial linkages and networks via research consortia. This section examines how Korea could improve their industrial commons by building an innovation-oriented, industrial ecosystem even in globalization.

In contrast to German social corporatist coordination, Korean labor did not have the capability to establish itself as a parapublic negotiator at the national level and equal social partner at the company level. Unlike liberal market economies, the Korean state has been actively involved in building a competitive industrial ecosystem in response to the hollowing-out of national industries in globalization.

Unlike the FDI-led development in Latin American countries like Mexico, the Korean state further emphasized its developmentalism as national corporations globalized. In contrast to the FDI-led development in Latin American countries including Mexico, Brazil, and Argentina, Korean development has been mainly through promotion of endogenous corporations (Amsden 2001: 238, 276–277). Due to FDI-led growth in globalization, these Latin American countries' liberalization and globalization meant abandonment of their existing industrial policies. In Latin American countries, industrial policies meant protectionism and import-substitution-industrialization (ISI), while export-oriented industrialization or liberalization meant free market fundamentalism with a laissez-faire neoliberal state, abandoning the developmental policies (Cypher and Wise 2010: 6–7, 45–46, 64–73; Calderon and Sanchez 2012: 9; Moreno-Brid 2013: 216–218). By contrast, due to developmentalism based on national firms, the Korean government continuously emphasized its developmental policy to improve the international competitiveness of national industries, even in liberalization. Paradoxically, the Korean government further reinforced its developmentalism by emphasizing the challenges resulting from globalization and liberalization, as shall be examined later.

How could the Korean state improve its innovation-oriented capabilities at home even in globalization? First, it should be noted that few large lead firms in Korea had interest in developing and collaborating with parts suppliers, unlike Japanese Original Equipment Manufacturers (OEMs). Traditionally, interfirm relations in Korea were not collaborative but adversarial and exploitative. Rather than developing collaborative relations with home suppliers, large Korean OEMs focused on free trade with foreigners, because key parts of their export products were imported from foreign countries, mainly Japan. This export-led growth based on imports of parts was due to the low development of parts and intermediate industries. Unlike Japanese industrialization, in which large OEMs sourced parts and intermediates from domestic suppliers, Korean industrialization had no parallel development of final products and parts industries. According to Korean economist Song (1990)'s calculation of interindustry linkages, the proportion of imported inputs directly needed for outputs across industries was 28.1% in Korea in 1985, whereas it was only 6.9% in Japan (Song 1990: 121–122).

For core export industries including electronics and auto, the dependence on imported parts was more serious.[8]

For example, Oh Wonchul, a key bureaucrat in the Park Chung Hee era, who built Korean heavy industries in the 1970s, remembers how strongly large assemblers like Shinjin automobile company opposed the government policy of import substitution of parts:

> [Shinjin automobile company earned great profits] but it did not contribute to the development of our automobile industry. All of their attention was engaged in importing chunks of parts as an SKD, and simply assembling and selling them.... The Ministry of Commerce and Industry could not leave the situation like this. Thus we ordered Shinjin to localize parts at least 32% until 1967, but Shinjin tried not to do it, giving one excuse or another. Finally it reached only 23.6% of localization of parts.... They were not interested in the localization of parts (*kooksanwha* in Korean). They were wholly immersed in making money.
>
> (Oh, Wonchul, 1996, vol. 4, 109–110)

Not only automobile companies, including Hyundai and Asia, but also electronics companies were not interested in localization of parts, and were absorbed in making money by assembly of imported parts (Oh, Wonchul 1996, vol.4: 112–113). Even up to the early 1990s, simply assembling the parts imported from foreign countries was more profitable for large companies than developing their own model and using domestic parts. That is why many people opposed Samsung entering the automobile industry, because Samsung would use foreign parts and ruin domestic efforts to improve the parts industry (KAMA 2005: 321).

Due to the underdevelopment of home suppliers, Korean lead firms initially globalized independently of home suppliers, as Americans did. According to a 1996 study by Korea Institute for Industrial Economics & Trade (KIET) of Korean automakers' internationalization, Korean automakers were most concerned with joint ventures or collaboration with local corporations in host countries (40%) and building sales networks (38.5%). Only 13.3% of Korean automakers believed that collaboration with home suppliers was important for success in globalization (KIET 1996).

However, due to the state-initiated development of Korean parts suppliers in the 2000s, Korean lead firms could collaborate with home suppliers in the course of building production networks on foreign soil, in contrast to initial stages of independent globalization. Actually, in the 2000s, Korean lead firms came to be

---

[8] For the exports depending on imported parts in electronics, see Song (1990; 119–122); for exports of automobile assemblers based on imports of parts, see Oh, Wonchul (1996; 94–95, 109–115); and KAMA (2005: 138–170).

interested in promoting home suppliers' capability and going abroad together, reflecting upon their own experience of failure on foreign soil. For instance, Hyundai in Canada, Samsung in the United States, and LG in Germany, closed their plants because they could not meet the high-level requirement of localization of parts due to increased costs.[9]

At first, Korean lead firms had difficulty in developing parts supply networks with local suppliers in developing countries as well. For example, Korean corporations such as Samsung, LG, Daewoo, and Hyundai faced problems with local suppliers in Mexico, including delivery time, volume, quality, and price. Korean corporations also had latecomers' disadvantage in using global suppliers. When Korean corporations in core export industries moved overseas, foreign competitors from advanced countries like Japan, the United States, and Germany already occupied the supply base of global suppliers and excellent locals. By using the same suppliers that competitors used, Korean firms believed they could not compete with foreign competitors.

According to a report of the Korean executive of the Industrial Development Agency in Northern Ireland, Korean lead firms like Samsung and LG had difficulty in building their parts supply networks in the UK because British electronics suppliers already had close relationships with Japanese corporations in the UK. The senior manager at the Procurement Planning & Strategy Team of Hyundai explains in a personal interview why Hyundai built nationally-oriented global networks instead of using global suppliers as well as locals in China:

> When we went to China, there were many global players [suppliers], but we strategically used our domestic partners in order to improve our competitiveness. Why did we bring our partners to China? It's because of *our differentiation strategy*. We purchase about 70% of parts from our partners. The price competitiveness of our cars depends on our partners. If we use the same companies that our competitors use, there is no difference with them. This year, we reached the production level of one million cars in China. By contrast, Volkswagen produced 40 or 50 million cars. We could not reduce price simply by volume. We need another strategy to compete with our competitors.   (Emphasis added)[10]

In order to contend with early movers in globalization, latecomer Korean lead firms could not use the same global suppliers as their competitors. Furthermore, Koreans have relatively small volume. Korean corporations had to reflect upon

---

[9] Personal interview with Korea Auto Industries Coop. Association, KAICA on May 13, 2010; Hankook Kyungjae (Korean), October 19, 1991; Segye Ilbo (Korean), October 20, 1994; Maeil Kyungjae (Korean), May 30, 1997.

[10] Personal interview with a senior manager at the Procurement Planning & Strategy Team of Hyundai on August 24, 2010.

their relative position as latecomers in globalization and search for a new differentiation strategy.

However, it was not easy for Korean lead firms to build nationally-oriented global networks with home suppliers on foreign soil, because of their home suppliers' small size and incapability, which mainly resulted from the traditional Korean developmentalism focusing exclusively on building national champions, as well as from the Korean OEMs' exploitative subcontracting system.[11] In order to build global networks with home suppliers, Korean lead corporations needed the relative improvement of home suppliers' capability, which was initiated by state-led developmentalism.

Actually, through Korea's transformation from classical developmentalism to inclusive developmentalism, it has achieved parallel development of parts and materials and upgraded collective capabilities in the course of globalization. In the mid-1990s, export competitiveness of parts suppliers (-27.7) was significantly lower than that of automakers (92.9).[12] However, Korean SMEs grew more rapidly than large corporations from 2000 to 2011, even according to research conducted by the leftist Economic Reform Research Institute (ERRI). Although the profit rate of large lead firms (6.84%) is higher than that of SMEs (5.33%), on average the growth of turnover and assets in SMEs is higher by 1.4 times and 2.3 times respectively than those of large corporations (We, Pyungryang 2011). The size of parts suppliers also grew. For example, in 1995, only 8% of auto parts suppliers employed more than 100 workers, whereas in 2009, approximately 49% of auto parts suppliers employed more than 100 (KAICA 2011: 27; Kim, Kwanghee 1998: 30). Suppliers also became more specialized. The number of specialized firms, which earn more than 50% of sales from parts and materials, increased from 483 in 2002 to 3,353 in 2010 (KIET 2012: 27). In addition, SMEs' R&D capabilities have significantly increased. The number of SMEs' research institutes increased from less than 100 in 1990, to 14,014 in 2007, and further, to 33,454 in 2015. The number of R&D researchers in the SMEs increased from almost nothing in 1990 to 62,792 in 2005, and more recently to 147,378. R&D researchers of SMEs now constitute approximately 48% of total private companies' researchers, on par with those of large assemblers (KISTEP 2015).

Due to this improvement of domestic industrial capabilities, Korean corporations' globalization has not generated deindustrialization at home, because Korean firms have built close connections between overseas and home production, in contrast to US globalization practices. As Korean parts suppliers

---

[11] The cause for underdevelopment of parts and materials suppliers in Korea was due mainly to the Korean developmental state's strategy of rapid industrialization as well as exploitative subcontracting relations by large corporations. For the Korean way of industrialization, see Kim, Eun Mee (1997: 97–167); Shin and Chang (2004: 33–40); Lim, Haeran (2010b).

[12] Export competitiveness = {(export-import)/(export + import)} x 100. See Park and Kim (1997: 30), table 3–1.

continuously develop their own capabilities at home, Korean lead firms have brought their home suppliers overseas, in contrast to their initial offshoring in which lead firms went abroad independently, as American lead firms did. Korean lead firms in electronics used joint-globalization slightly earlier in the mid-1990s than automakers did.

Many Korean suppliers whom I interviewed reported that their overseas production does not reduce their domestic operations; on the contrary, it increases domestic volume of production, because they still make the technologically-advanced core parts in Korea, while foreign plants produce relatively simple parts and assemble them with parts imported from Korea.[13] Korean firms keep their production at home and are interested in further upgrading because most Korean suppliers believe that their competitiveness lies in their close relations with customers, sub-tier suppliers, and neighboring research institutes at home. In a personal interview, a senior manager of a car-seat manufacturer explains why it keeps and upgrades home production while expanding overseas production:

> The reason is that our competitiveness comes from here. Technological capabilities matter for competitiveness. Foreign countries, where we produce, are less prepared for the good infrastructure we want. I traveled for research in more than 20 countries. But few countries are fully equipped with all parts including materials, components, and assembly. For example, China may be proud of making satellites, but they do not make a specific strong bolt that we want for our seat. There are many missing parts, including antistatic seat fabric, and so on.[14]

How could Koreans upgrade their home base in the course of globalization? The Korean state initiated and coordinated the upgrading of the industrial commons at home. Korea's upgrading was not a natural result of private companies' voluntary actions in the free market, but an outcome of the state's conscious efforts to upgrade, and private companies' adaptation in their interaction with state and other actors. The free market, in which large assemblers pursued their own interests, could not change the traditional system of exports of final products based on imported parts. The state initiated and drove the changes, and reflexive actors redefined their interests in interactions with other actors.

Also in the course of liberalization and globalization, the Korean government did not discard its industrial policies, unlike Latin American countries. Rather, the Korean government has continuously used strategic industrial policies of promoting domestic industries. More importantly, the Korean government's priority in industrial policies shifted in the late 1990s and 2000s from exclusive allocation of physical inputs to nurturing inclusive and collaborative networks. In the past,

---

[13] Personal interviews with Engine parts makers on June 23, 2010; personal interview with a muffler-maker in China on July 12, 2011.

[14] Personal interview with a senior manager of a car-seat maker Dae Won on July 6, 2010.

the Korean government focused on accumulation of large capital which was provided exclusively to large export corporations to realize economy of scale. However, the government's direct financial support for large conglomerations no longer exists, although offices remain for key industries in the Ministry of Industry (MoI).[15] More noteworthy is that the Korean state developed a new version of developmentalism which expands and improves collaborative networks via innovation consortia, rather than simply giving R&D tax credits and cash directly to individual corporations, as in the US model (Story 2012).

Why has the Korean state changed its priority of industrial policy, from nurturing large assemblers of export products to upgrading the industrial ecosystem for an innovation-oriented economy? First, since the late 1980s, the industrial policy-makers and political leaders began to recognize the problem of final assembly-oriented industrialization based on foreign inputs including parts, materials, and machines. In this foreign input-dependent and large assemblers-centered industrialization, export of final assembled products such as automobiles caused a chronic foreign trade deficit of intermediate inputs (Kim, Dohoon 2014: 20). In addition, the Korean government began to recognize the limits of a physical input-oriented economy based on low wages and low technology. Particularly as China and Southeast Asian countries were catching up rapidly by using low wages and assembly jobs, Korean industrial experts began to think that Korea needed to upgrade its industries to a more technology-intensive and value-added system, as we will explore.

How has the Korean government implemented its policies to change from an inputs-oriented to an innovation-oriented system? First, the government focused on support for R&D activity, instead of mobilizing physical inputs. As we show in Figure 3.1, Korea increased its R&D activity more dramatically than any other advanced country, from 0.56% of GDP in 1979 to 1.7% in 1991, and to 4.29% in 2014, the highest percentage in the OECD countries. In the 1970s, R&D activity in Korea was insignificant because the traditional growth strategy in Korea was input-oriented, particularly capital-input-oriented growth based on simple technology. However, since the mid-1980s, Korea began to focus on technology-oriented growth and dramatically increased its R&D spending in the 2000s.

However, the total R&D growth in Korea is mainly related to the government's shift in the priority of industrial policy to build innovation-oriented systems. The Korean government has rapidly increased its R&D investment, particularly since 2000, by 10.1% on average per year. The share of small and medium-sized firms in the Korean government R&D support significantly increased from 15% in 1991 to 62% in 2009.[16] In addition, government R&D support engendered private R&D activities rather than replaced them. As many empirical studies show, growth of

[15] Personal interview with former Vice Minister of Knowledge Economy on June 22, 2015.
[16] Ministry of Science, ICT, and Future Planning, *Yungugaebalhwaldong Josa Bogoso* (Korean) [Survey of Research and Development in Korea] (Years. Seoul: MSIFP).

government R&D spending is closely related to growth of private firms' R&D investment (Kim, Kiwan 2007: 227; Choi, Daesung 2014: 5). Many corporations in my personal interviews reported that in order to get government R&D support, they also had to invest in R&D and employ more engineers and researchers, not only because they had to develop a preliminary idea and proposal, but also because they needed to implement their own proposals.[17]

More importantly for building an innovation-oriented industrial ecosystem in the course of globalization, the Korean government focused on expanding and reinforcing industrial linkages by promoting collaborative R&D consortia among large corporations and SMEs. The Korean government mainly use research consortia, in which public research institutes, Original Equipment Manufacturers (OEMs), parts suppliers, and universities worked together. The Korean government and public research institutes work as convener, although private companies are in the driver's seat in the consortia research project. In order to develop the industrial ecosystem, the government first conducts a study on demands, and then invites public research institutes such as the Korean Evaluation Institute of Industrial Technology (KEIT) to recruit participants and coordinate projects, such as development of a chassis module corner. Even in the process of a demand survey, industrial technocrats work together with trade associations and industrial experts at universities.

According to personal interviews of then-participants in the process of drafting the Special Law for Promotion of Parts and Materials, officials and industrial experts in trade associations, government research institutes, and universities worked together, analyzing the value chains of every product in detail, to determine how much value belongs to Korea when a Korean final product is exported. They then sought solutions to questions, such as who can make the parts, which parts are more important, what kinds of technology and skills do Korean parts-makers need, and what kinds of support do they need.[18]

Notably, the Korean government has connected large customers and parts suppliers in so-called "customer-related" projects of developing parts and materials. For example, a senior manager of the Materials & Components Planning Team in the Korea Institute for Advanced Technology (KIAT) identifies the "customer-related" method as one cause of success:

We have conducted many customer-related projects since the early 2000s. Only when parts makers have their customer's firm commitment of purchasing the parts that they will develop do we support the project. In the past, parts makers

---

[17] Personal interview with a senior manager at the MK Electron, Co. LTD on November 19, 2015.

[18] Personal interview with a senior manager of Korean Association of Machinery Industry on June 24, 2015; personal interview with then-directors of Ministry of Commerce, Industry and Energy on May 27, 2015.

developed without any plan of how to commercialize....In these customer-related projects, we assess the performance and market situation, particularly foreign competitors' situation, with the part-maker together and sometimes change the proposal and target.[19]

Actually, customer-related projects achieved greater success at commercialization than simply providing financial support for R&D. For example, the rate of commercialization in Korean government supported R&D projects for SMEs is approximately 40%, whereas the rate of commercialization of customer-related R&D projects is 77.8%.

More notably, the collective learning and innovation capabilities of the Korean R&D consortia surpass American R&D tax credits and cash awarded directly to companies. Consortia participants in Korea report that most important for them is not simply the size of the R&D fund, but the collaborative networks developed through the consortia. A medium-sized lens maker for Samsung smartphones emphasized in my personal interview the importance of participation in the government research consortia:

> The reason we participate in the public R&D projects is not simply the amount of cash, but we want to enter and keep the close networks available through government research institutes and the many customers and related research institutes. Once we conduct a collective project, they may offer another project related to us.[20]

The formal innovation networks supported by the Korean government and informal networks of private firms and research institutes are mutually reinforcing and tend to improve the industrial commons in the collective ecosystem. For example, a semiconductor parts-maker with long-term relations with Samsung could participate in a new government World Premium Materials (WPM) project with Samsung SDI because other participants recognize this company's specialty of melting and alloying materials.[21] A senior manager of a supplier that originally made Samsung electronics parts reports how participation developed in a new consortium for development of automobile parts due to their existing industrial networks:

> As we keep contacts with public research institutes to conduct government projects, they know what we are doing. Thus they came to know our work on developing an anti-drowsiness camera. Because the government considers this

[19] Personal interview at KIAT on June 4, 2015.
[20] Personal interview at Sekonix Co., Ltd on November 12, 2015.
[21] Personal interview at MK Electron, Co. LTD on November 17, 2015.

technology important for our industries, they offered us research support....In this project, Hyundai MOBIS and other automobile suppliers participate because our firm alone cannot develop the part. We need an automobile, and then we need to develop software. That is why and how we collaborate.[22]

In contrast to simple R&D tax credits and cash giveaways directly channeled to individual firms, the new version of Korean developmentalism focuses on nurturing learning and innovation abilities by expanding collaborative networks in which formal and informal networks reinforce each other. Both Korean government and public institutes work as conveners and coordinators of these networks. With these domestic networks nurtured by the government, Korean lead firms bring their home suppliers overseas, while Korean firms on foreign soil have connections with their home base, continuously upgrading their home production.

---

[22] Personal interview at Sekonix Co., Ltd on November 12, 2015.

3

Locating Korea Historically

Korea's economic system has significantly changed since the 1980s, from total mobilization and *dirigisme* by the authoritarian state to a cogovernance system based on private initiatives in investment decisions. The state's role also changed, from direct husbandry of national champions equipped to compete in the international market to more indirect support of firm-led investments and nurturing industrial linkages for an innovation-led economy. Now, the Korean state focuses more on developing an industrial ecosystem rather than directly targeting a few large national champions. However, the Korean state still plays an active role in building and upgrading national strategic industries for export-led growth. Before examining in detail what makes for continuity and change in the evolution of Korean capitalism, this chapter provides an overview of changes and continuity in Korean capitalism, focusing first on changes in developmental strategy from input-oriented to innovation-based growth; second, changes in class alliances; and third, changes in policy instruments and governance methods.

Changes in Developmental Strategy

The Korean economy has rapidly grown since the 1960s. Yet this growth was not due to mobilization of cheap labor or massive capital inputs, but due to changes in developmental strategies, from highly input-oriented to high value-added and innovation-oriented growth. This transformation occurred not by voluntary actions in the free market, but by the state's initiatives and private firms' responses.

The Korean economy has grown more rapidly than any other state. In order to measure how well the Korean economy performed, we use the percentile ranks of GDP per capita as seen in Figure 3.1.[1] GDP per capita is normally used to measure how well a country performed economically, especially to measure a country's relative performance in comparison to other countries. But absolute ranking of GDP per capita has problems in indicating its relative performance. For example, 5th highest score among 10 examinees is different from 5th highest score among

---

[1] I thank my friend Jaehong Yi for this idea.

Changes by Competition: The Evolution of the South Korean Developmental State. Hyeong-ki Kwon, Oxford University Press (2021). © Hyeong-ki Kwon. DOI: 10.1093/oso/9780198866060.003.0003

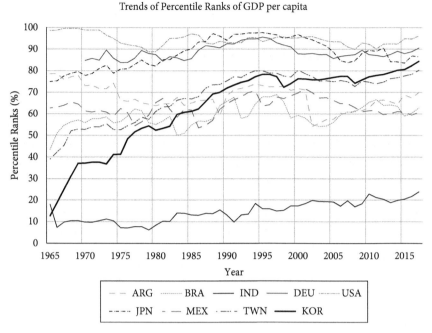

Figure 3.1. Trends of Percentile Ranks of GDP Per Capita
Source: Calculated from GDP per capita data of the World Bank.

100 examinees. To fix this problem, we use the percentile rankings. The percentile rank of a raw score is interpreted as the percentage of examinees in the norm group who scored at or below the score of interest. The mathematical formula is

$$\frac{Fb + 0.5 * Fa}{N} * 100\%$$

where *Fb* (frequency below) is the frequency of all scores below the score of interest, *Fa* (frequency at) is the frequency of the score of interest, and *N* is the number of examinees in the sample. For example, when there is only one 5th highest score, 5th highest score among 10 examinees is calculated as 55%, and 5th highest score among 100 examinees as 95.5%. Now that percentile ranks can be a consistent measure irrespective of examinees' size (total number of countries), percentile ranks can keep track of relative economic performances of a country through years.

As seen in Figure 3.1, the percentile growth of the Korean economy in GDP per capita is striking, from one of the lowest ranking worldwide at 12% in 1965 to one of the highest at 84.4% in 2017. In contrast to other countries' performance: India remained among the lower-ranking groups, from 18.0% in 1965 to 23.9% in

2017, while Argentina and Mexico declined, from 78.5% in 1965 to 70.0% in 2017, and from 62.7% in 1965 to 60.8% in 2017, respectively. Although Japan and Taiwan performed well, their growth is not as large as Korea's: Japan rose from 75.0% in 1965 to 86.4% in 2017, while Taiwan rose from 39.0% in 1965 to 80.3% in 2017. Germany and the United States stayed relatively in the highest-ranking group: Germany rising from 84.8% in 1970 to 90.5% in 2017; the United States from 98.7% in 1965 to 96.2% in 2017.

However, Korea has economically grown using not the same methods, including low wages and an input-oriented strategy. On the contrary, due to changes in its developmentalism, Korea could achieve rapid economic growth successfully for such a long time. In its early phases of industrialization, Korea pursued large-scale assembly production of final products using cheap labor, disciplined by the state, while importing intermediate inputs including machines, parts, and materials. As Eichengreen and Chung (2004) point out, the Korean growth strategy until the 1980s showed only quantitatively extensional growth in which Korean firms adopted proven technology from foreign countries and operated with large-scale inputs of capital and cheap labor. They did not need special efforts to innovate, although they could effectively learn the production skills through large-scale operation. Their effective strategies were to copy or modify, rather than innovate. Korean large firms were interested in the government policy and increasing market shares, rather than profitability in the market because they heavily relied on the state's control over finance and strategic allocation of credit (Park, Taegyeon 1997: 179–181; Ko, Youngsun 2007: 6–66).

While pursuing an input-oriented growth strategy, the Korean state mobilized massive capital not only from domestic savings but from abroad, and funneled it exclusively to a few strategically selected firms to maximize its effectiveness, given the limited resources. For example, in order to build the heavy chemical industries (HCI), the Korean government used financial support, including public financial investment and loans, private bank lending, and foreign loans. Particularly, the government established the National Investment Fund (NIF) in 1974. Domestic financial institutions were legally forced to buy the NIF bonds. Approximately 60% of the NIF was invested in strategically targeted HCI industries from 1974 to 1979. In addition, the Korean Developmental Bank (KDB)'s share of total equipment investment lending was almost 50% in 1979; and approximately 63% of total bank loans were provided as preferential policy loans in that year. Most domestic financing funds had been funneled exclusively into large corporations in strategically selected industries. The excessively skewed allocation of credit, controlled by the state, was targeted at firms in most cases to realize the economy of scale (Amsden 1989: 68–72, 88–112; Koo and Kim 1992: 128, 134–138; Rhee 1994: 71–76).

Table 3.1. Changes of Contributors to Economic Growth in Korea (unit: %)

		1971–1980	1981–1990	1991–1995	1996–2000	2001–2006
GDP growth rate		7.0	8.4	7.5	4.3	4.5
Growth Rate	Capital Stock	13.0	10.8	13.0	8.1	5.3
	Labor	3.5	2.1	2.2	0.6	0.3
	TFP	0.6	4.0	2.5	1.8	2.8
Contribution	Capital Stock	57.1	34.2	44.8	47.8	33.6
Rate	Labor	34.4	18.3	21.9	9.9	4.7
	TFP	8.5	47.4	33.3	42.3	61.7

Source: KIET (2008) e-KIET, table 2.

In order to realize this economy of scale, the state, particularly the Ministry of Industry (MoI),[2] controlled market entry before 1995, for example when Samsung was restricted to enter the automobile industry. After selecting the best performers or followers of the state developmental policy, the Korean state provided these large corporations with significant policy finance for building facilities and operation, and with production sites, energy, and skilled labor. The corporations worked by government policies, not by market profits. Hence, they were most concerned with the government's policy direction and selection, rather than with profitability in the market (Kim, Dohoon 2014: 21–23).

However, Korea now has changed from an input-oriented economy, based on the massive capital inputs and cheap labor of the 1970s, to more qualitative, innovation-oriented growth based on total factor productivity (TFP), mostly realized by R&D and innovation. As seen in Table 3.1, the contribution rate of capital inputs to Korean economic growth changed from 57.1% on average in the 1970s to only 33.6% in the 2000s, whereas the contribution rate of the TFP significantly increased from only 8.5% in the 1970s to 61.7% in the 2000s. Since the mid-1990s, Korean firms began to shift from quantitative expansion growth to endogenous growth based on productivity and innovation. Now, rather than selecting a few large firms and building national champions to realize the economy of scale, the Korean state is more concerned with building an industrial ecosystem or idea-generating innovation networks of multiple actors. The developmental

---

[2] The Ministry of Industry (MoI) has changed its name several times in Korea, as follows: the Ministry of Commerce and Industry (MCI) in 1948–93, the Ministry of Trade, Industry and Energy (MTIE) in 1993–4, the Ministry of Trade and Industry (MTI) in 1994–8, the Ministry of Commerce, Industry and Energy in 1998–2008, the Ministry of Knowledge Economy (MKE) in 2008–13, and the Ministry of Trade, Industry, and Energy (MTIE) in 2013–present. However, in order to simplify these names, this book uses MCI in 1948–93 and MoI in general.

policy turned from the traditional exclusive system to a more decentralized and inclusive system of governance.

The shift from a traditional input-oriented strategy to a high value-added, innovation-oriented strategy is due to the state's intentional efforts and firms' reactions, as shall be examined in later chapters. State policymakers in Korea do not currently believe that the traditional input-oriented policies are still effective. They believe, rather, that the input-oriented and quantitative expansion strategy can deter their competitiveness in the international market, thus engendering nonperforming loans and over investments. For more than decade, as we will examine in greater detail later, considering the catch-up of Asian low-wage countries as well as advanced countries' technology protectionism since the mid-1980s, Korean policymakers tried to change the chaebols' input-oriented growth strategy to more value-added production specialization. But due to a special economic boom in 1986–88, the efforts to reform the quantitative growth strategy were put off.

Meanwhile, in order to overcome the limitation of input-oriented growth, large corporations diversified their businesses horizontally. For example, Samsung diversified its business to petrochemicals, rather than improving its profitability by R&D and innovation.[3] Protracted conflicts occurred between the state's specialization policy and the chaebols' octopus-like diversification. After the Asian financial crisis of 1997, the Korean state successfully disciplined the chaebols to change their debt-based expansion strategy to high-value-added, qualitative specialization by letting many large corporations like Daewoo go out of business.

Changes in developmental strategy, from input-oriented to highly value-added, innovation-oriented growth strategy, incurred changes not only in policy instruments and methods, but also in developmental governance and class alliances. From the Fifth Five-Year Economic Plan of 1987–91, for example, the state turned its developmental method from the existing quantitative planning to a strategy emphasizing private firms' creative initiatives and the state's indirect role in firms' innovation and technology development (Kim, Linsu 1993: 357, 367–374; Yoon, D. 2011: 119–121). The Korean developmental state changed its policy instruments, from massive mobilization of capital and exclusive investment in large-scale facilities to improvement of technology development through R&D. Despite changes in the methods and instruments, the Korean state still continues its developmentalism by which it selects strategic industries and provides many incentives to improve national competitiveness.

[3] Personal interview with former Vice Minister of Knowledge Economy (MKE) on June 22, 2015.

Changes in Class Alliances

As the developmental strategy in Korea has changed from input-oriented to more innovation-based growth, class alliances in the Korean developmental state have changed from exclusive alliance with large corporations to a more inclusive alliance including small and medium-sized enterprises (SMEs) as well as large corporations. Korea can no longer support chaebols exclusively or apparently, as the traditional 1970s developmental state did without incurring the political cost of public criticism due to democratization in 1987. Now, the Korean state developmental policy focuses on nurturing SMEs and building interfirm networks for innovation, rather than building a few national champions to realize an economy of scale. However, shifting its priority to SMEs, Korean developmentalism still maintains alliance with chaebols rather than replacing them. The Korean state's alliance with chaebols continues for securing home market and a new version of developmentalism, although the current Korean developmentalism lost "some of the intimacy and exclusivity" between the state and chaebols which characterized the traditional developmental state (Hundt 2009: 105; Amsden 2013: 17).

In the early phases of Korean state-led development, developmental policy-makers focused on building large corporations in strategic industries, such as heavy chemical industries, to realize an economy of scale. Hence, the Korean state excluded SMEs and nonstrategic industries in credit rationing and funneled massive capital exclusively to a few large corporations. Although there were some policies that supported SMEs in the 1960s and 1970s, SMEs were essentially excluded in the developmental policy (Kienzle and Shadur 1997: 23–32; Jun, Changwan 2004: 99; Ko Youngsun 2007: 49; Kwon, O. Y. 2010: 233–235). In particular, through the HCI drive of the 1970s, economic concentration worsened because the state mobilized massive capital and funneled it to a few large corporations and intentionally controlled market entry. As a result, Korean SMEs were underdeveloped.

However, from the mid-1980s Korean policymakers began to pay attention to the serious imbalance between SME development and large corporations.[4] Following the change in the 1970s to nurture SMEs, Korean governments in the 2000s spent most of the state's policy finance to develop and to support SMEs. From 1971 to 1991, approximately 65% of total Korean bank loans was for policy finance, to build large corporations in strategic industries including steel, oil and chemicals, automobile and semiconductor industries (Park, Taegyeon 1997: 179–181). With this government support, large corporations expanded in size, and thus their debt-equity ratio reached about 400%. After the 1997 crisis, the Korean government has reduced policy finance to 25% of total bank loans in

---

[4] Personal interview with former Minister of the Industry & Energy on April 23, 2013.

Table 3.2. External Financing by Korean Manufacturing SMEs (unit: %)

	Bank loans	Policy Finance	Non-bank Finance	stocks	Corporate Bond	Private Loans	Others
2001	66.2	24.4	2.6	2.2	0.6	2.5	1.5
2002	70.7	23.4	3.1	0.3	0.2	1.9	0.4
2003	73.2	19.4	3.4	0.5	0.5	2.1	0.9
2004	72.7	19.8	3.3	0.6	0.3	3.1	0.2
2005	72.2	22.7	2.8	0.0	0.3	1.3	0.8
2006	71.9	24.8	1.5	0.3	0.4	0.9	0.2
2007	74.3	21.7	2.1	0.0	0.4	1.2	0.2
2008	71.5	21.8	3.9	0.2	0.1	1.8	0.5
2009	62.1	30.8	3.1	0.3	0.8	2.8	0.1
2010	65.9	26.5	3.4	0.2	0.8	1.5	1.6
2011	83.3	10.6	0.9	1.1	3.2	0.4	0.6
2012	80.3	14.2	1.3	0.7	3.4	0.1	0.0

Source: Korea Federation of Small and Medium Business (years) *Survey on SME Financing Problems*; Sohn and Kim 2013: 10.

2012, and policy finance now goes by and large toward SMEs.[5] Large corporations have reduced their reliance on debt down to 86.32% in 2012, relying mostly on internal savings and direct market capital. By contrast, SMEs' debt ratio increased to 134.41% in 2012, relying on policy funds as well as banks (Sohn and Kim 2013: 10; Kang, Seojin 2014: 3).

As seen in Table 3.2, in the 2000s Korean manufacturing SMEs relied on policy finance for approximately 15–30% of total financing, while relying on banks by 60–80%. Notably, the government's policy finance moves in opposite directions with private bank loans to complement them and continuously cover 90–96% of SMEs' external debt with private bank loans. Policy finance for SMEs in GDP is very large in Korea at 6%, compared with the UK, Sweden, Denmark, the United States, Italy, and France, by 0–1% (Sohn and Kim 2013: 22).

The methods of SMEs policy also have changed from simply financing support to nurturing innovation capabilities and building industrial ecosystem for innovation. In the 2000s, the Korean developmental policy for SMEs focuses on R&D assistance, with SME start-ups and financing, building and strengthening technological innovation capabilities, fostering venture businesses, as well as nurturing collaboration with large corporations, like R&D consortia (Kim, Jongil 2007: 124–125, 140; Kwon 2010: 234–235; Yoon, D. 2011: 213; Amsden 2013: 2). For example, state-funded research institutes like the Electronics and Telecommunications Research Institute (ETRI) have focused on helping SMEs to

---

[5] This Korean policy finance is the largest size among those of developed countries. Even Japan's policy finance is 11% of total bank loans in 2010. Only Germany ties at 25%, the highest percentage. See Fitch (2013: 3) and Thurbon (2016: 169, endnote 2).

develop their innovation capabilities since the late 1990s, although large corporations also participate in the collective research consortia. Until the 1990s, the ETRI focused on large national projects to develop cutting-edge technologies with large corporations, including development of automatic telephone switching devices like TDXs, semiconductor DRAMs, and CDMA. However, now the ETRI focuses on developing small projects with SMEs and coordinating the R&D consortia. A senior manager at the ETRI reports its policy change in a personal interview as follows:

> We are still working on the large projects like development of advanced LTE technology. However, our main jobs have changed. Now, we have handed development of cutting-edge technologies over to private companies and we are going to focus more on seed technologies which they commonly use....In addition, rather than going to grand projects as we did in the past, we now go to smaller projects. However, it does not mean a decrease of the ETRI budget. By contrast, the budget has increased continuously. What I am saying is that the priority and shares have changed. In the past, we targeted grand projects with large corporations, but now the target has moved toward SMEs. We now try to do more small projects with SMEs while continuing the development of original technology with large firms.[6]

After the 1997 Asian financial crisis, the Korean government began to focus on nurturing SME capabilities for innovation and research, not only to increase employment, but more importantly, to upgrade Korean industrial competitiveness by developing knowledge-intensive industries.

In Korea of the 2000s, the state could hardly directly provide chaebols with preferential support, not simply because of public criticism, but more importantly, because policymakers themselves believed that the traditional developmental methods of funneling massive inputs exclusively to a few large corporations and pursuing debt-based expansion are no longer effective for national competitiveness.[7]

However, despite the shift of policy priority to SMEs, the Korean state still continues its basic alliance with large corporations. Even in the process of liberalization and democratization in the 1980s and 1990s, the Korean state continued the industrial structure dominated by large corporations, enduring the criticism of fair trade for market competition, because policymakers believed that without large corporations, they could not achieve the effectiveness of their

---

[6] Personal interview with a senior manager at the Intellectual Property Management Department of ETRI, on April 18, 2013.

[7] Personal interview with a senior official of the R&D Strategy Planning Bureau in the Ministry of Industry on June 18, 2018; Thurbon (2016: 152).

developmental policy (Lim, Haeran 1998: 8–9; Amsden 2013; Hundt 2014: 5–7; Zhang 2014: 226–227). Even in the Asian financial crisis of 1997, which we will explore later, when large corporations' reckless, debt-based expansion was regarded as a major cause for the crisis and chaebols became the target of society-wide reform, the state tried to correct the chaebols' bad practices rather than fundamentally change the chaebol-dominant structure. The state utilized large corporations for its developmental strategy rather than discard them. Now, the Korean state focused on promotion of more collaborative interfirm relations for an innovation-oriented economy. The government needed large corporations for their legitimacy based on economic growth, whereas large corporations collaborated with the state for their business (Shin 1994: 32; Yoon, D. 2011: 61, 250).

Korea's support of SMEs does not mean the demise of developmentalism, contrary to DS demise theorists' argument that even neoliberal states like the United States support SMEs. In contrast to the US SME policy, which focuses on the just provision of general services available to every SME, the Korean state's SME policies are more strategic and selective for developmentalism. For example, the special policy for promotion of venture firms in the Kim Dae-jung administration (1998–2002) targeted the nurturing of hi-tech startups, particularly in the ICT industries (Chang, Jiho 2005; Kim, Jongil 2007: 125). Venture firms were selected not by the market but by the government's selection criteria. The Kim Dae-jung administration also enacted the then-year Special Law for Promotion of Parts and Materials in 2001. The Special Law was extended another ten years, from 2012 to 2022, based on evaluation of its successful effects. The Special Law was also extended into the Special Act for the Promotion of Material, Parts, and Equipment Industries as a constant law in December 2019 by the Moon Jae-in administration (2017–present). The special law aimed at both reversing the trade deficit of parts and developing more collaborative and innovative industrial networks between the large Original Equipment Manufacturers (OEMs) and parts suppliers in a national economy, particularly in the automobile and electronics industries.

The Roh Moo-hyun administration (2003–08) also emphasized the "selection and concentration" strategy in nurturing SMEs. For example, this administration strategically aimed at building the "innovation business SMEs." Government support targeted the approximately 10,000 venture and innovation firms and 40,000 innovation candidates, recognized and selected by the government, not by the free market. The government's innovation-oriented activities included development of new technology and products, their commercialization, technology assistance, and technology funding, and building regional networks (MoFE 2006; Chamyeo Jungboo Special Briefing Team of State Affairs 2008: 160–169, 180).

The conservative governments, including the Lee Myung-bak (2008–13) and Park Geun-hye (2013–17) administrations, continued the industrial policy laws enacted by the former progressive governments, including the Special Laws for

Promotion of Parts and Materials, and developed similar but differently-named developmental policies for SMEs, such as "Promotion of Korean Hidden Champions" in the Lee administration and the Innovation Center for Creative Economy in the Park administration. The Lee Myung-bak administration emphasized globalization of parts suppliers, making new technologies into flagship industries, upgrading SMEs' innovation capabilities, while the Park Geun-hye administration emphasized the innovation cluster for creative economy by matching and supporting collaborative relations between SMEs and large corporations.[8]

Finally, unlike German social corporatism, Korean labor is still excluded in the core policy alliance at the national level, although it has increased its political voice significantly since the democratization of 1987. Actually, more than any other groups, Korean labor and civil associations increased their independent power through political competition in elections after democratization. Throughout industrialization of 1960s and 1980s, Korean labor was severely repressed to secure the competitiveness of national industries with low wages and disciplined labor. Under Korea's authoritarian regimes, workers were restricted from establishing independent trade unions. Following the revision of labor law in 1963, authoritarian governments in Korea directly intervened in labor disputes and repressed collective actions by workers. In the 1960s and 1970s productivity grew, while real wages declined. Until the late 1980s, labor in Korea was the object in economic administration, not the subject in economic decisions (Deyo 1987; Choi, Jang Jip 1989: 299–300; Bello and Rosenfeld 1990; Kim, E. M. 1997: 171, 204; Lee, Jangkyu 2008: 151).

Despite state repression, the labor movement in Korea grew slowly due to the success of Korean industrialization. In particular, the heavy chemical industrialization of the 1970s produced an abundance of collective workers in large-scale workplaces. Workers in the heavy chemical industries were more highly-educated male workers, compared with female workers in the textile industry of the 1960s, creating fertile conditions for a labor movement. Actually, as the political space was opened with democratization in 1987, the Korean labor movement came to explode. The number of strikes skyrocketed from almost zero in 1973, and 98 in 1983, to 3,749 in 1987, while unionization rose from 12.28% in 1986 to 18.60% in 1989 (Gray 2015: 93).

However, Korean labor failed to establish itself as a parapublic partner in the socio-economic decision making at the national level, although it could gain the formal rights of labor, including independent unionism and economic benefits including wage growth and reduced work time (Lee, Yoonkyung 2009; Whitley 2016: 43). Korean labor could not provide a competitive alternative to the existing

---

[8] Personal interview with staff reporter at the business desk in Dong-A Ilbo on September 25, 2014. See also KIET (2008 and Thurbon (2016: 111, 136).

state-led developmentalism even in the economic crisis of the late 1990s, a failure we will explore later. Because Korean labor was organized as company unions, rather than as German-style industry unions, it had difficulty in developing a unified class voice, particularly suffering from the inside-outsider problem with irregular workers. Furthermore, Korean labor called for legal guarantees of labor rights, welfare states, and correction of the skewed distribution of wealth, but they failed to gain public support with a persuasive alternative for economic development (Deyo 1987; Kim, E. M. 1997: 209–210; Jun, B.Y. 2008).

Even at the company level, Korean labor has been excluded in key decision making, unlike Germany's unions and works councils (Kim and Shin 2004; Kong 2012; Song, Jiyeoun 2014; Witt 2014b; Jo, Hyungjae 2016). Against workers' aggressive confrontation in the course of democratization, Korean employers developed a more engineer-oriented production system, excluding general workers in the decision-making of how to organize work, as seen in the Hyundai automobile (Song, Jiyeoun 2014; Jo, Hyungjae 2016: 25–31, 50–80). This is in contrast to German social corporatism in which labor gained a legitimate voice in work organization, while proposing a relevant vision of how to create national wealth, as seen in the Volkswagen 5000 project in the course of globalization. Although Korean firms adopted high-performance work organizations, such as employee participation in production improvement, a more top-down organization based on production engineers has been adopted, different from collaborative deliberation with employee representatives (Kim and Bae 2005; Kong 2012; Jo, Hyungjae 2016; Whitley 2016: 53). Even after democratization, Korean labor failed to gain parapublic status, as German labor did in social corporatism.

Changes in the Policy Instruments and Governance Methods

Not only liberals but also many classical DS theorists hold that the Korean developmental state came to demise because it lost its strong power instruments, such as state control over finance and pilot agencies like the Economic Planning Board (EPB), to unilaterally discipline businesses, while assuming some institutional elements as criteria to measure strength relative to business (Moon 1994; Moon and Kim 1996; Kim, E.M. 1997; Chang and Evans 2005; Chang, Chung and Lee 2012). In the past, the Korean state's developmental policy instruments were mainly the state's control over finance and credit allocation, as well as various state regulations on firms' market entry and their imports of foreign technology and parts. Now Korean financial and trade markets have been liberalized. The Korean state both deregulated the rules on market entry and dissolved the EPB, which many DS theorists and neoliberals regarded as a symbol for the demise of Korean DS (Fields 2014: 54–55; Chang, Park, and Yoo 1998; Wade and Veneroso 1998).

However, liberalization and deregulation do not mean the demise of Korean state developmentalism. Traditional policy instruments such as state control over finance and regulations on market entry are no longer effective for developmentalism, as developmental strategy changes from input-oriented to innovation-driven growth, and policy goals shift from building national champions to nurturing industrial ecosystems for innovation. Although a centralized pilot agency like the EPB dissolved in 1994, the state governing system for industrial developmentalism has expanded through competition among industry-related ministries inside the government, as we will examine later in Chapters 6 and 7. Now the Korean state utilizes more R&D expenditures to improve firms' innovation capabilities, rather than controlling direct investments in facilities. It focuses on collaborative R&D consortia of firms, research institutes, and universities, rather than building individual firms to realize the economy of scale.

Concerning changes in policy instruments, the Korean state abandoned many regulations, particularly the market entry regulation, control of imports, and price controls through liberalization of the 1980s–1990s. Actually, state control over market entry and parts imports was a key instrument for the Korean developmental state of the 1970s. Based on seven individual industry promotion laws, such as the Automobile Industry Promotion Law and the Shipbuilding Promotion Law, the Ministry of Commerce and Industry (MCI) had permission of market entry and imports of foreign technology, and even allocation of production volume in the cause of nurturing large-scale production. A former senior official of MCI comments on MCI's power in a personal interview as follows:

Was it determined by the market when Samsung and LG tried to decide the prices of TVs and refrigerators? Until 1982, I decided it in the department of home electronics of the MCI, based on the costs of parts and assembly. The price control bureau of the EPB supervised it later. That was almost a planned economy. Of course, we did it because they were monopolistic items. Later, the price control was removed. We changed to a report system. That was a kind of revolution. Although we were basically a market economy, we controlled a lot. In our MCI, we controlled the price; the sales volume, we also decided it; whether we would sell the color TV in domestic market or not, we decided it; and we also decided the imports of parts and materials. Even when executives of Samsung would go abroad, they needed our permission.[9]

As former bureaucrats in the MCI say, the government had almost life-or-death authority on private firms. According to the memoirs of former CEO of Hyundai

---

[9] Personal interview with a senior official of R&D Strategy Planning Bureau in the Ministry of Industry on June 18, 2018. He had worked in the Ministry of Industry from 1978 to 1999, and after that, recently got the job in the Ministry of Industry again.

(Korea's largest automobile corporation), in the 1970s automotive corporations should not only get state approval of business, but also compete against each other for the number of cars allocated by the government (Jung 2000: 144–148).[10] Even in 1994, when Samsung tried to enter the automobile industry, the Korean government prohibited it by the introduction of technology permits, although thereafter the government liberalized market entry regulation (Kim, Yong-bok 1996: 207–222). As the MCI liberalized the key instrument of market regulations, it had to find another instrument and new role for developmentalism to improve the competitiveness of national industries: indirect support by R&D incentives to nurture industrial ecosystems for innovation, rather than giving up its developmental policy.

Meanwhile, another key policy instrument was policy finance to build national champions based on input-oriented strategy. In actuality, state-led capitalism at its height in the 1970s meant the state's total mobilization of almost 65% of domestic capital and rationing it exclusively to the strategic heavy chemical industries by its control over banks and financial institutes. State control of finance in the 1970s consisted mainly of commercial banks and state-owned special banks. Through these financial institutes, the Korean state used preferential bank loans and differential access to domestic and foreign credit in favor of large corporations as policy instruments for developmentalism (Rhee 1994: 66, 71–75). By its institutional capability to mobilize and distribute capital, the state could discipline the large corporations in a reciprocal exchange of firms' compliance and favorable state support (Amsden 1989, 2001).

However, the Korean state now liberalized its financial control system by making central banks independent, privatizing state-owned banks, adopting global standards in lending, and opening financial markets. In addition, the amount of policy finance was significantly reduced. Even up until 1992, the size of policy finance reached approximately 50% of total bank lending, on which private firms heavily relied. However, starting with the Kim Young-sam administration (1993–97), policy loans began to reform. As the size of policy finance declined with financial deregulation, large corporations began to seek out foreign financial markets with lower interest rates, which resulted in the Asian financial crisis of 1997.[11]

However, unlike the DS demise theorist arguments, the reduction of policy finance does not mean the demise of Korean state-led developmentalism. For example, the national pension fund in Korea was established not for the purpose of civil welfare, but for development to build the heavy chemical industries in the

---

[10] CEOs of the automobile corporations were also concerned with their personal confinements and frequent commands by the government, particularly the KCIA (Jung 2000: 144–145).
[11] Personal interview with a former senior official in the MoI, on June 11, 2018; Yoon, D. (2011: 256).

1970s. However, after the Asian financial crisis of 1997, the Korean government reformed pension fund governance, seemingly following the neoliberal IMF's conditional requests. The Korean government introduced private pensions and repealed the compulsory deposit system for national pension funds, while investing the funds in the financial market. However, these reforms do not mean a wholesale transformation to a neoliberal free market system and abandoning developmentalism. On the contrary, the Korean government still maintains its developmentalism even in the changed methods.

For example, although almost all Korean national pension funds (98%) were invested in the financial market in 2009, its largest share by approximately 80% was invested in buying government and public bonds, including Industry Finance Bonds and SME Finance Bonds, as well as Public Power Corporate Bonds, Telegraph and Telephone Bonds, and Currency Stabilization Bonds. They are still used for state developmentalism to complement the government budget. In addition, 7% of the National Pension Fund was used to buy corporate bonds, but they still have developmentalist characteristics because the corporate bonds aim to protect Korean large corporations from foreign M&As. For example, the national pension fund has more than 5% of shares of Korea's 100 largest corporations, including Samsung Electronics, POSCO, Hyundai Automobiles, LG Chemicals, Shinhan Finance, Kia Automobiles, and SK Innovation. Most Korean large corporations still rely on the Korean government to stabilize their ownership as well as provide cashflow (Kim, Chung-soo 1998: 53; Joo, E. 2009; Kim and Joo 2010; 11; Eun, Min Su 2011: 138–139, 159–164).

Although state control of private banks became deregulated, the Korean state still has significant financial instruments enough to intervene in strategic industries, such as government treasury investments and loans and government-owned special developmental banks, including the Korea Development Bank (KDB), the Korea Exchange Bank (KEB), and the Industry Bank of Korea (IBK). The Korean government also offers new tax incentives and nonfinancial instruments, including regulations like Seoul Metropolitan Area Development, tax investigation, and overseas market development.[12] In particular, tax incentives became an important instrument, as the effectiveness of direct policy finance came to decline. In the 1970s, the temporary tax credit system for investment was introduced, but was ineffective because a large amount of policy finance was provided. However, from 1998 to 2007 the amount of tax reduction increased by five times, enabling the state to support firms' investment in facility and R&D. Particularly, the Roh Moo-hyun administration (2003–07) increased tax cut rates by 15% and expanded its targets (Yoon, D. 2011: 64, 256).

The Korean state still has power to coordinate the liquidation of faltering large corporations. Until the 1980s, the state directly intervened in the liquidation of

---

[12] Personal interview with former Minister of Industry and Energy on April 23, 2013.

insolvent large corporations in an informal and discretionary way (Lee, Kim, and Han 1989; Han, S. 1994: 206–230). The state unilaterally decided the liquidation and the M&A with the justification of improving the competitiveness of national industries. Through state-led liquidation, the Korean government increased the scale of chaebols and disciplined the businesses. After the 1997 Asian financial crisis, the state's intervention in the liquidation process became more formally and legally institutionalized, compared with the state intervention in the military-authoritarian periods. However, this does not mean that state intervention in the liquidation process of large corporations disappeared. Under the justification that large corporations' insolvency can have significant impacts on the national economy, the Korean government continues its intervention in the liquidation process. For example, the Kim Daejung administration actively intervened in liquidation of banks and large corporations, particularly in the so-called Big Deal corporate swap, although unlike in the past, the Kim government coordinated the liquidation and corporate swap process through a formal procedure seemingly led by creditor financial institutions (Kim, Lee, Jung, and Lee 2003: 47–48, 170, 176–178; Kim, K.W. 2001: 110; 120). In 2000, the Kim Dae-jung government enacted the Corporate Restructuring Promotion Act. Based on this law, the Lee Myung-bak administration (2008–13) also intervened in corporate restructuring (Yoon 2011: 256–258).

The Korean state did not shrink or retreat, even in the course of liberalization. On the contrary, it expanded its developmental capabilities, although the pilot agency EPB came to dissolve. Ironically, as the influence of traditional developmental agencies like EPB and the MCI retreated, new agencies including the Ministry of Information and Communication (MIC) and the Ministry of Science and Technology (MoST) emerged to fill the vacuum, in competition with existing developmental agencies including the EPB and the Ministry of Industry (MoI). Contrary to many DS demise accounts, competition among industry-related ministries resulted in expansion of policy capabilities and affiliates, through the 1980s and 2000s, in the process of liberalization and globalization.

As seen in Table 3.3, in order to lead the initiative in the national developmental agenda, the MoI, the MIC, and the MoST built competitively many affiliates including policy research institutes, research institutes of industrial science and technology, as well as industry-related associations. In the 1960s, the Korean state had only two R&D-related institutes, but later the industry-related ministries competitively built their policy and R&D institutes, 18 affiliates in the 1980s and 9 affiliates in the 1990s. A chief of the R&D strategy team in the MoI recalls how the industry-related ministries built their affiliate organizations as follows:

The Korea Institute of Industrial Technology (KIIT) is actually established by the MoI, in the process of its competition with the MoST, which had the Korea Institute of Machinery and Metals (KIMM), Korea Institute of Science and

Table 3.3.   Establishments of Affiliate Institutes for Policy and Technology Research

	Policy Research Institute	R&D Institute for Industrial Innovations	R&D Institute for Science & Technology
1980s	Korea Institute for Industrial Economics and Technology (KIET, 1981)	National Construction Laboratory Institute (NCLI, 1983)	Korea Research Institute of Bioscience and Biotechnology (KRIBB, 1985)
	Institutes for Communications Research (ICR, 1985)	Electronics and Telecommunications Research Institute (ETRI, 1985)	Korea Basic Science Center (KBSC, 1988)
	Center for Science and Technology Policy (CSTP, 1987)	Korea Electrotechnology Research Institute (KERI, 1985)	Institute of Space Science and Astronomy (ISSA, 1986)
	Korea Energy Economics Institute (KEEI, 1986)	Korea Center for Machinery and Materials (KIMM, 1986)	Korea Aerospace Research Institute (KARI, 1989)
	Korea Labor Institute (KLI, 1988)	Korea Food Research Institute (KFRI, 1987)	Korea Polar Research Institute (KOPRI, 1987)
	Korea Institute for International Economic Policy (KIEP, 1989)	Korea Institute of Industrial Technology (KIIT, 1989)	
1990s	Korea Institute of Public Administration (KIPA, 1991)	Korea Institute of Energy Conservation (KIER, 1991)	Korea Institute of Technology and Technology Information (KIST, 1991)
	Science and Technology Policy Institute (STEPI)	Korea Railroad Research Institute (KRRI, 1996)	National Fusion R&D Center (NFRI, 1996)
	Korea Environmental Industry and Technology Institute (KEITI, 1992)	Korea Maritime Institute (KMI)	Korea Institute of Oriental Medicine (KIOM, 1994)
	Korea Research Institute for Vocational Education and Training (KRIVET, 1997)		

*The parenthesis includes the acronym of the institute and the year of its establishment.
Source: Yoon, D. 2011, pp. 114, 164.

Technology (KIST), and the Electronics and Telecommunications Research Institute (ETRI). The MoI made it in 1989 by emphasizing the necessity of industry-related application technology, because the MoI did not have the institutional instruments, when it began to focus on technology innovation policy as a new industrial policy. In addition, while developing technology policies based on the KIIT, the MoI established more affiliate research institutes, such as the Korea Institute for Advancement of Technology (KIAT), and the Korea Institute of Industrial Technology Evaluation and Planning (KIITEP).... Under the KIIT, there had been a skill training center, based on which we established the Korea Polytechnic University.[13]

These affiliates expanded the industry-related ministries' industrial functions and capabilities by providing information on companies and directly coordinating the public-private R&D consortia.

For example, the Korea Core Industrial Technology Investment Association (KITIA) was established in 2001 by the initiation of the Ministry of Industry (MoI) in order to connect capital investors with parts suppliers. The KITIA as a nonprofit corporation of investors is seemingly independent of the MoI, because its seed money comes from membership. However, as a senior manager of M&A Desk at the KITIA reports in a personal interview, "its actual operation relies on the MoI 100%" by running the MoI's programs, such as investor-related technology developments, and inbound and outbound M&A, which the MoI supported financially under the Special Law for Parts and Material Industry Promotion in 2001–22.[14]

Meanwhile, as mentioned earlier, a major alternative instrument for new strategy of developmentalism, based on innovation-led growth, is the R&D incentives and tax incentives. In particular, the R&D support became the MoI's key alternative to traditional instruments like market entry regulations and permission of imports of foreign technology. Actually the MoI gave up the traditional methods of market regulation because those policy instruments and methods were no longer effective for new developmental strategy. A chief of the MoI R&D strategy team says in a personal interview:

> In the past, we enjoyed the permission rights based on the seven individual industry promotion laws. However, how can firms be competitive now if the CEOs should get a permission from a section head to proceed?...In the early 1980s, even Samsung and LG were relatively small and less globalized. They wanted to rely on the government to somehow survive in the global market. However, from a certain time, we began to think inside the MoI how we could decide the price, and how absurd it was to decide whether we would permit or not the introduction of foreign technology. They should decide it based on their own market situation. As they globalize, they have more information than the government....However, we could not do nothing. We found a new role. That is

---

[13] Personal interview with a senior official of the R&D Strategy Planning Bureau in the MoI on June 18, 2018.
[14] Personal interview with a senior manager of the M&A Desk in the Korea Core Industrial Technology Investment Association on June 2, 2015.

R&D. When we saw Japan, they did R&D consortia for development of, say, one mega or two mega DRAM or 5-generation computer and so on.[15]

As seen in Figure 3.2, the Korean government began to focus on R&D in the mid-1980s. The Korean government has increased its R&D expenditure and many R&D-related, indirect incentives, such as preferential finance for R&D to induce private firms' R&D investment since the mid-1980s. For example, total R&D expenditure of GDP in Korea was only 0.32% in 1971 and 0.6% even in 1981, lowest ranking among the countries. But it increased dramatically to 2.6% in 1994, and after the crisis of the late 1990s it further grew to 4.4% in 2014, highest ranking worldwide, although it ranked at about 6th in the sense of absolute amount of R&D.

Unlike many political economists' expectation that state-led developmentalism would recede as the desire for social welfare grew (Levy 2015; Yeung 2017), the

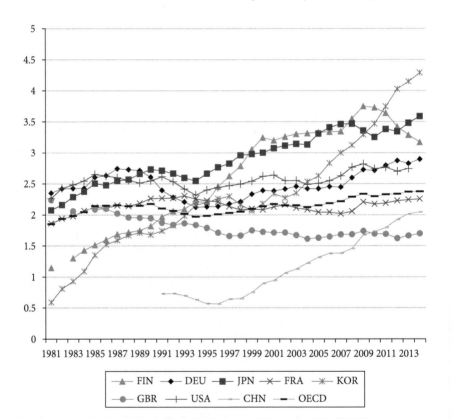

Figure 3.2. R&D Expenditure Trend of Advanced Countries (% of GDP)
Source: OECD Data; https://data.oecd.org/rd/gross-domestic-spending-on-r-d.htm

[15] Personal interview with a senior official of R&D Strategy Planning in the Ministry of Industry on June 18, 2018.

government R&D expenditure as a Korean industrial policy did not decline, as the social welfare expenditure grew. For example, even in the progressive government of Roh Moo-hyun (2003–07), the annual growth rates of government R&D investments was 10.6% on average, higher than the annual growth rates of government budget by 9.9%. If policy funds for R&D are added, the public expenditure is much bigger, because the policy funds for R&D independent of budget, including the Strategic Industry Promotion Fund, the Informatization Promotion Fund, the Science and Technology Promotion Fund, and the Atomic Energy R&D Fund, annually increased by 14.7% on average (Kim, Kiwan 2007: 279).

More importantly, the Korean government's R&D policy differs from those of other advanced economies like the United States in the sense that Korean R&D policy aims mainly at commercialization of industrial technology as a key instrument of selective developmentalism, rather than general services for pure science. For example, in the Korean government's total R&D expenditure in 2007, the R&D for defense is only 13.3%, while the rest, 86.7%, is for non-defense purposes. More noteworthy is that most R&D for nondefense is used for economic development, at 52.9% of the total R&D expenditure. By contrast, in the total R&D expenditure of the US federal government in 2005, the R&D for military defense was 57.1%, while non-defense R&D was only 43% of the total R&D budget, of which health and environment are the largest shares.

As seen in Figure 3.3, this trend in the comparison of government R&D expenditure by countries continues more or less. The Korean government spent more or less 45–50% of its total R&D expenditure for economic development throughout the 2000s. By contrast, in 2018 the US federal government spent most of its R&D budget, at 60% for defense, while using only 38.2% for nondefense, of which health and general science are the largest by 18.7% and 6.6% respectively (Kim, Kiwan 2007: 282–287; Choi Daesung 2014; 34; Hourihan and Pakes 2018).

Although the Korean state changed its goal and method from massive investment in facilities to development of technology and improvement of R&D capabilities, it continues its developmentalism of strategically allocating resources to strategic industries. As Lall (2004) rightly points out, the dramatic growth of R&D in Korea in the last two decades resulted from state developmentalism: "All this was an integral part of its selective industrial policy" (Lall 2004: 21). Although it gave up its traditional quantitative growth strategy, it did not discard the developmental policy to promote strategic industries.

For example, most Korean R&D expenditure aimed at development of industry-related technology by more or less 50%, rather than basic science research as the United States does (KISTEP 2015). Even after giving up specific industrial promotion laws in the mid-1980s, the Korean state set many developmental policies for long-term projects, including the Industry Base Technology Development Project in 1987, the Advanced Technology Development Project called G7 in 1992, the New Industry Promotion Strategy in 1999, the Parts and

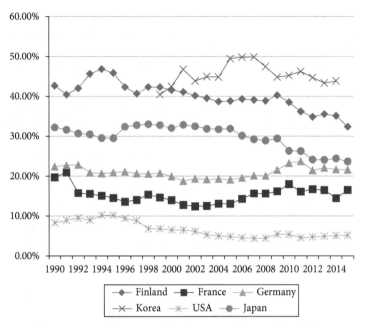

Figure 3.3. Comparison of Economic Development Shares in Total Government R&D Expenditure

Source: OECD Data; http://stats.oecd.org/

Materials Promotion Project in 2001, the Next Generation Growth Engine Project in 2003, and so on. Those projects lasted by and large more than five years, sometimes across different administrations. These new developmental projects selected the strategic industries and intensively supported them under the principle of "selection and concentration" (Kim, Linsu 1997; Lim, Youngil 1999; Yoon, D. 2011: 255). As private corporations grew, the relative share by government expenditure in the total economy declined, although the absolute size increased. Policymakers recognized this shift, and became concerned about effective and strategic usages of the expenditure. For instance, both public and private R&D investments concentrate on specific industries, including electronics, semiconductors, machine, and automobile industries because the government strategically selected them and led the development consortia such as the public-private consortium of CMMA development (Lee and Lim 2001; Kim, Kiwan 2007: 289–292; Kim and Kwon 2017).

Even large Korean corporations which maintain big R&D institutes are concerned with the government's R&D policy, because public R&D support are still significant incentives to them. A senior manager of the Federation of Korean Industries (FKI, trade association of large corporations in Korea) comments on the importance of public R&D incentives in a personal interview:

Korean governments have significantly contributed to the corporations' R&D activities through R&D tax-cut measures. That is why our R&D size of GDP is the world's top, similar with that of Israel. Private corporations began to think that building facilities was not enough; we needed R&D for our competitiveness. That is why companies established their own R&D institutes. Samsung made several big R&D centers. However, against the background of corporations' investment in R&D, there are the government R&D support, particularly R&D tax incentives. I cannot measure the exact amount of government support, but those are very large incentives to large corporations because even our large corporations do not have a big margin in their profits. Even small cuts to their costs can work as big incentives to them.[16]

In the current Korea of 2018, even large corporations which globalize intensively are still very sensitive to the Korean government's indicative planning and industrial policies, not only because the state's R&D support, including tax incentives, contributed to cost cutting, but more importantly, because the Korean state provides many industrial commons, such as large test beds, parts supplier networks, and R&D consortia, which even global corporations cannot create inside their company walls. A director of the FKI (trade association of large corporations) in a personal interview requests more active roles from the Korean government, while complaining that the current progressive Moon Jaein government may reduce the support to them due to economic democratization:

We need the government's increased attention to the policies, such as finding together the next generation growth engines, providing R&D support, providing test beds, and deregulation,...and providing infrastructure....Individual companies needs them, but they cannot make them....Our country is small and thus we cannot separate economy from politics. We need win-win.[17]

Even globalized, large corporations in Korea are concerned about what directions the government emphasizes as industrial policy and what kinds of support, such as tax incentives, they provide, because they need their own competitive sources at home—industrial commons and domestic ecosystem, which individual firms cannot build. Actually, instead of mobilizing large capital and authoritatively allocating it, now the Korean state is actively involved in building the industrial ecosystem for innovation by selective incentives including R&D support. In order to intensively concentrate on the promotion of strategic industries, the Korean state

---

[16] Personal interview with a senior manager of the Federation of Korean Industries (FKI) on May 17, 2018.
[17] Personal interview with a senior manager of the Federation of Korean Industries (FKI) on May 8, 2018.

has used many other policy methods, including tax breaks and technology development support, as well as reducing early investment risks and channeling the financial flow to the selected industries.

To sum up, the Korean state still continues its state developmentalism even in the course of liberalization and globalization. As seen in the policy of promotion of venture firms in the Kim Dae-jung administration (1998–2002), the government, not the market, selected the criteria of the venture firms (Chang, Jiho 2005). When it selects the targeted firms and industries, the Korean government now consults more private specialists and industrialists in the forms of seemingly bottom-up information, including advisory committees, compared with the past. But the state still leads the selection; the collective deliberation with private actors are not equal negotiations but simple consulting.[18] As Witt (2014b: 231) confirms through comparison of national economic systems, the Korean state still strategically coordinates and decides its directions of change for Korean industrial development.

---

[18] Personal interview with Director at General Services Division in the Ministry of Science, ICT, and Future Planning on May 12, 2015.

4

The Classical Developmental State in Korea

This chapter explores the characteristics of the classical developmental state in Korea in the Park Chung Hee era of the 1960s and 1970s, how it was established, and how it evolved. Neoclassical economists and neoliberals emphasize the discontinuity between the 1960s and the 1970s of Korean capitalism in the Park Chung Hee era. They hold that in the 1960s, the Korean economy grew rapidly due to its market orientation and exports based on international comparative advantages, whereas in the 1970s, it moved toward the developmental state by its strategic industry promotion in the heavy chemical industries (HCI) which resulted in the economic crisis of the late 1970s (Stern et al. 1995; Lee, Man-Hee 2010). Most DS scholars also focus on the HCI drive of the 1970s to identify the typical developmental state in Korea (Amsden 1989; Kim, Hyung-A 2004). However, unlike the arguments of neoliberals and some DS theorists, this chapter reveals that the basic characteristics of the Korean classical developmental state, including state-guided capitalism, input-oriented growth strategy by mobilization of domestic and foreign capital, and export-led industrialization, were already established in the 1960s, although the 1970s saw a shift to an extreme variant of developmental state.

Meanwhile, many historical institutionalists hold that Korean state-led developmentalism came from the historical legacy of Japanese colonialism (Comings 1987; Woo 1991; Ahn, Byung-Jik 1993, 1995, 2001; Lee, Dae Kun 1997; Kohli 1999). For example, Kohli holds that the South Korean model of developmental state, authoritarian and architectonic, with state-dominated alliance with business and repressive control of labor, "can be argued to have fallen back into the grooves of an earlier origin and traversed along them, well into the 1980s" (Kohli 1999: 96, 128). Recently, some scholars like Thurbon (2016) also emphasize the historical origin of Korean developmentalism by saying that the developmental mindset was formed by the shared experience of "military training and service under Japanese colonial rule" (2016: 28). She holds that the Korean developmental mindset is inherited from "Japan's approach to nation building through heavy-handed, state-led industrial development" (2016: 29) and continues even up to now.

However, even under the legacy of Japanese colonialism, the Korean economy of the Rhee Syngman administration (1948–60) was not developmentalism but a kind of predatory state (Amsden 1989; Eckert et al. 1990; Chibber 2002: 57–61).

Changes by Competition: The Evolution of the South Korean Developmental State. Hyeong-ki Kwon, Oxford University Press (2021). © Hyeong-ki Kwon. DOI: 10.1093/oso/9780198866060.003.0004

The Rhee Syngman administration did have a strong state capability to control massive capital, including control over the allocation of foreign aid, but it did not have the will of economic developmentalism. Korea could build a model of state-led developmentalism like the export-oriented industrialization (EOI), unlike the import substitution industrialization (ISI) of Latin American countries, not because of historical inheritance of Japanese colonialism, but because even the Park Chung Hee administration reflected upon the failure of its initial import-substitution strategy. Although Japanese developmental methods might provide ideas and insights for Korean developmentalists, they were one of many possible and available ideas for developmentalism. To better understanding the real formation of Korean developmentalism as a distinctive model, this chapter emphasizes the dynamic politics in which key actors make choices and put them into action, while recomposing their identity as well as their strategies through elite competition and rivalry. This chapter examines first how classical Korean state-led developmentalism was formed through dynamic politics in the 1960s, and second, why it evolved to another extreme variant of developmental state in the 1970s.

Formation of Korean Classical Developmentalism

Korea's classical state-led developmentalism had already been established in the 1960s, contrary to the neoclassical economists' discontinuity thesis of a liberal market system in the 1960s and state developmentalism in the 1970s. The idea of the state-led developmentalism prevailed even in the 1950s in Korea, as well as in other developing countries like India and Latin American countries. Unlike India and Latin American countries, Korea pursued export-led industrialization. In order to build national industries for exports, the Korean state focused on nurturing private companies with massive inputs of capital, rather than building pubic corporations as many other developing countries did. Unlike Taiwan and many Latin American countries, Korea established centralized state control over finances, including domestic savings and foreign loans, plus authoritarian power to discipline private firms to invest productively to realize input-oriented growth (Haggard 1990; Amsden 2001).

However, these characteristics of Korean classical developmentalism, including export-oriented industrialization and state-led mobilization and allocation of credit, were constructed by dynamic politics inside and outside the state, and not by the historical inheritance of Japanese colonialism, nor by the domestic market size suggested by the many scholars such as Haggard (1990). Hence formation of the Korean developmental state is the process of formation of key organizational actors, such as leading economic bureaucrats of the Economic Planning Board

(EPB) and the Ministry of Commerce and Industry (MCI), who could form and materialize their ideas in political interaction.

Developmental Ideas and Organizational Agencies

The idea of state-led developmentalism prevailed even in Korea of the 1950s, although it did not materialize due to lack of organizational agency to put it into action. In Korea of the 1950s, almost all political parties, socialist as well as right-wing parties, shared the idea of state-led developmentalism, although they conflicted with one another ideologically (Kang, Lee, and Choi 2008: 14). For example, according to Chung Jina (2007: 25–32), who studied the programs of the political parties under the US Military Government in Korea (1945–8), almost all political parties not only in the taskforce committee to establish a provisional government, but also in the Korean interim government, constituted of right-wing and the neutralparties, shared two basic ideas: first, the state should play an active role in dissolving the feudal system and transforming the landlords' capital to industrial capital; second, the state should lead the industrialization. In addition, throughout the 1950s and 1960s, there were three main alternatives of economic development in Korea, including economic development by private initiatives, state-led development, and social-democratic development. However, the proponents of private initiatives also agreed on the necessity of "state-led economic development plans" (Park, Tae-gyun 2007: 50–65, 100, endnote 161).

Even before Park Chung Hee seized power through a military coup in May 1961, several economic development plans were in motion, including the 1954 Nathan report, the 1959 Three-Year Economic Development Plan, and the Five Year Plan of the Chang Myon administration (1960–1). However, these plans were not materialized due to the lack of organizational agency and developmental will in the government. For example, the Rhee Syngman administration (1948–60) had sufficient power to control businesses because it held monopoly power to allocate foreign aid, the largest sources of finances in 1950s Korea, given the industrialists' weakness and capital shortages. However, President Rhee Syngman succumbed to political consideration, rather than economic development, in allocation of foreign aid (Song, Insang 1994: 149–150; Kim, Jungjoo 2005: 168–169; KEMHCC 2013: 38).

The Rhee administration's basic economic policies were import substitution of consumer products, and upward revaluation of Korean currency to earn more US foreign aid. In the late 1950s, as US aid decreased, the Department of Economic Reconstruction launched a three-year economic plan, but it was driven by the Reconstruction Minister's personal ambition amidst President Rhee's neglect (Kim, Jinhyun 1964: 104–105; Kim, Jungjoo 2005: 173). The three-year plan was announced in December 1959, three months short of the collapse of the Rhee government. President Rhee was basically not interested in economic development, but in economic stabilization and earning more aid from the United States, whose main policy also was economic stabilization (Park, Dongchul 1993: 94–95; Yu, Ho-yul 1996: 86; Lee, Wanbum 2006: 39–45; Kang, Lee, and Choi 2008: 24–29).

Unlike Thurbon (2016)'s definition of DS, the ambition of developmentalism alone was insufficient for state-led developmentalism. Not only ambition but also the capabilities of leading agencies are needed to carry ideas into effective action. With greater ambition for economic development, the military government immediately announced the First Five-Year Economic Development Plan in the late May of 1961, based on the 1959 and 1961 plans of former governments. However, lacking popular support, the military government announced another plan, the Comprehensive Economic Reconstruction Plan made by the Supreme Council for National Reconstruction (so-called Supreme Council Plan) in July 1961, and made another plan, the First Five-Year Economic Development Plan by the Economic Planning Board (EPB) (so-called the EPB plan) in October 1961 (Lee, Kunmi 1996: 537; Lee, Wanbum 2006: 53–54, 95–104, 123; Park, Tae-gyun 2000b: 114–119). However, with the lack of an appropriate leading agency and finance shortage, the military government could not continue its First Five-Year Economic Development Plan.

Formation of Leading Organizations

Park's military government made serious mistakes in initial developmentalism, especially in currency reform, which resulted in economic crisis. Despite its economic blunder, however, Park's military government continued its state-led developmentalism by changing developmental strategy from existing "balanced and comprehensive" and import-substitution industrialization (ISI) to an imbalanced and export-oriented industrialization (EOI). However, these changes to a new version of developmentalism meant changing the leading agencies from revolutionary officers of the Supreme Council to civilian economic bureaucrats around EPB and the Ministry of Commerce and Industry (MCI) (Lee, Byungchun 1999: 154–157; Park, Tae-gyun 2000b: 126, 133). These changes in developmental strategy resulted from power politics inside the state. Changes in developmentalism required both changes in policymakers inside the state and reorganization of relations between state and businesses through a political process.

Initially following the military coup of May 1961, the new military revolutionaries seized the initiative in policymaking by excluding old bureaucrats, United States Agency for International Development (US AID), and chaebols, and recruiting new reform-oriented scholars like Park Heebum (Lee, Sangwoo 1985: 202). However, as their impatient economic policies such as removal of usurious loans and currency reform blundered, the existing relations and relative power of military revolutionaries changed vis-à-vis the United States, chaebols, and civilian economic bureaucrats. Economic bureaucrats gained influence through the process of revising the original Plan in 1962–4.

First, the military government moved in its relationship with the United States from arm's length to collaborative relations. In the early stage of the military government, the United States lost its influence in Korea, as the US News reports:

> With the Army running things in South Korea, the United States finds itself in a changing role. This doesn't mean Korea is lost as an ally. In fact, Korea is more strongly anti-Communist than before the recent coup. New rulers welcome US help, but they have ideas of their own. The day is gone when the United States can control Korea's Army or supervise Korean affairs.... Already, American diplomats, generals, and economic experts have lost a great deal of their power to tell the South Korean government what to do and how to behave in conducting its affairs.   (US News & World Report, June 19, 1961, pp. 50–51)

As all standing committees under the Korea-United States Combined Economic Bureau (CEB) were revoked, the United States lost its voice in Korean economic affairs (Yu, Hoyul 1996: 95). However, Korea-United States relations began to turn around in November 1961 when US President Kennedy formally invited Park Chung Hee to the White House. Park wanted to get US sanctions on the military coup and increase financial aid for economic development, while the US government intended to probe the real intention of the military government.

The Korean military government also changed its relationship with large capitalists. In the face of economic difficulties the military government opted for practical solutions rather than revolutionary fervor, as more pragmatic forces inside the military government gained voice. Thus, the government shifted from its anti-chaebols stance to cooperative partnership for economic development. While confiscating chaebols' private banks, the government induced them to work for economic development by mitigating their crimes (Kim, Jinhyun 1964: 158–177).

Initially, the government, directed by military revolutionaries, was impatient to achieve economic development in order to claim the legitimacy of their power undermined by their military coup. They justified their coup through independent national economic development, and recognized that to achieve economic development, they had to mobilize financial resources. They first nationalized commercial banks owned by large capitalists (called illegal fortune amassers), and the government restricted the voting rights of civil shareholders to not exceed the 10% ceiling, enabling the military government to seize full control over domestic banks (Kim, Sangjo 1993: 110–112; Lee, Sangchul 2003: 328–329; 2002: 120–121).

In addition to nationalization of commercial banks, the military government seized control over introduction and allocation of foreign capital. In September 1961, the military government announced the criteria for selecting importers of foreign capital, and in July 1962, it proclaimed the law on government payment assurance of private foreign loans. Although the Korean government transferred the payment assurance of private foreign loans to banks, it could still hold a full control over introduction and allocation of foreign capital because it had control over banks (Lee, Sangchul 2002: 115, 120–125).

However, the most significant change inside the government was the shift of authority in economic policy decision-making from military revolutionaries to economic bureaucrats, and formation of an appropriate leading agency for economic development to put their ideas into action. Despite the great ambition and desire for economic development, and strong, autonomous state capabilities, Park's military government faltered with many policy mistakes. The government had no leading organizational forces like EPB to define proper strategy.

EPB, established in early July of 1961, had significant institutional powers to devise a development plan, supervise its implementation, provide its policy instruments, and coordinate other ministries due to its centralized economic functions, including budget allocation function and control of flows of foreign capital and technology.[1] For example, through control of foreign loans, EPB could execute economic plans for government investments and private projects, in which approximately 44% relied on foreign loans in the total investments of 1962–9 in Korea (Kim, Hungki 1999: 192–193).

However, EPB could not serve as an economic control tower. Ministers of EPB changed frequently—seven times over two years and 10 months. After May 1964, when Chang Kiyoung became the EPB Minister, EPB stabilized its economic authority. Minister Chang worked as Minister of EPB for three years and five months (Lee, Manhee 2010: 86; Oh, Wonchul 1995, vol. 1: 68–69). More importantly, initiatives for economic development in the Korean military government changed. Initially the initiatives were in the hands of military revolutionaries like General Yu Wonsik in the Supreme Council for National Reconstruction. But after the economic blunder of 1962, significant changes occurred in the developmental leading agencies, from military revolutionaries to economic bureaucrats

---

[1] EPB took over the budget function from the Ministry of Finance and the statistics function from the Ministry of Interior Affairs. It also inherited economic planning and coordinating function from the Ministry of Construction. For EPB institutional capabilities and its formation, see Kim, Hungki (1999, 42–43, 192–193) and Lee, Manhee (2010: 91).

on EPB.[2] Thereafter through debates and competition EPB staff had to search for proper developmental strategies, particular in the period of 1962 to 1964 when the First Five-Year Plan underwent revision due to blundered economic policies and US pressure to reform. Classical developmentalism in Korea was formed in this political process.

Initially, the military government's developmental strategy was led by the military revolutionaries like General Yu Wonsik in the Supreme Council for National Reconstruction, not by EPB.[3] The Supreme Council's developmental strategy was a balanced and comprehensive industrialization called *Naepojuk gonguphwa* allowing for balanced and simultaneous development of industries of both producer goods such as steel, machines and automobiles, and consumer goods such as clothing and foods (Lee, Wanbum 2006: 106–108). Criticizing the consumer products-oriented industrialization of former administrations, military revolutionaries preferred to put first priority on construction of the steel industry in order to overcome its dependence on foreign products, although economic bureaucrats in MCI argued for development of light industries based on comparative advantages. Focusing on the independence of a national economy, proponents of the *Naepojuk gonguphwa* emphasized mobilization of national capital rather than foreign capital. They wanted to differentiate their strategy from the ISI of the Latin American countries which they believed relied mostly on foreign capital (Park, Heebum 1968: 72–73; 1962a; 1962b; Lee, Dae Kun 1987: 172).

To mobilize domestic savings, military revolutionaries propelled the currency reform in June 1962 and planned to put domestic savings under the control of the newly established Industry Development Agency (Park, Tae-gyun 2000b: 123). But the currency reform, as well as many other economic policies, resulted in a debacle. Foreign exchange reserves significantly declined as the relationship between the military government and the US government deteriorated. Thus, in the process of revising the original First Five-Year Economic Development Plan, the initiatives in the economic policy-making shifted from military revolutionaries in the Supreme Council to economic bureaucrats, particularly EPB. Recognizing that desire and will alone were insufficient for economic development, the military revolutionaries delegated the decision-making authority regarding economic affairs to economic bureaucrats (Kang et al. 2008: 81, 133).

Due to domestic problems including the failure of currency reform, the underperformance of economic growth, shortage of foreign exchanges, and high

---

[2] After the failure of currency reform, US AID regained its voice in Korean domestic affairs and requested to replace the key radical reformers, including Yu Wonsik, Park Heebum, and military Song Yochan, and Baek Sunjin, with economic bureaucrats including Kim Youtaek, Cha Kyunhee, and Kim Chung-yum (Park, Taegyun 2000b: 133).

[3] Park Chung Hee also agreed on the Yu Wonsik's developmental strategy initially. The representative theorist for the military revolutionaries was professor Park Heebum (Chun, Byungkyu 1988: 198–199; Park, Tae-gyun 2007: 56–59, 99).

inflation, as well as US pressure to reform, the military government could not but revise the original plan.[4] However, Park Chung Hee's military government did not discard all the state-led developmentalism by simply following US demands and turning toward a free market system. Following the US request to revise its inward-looking and overambitious plan, the Korean government reduced its goal of growth rates from 7.1% to 5%, and discarded the construction plan of comprehensive steel and machine industries and strengthened private initiatives (Park, Tae-gyun 2000b: 135). However, the Korean government's new developmental strategy differed from what the United States had in mind. For example, the exports that the United States emphasized did not mean the new Korean strategy of export-led industrialization, but a simple method to reduce the budget deficit in the Korean government and to reduce its aid (Lee, Wanbum 2006: 161–163; Park, Tae-gyun 2000b: 136). Export-led industrialization, as we will explore later, is a strategy found and confirmed by the practices of the economic bureaucrats, particularly bureaucrats of MCI.

In addition, unlike the American free market idea, the Korean military government still maintained the state-led allocation of credits, even discarding the Industry Development Agency plan of the 1962 currency reform. Throughout the process of revising the original plan from November 1962 to early 1964, the Park government created the new developmentalism, as with the export-oriented industrialization, through trial and error in the leeway allowed by the US government. It also formed leading agencies like EPB and MCI to put their developmentalism into action. This was the birth of classical Korean developmentalism.

The first notable change in the revised plan was to integrate the Korean economy in the international market. This shift from existing import-substitution industrialization (ISI) to export-oriented industrialization (EOI) utilized foreign loans fully. From the perspective of military revolutionaries like Yu Wonsik, the transformation to export-led industrialization with foreign loans was a kind of dependent development. After losing his power, he evaluated the Korean developmentalism of Park Chung Hee as follows: "The Korean economy turned from pursuing an independent national economy to a colonial, in other words, dependent economy" (Yu, Wonsik 1987: 340). Yet contrary to the criticism of the military revolutionaries and progressive scholars, the Korean economy differs from many Latin American economies based on foreign direct investments (FDI). By utilizing foreign loans, not FDI, Korea built independent national industries.[5]

---

[4] The original Developmental Plan aimed at 5.7% growth rate, but the actual growth reached only 2.8%. Due to the government's ambitious investments, the foreign exchange reserves became exhausted. The government could not continue its original investment plan. In addition, poor harvests in 1962 and 1963 also contributed to the economic crisis (Lee, Wanbum 2006: 154–155).

[5] Unlike in Latin American countries, FDI played a limited role in Korea. FDI contributed only 1.2% on average to gross domestic capital formation from 1962 to 1979 (Korea Exchange Bank 1980: 8).

Second, the Korean state changed its developmental strategy from a balanced growth to an imbalanced and strategically targeting industrialization to promote export industries (Lee, Wanbum 2006: 60–61). Proponents of balanced and comprehensive industrialization, such as Park Heebum, argued that their original plan was to build the heavy industries of producer goods, including iron and steel, locomotives, ships, automobiles, and machine tools, but their plans were wholly discarded in the revised plan of 1964 (Park, Heebum 1968: 23).[6] Instead, the Korean government began to focus on selectively promoting 13 exportable industries, including raw silks, cotton, rubber, and plywood, considering comparative advantages as well as the effects of industrial linkages and employments (Lee, Byungchun 1999: 152; Kim, Chung-yum 2006: 153).[7]

Export-oriented Industrialization and MCI as a Main Agency

Throughout the process of revising the original First Five-Year Plan in 1962–4, Korea changed from the existing import-substitution (ISI) to export-oriented industrialization (EOI), in contrast to the then-prevalent paradigm of ISI in developing regions including Latin American countries and India. Although Brazil, Argentina, and Mexico turned their ISI toward EOI in the 1970s and 1980s, unlike Korea, they did not develop the industrial policy to selectively and strategically nurture national industries. The Korean state did not change from ISI to EOI due to its small size, as many DS theorists including Amsden (2001: 161) argue, nor due to the external pressure of the US government or the strong state to overcome the opposition of social forces (Haggard 1990: 40, 60–61, 68). If we consider that small states, Costa Rica and Uruguay, pursued ISI rather than EOI, the size of domestic market is not the decisive factor for EOI. Korean EOI based on strategic developmentalism was not built by the US influence. Instead, export-led industrialization in Korea was developed by economic bureaucrats' learning through trial and error, as well as through competition between MCI and EPB, in which MCI identified exports as their own organizational rationale.

The US advice to the Korean government was merely to consider exports to balance budget, not for export-driven industrialization. The United States did not advise selective targeting as industrial policy, but price incentives such as exchange rate, export credit, and access to imports on a nondiscretionary basis (Haggard et al. 1991: 865). The Korean transformation toward EOI was formed by

---

[6] The balanced growth strategy was prevalent and in some sense a kind of obsession in the economic discourse in Korea of the 1950s and 1960s although it changed to the imbalanced and export-oriented growth in the late 1960s (Park, Taegyun 2004: 38).

[7] In the late 1960s, the problems of state-led development based on the imbalanced growth strategy came to occur. That is mainly too much dependence on foreign loans and the insolvency of firms based on foreign loans (Kim, Hungki 1999: 126).

the economic bureaucrats, particularly in MCI, in the process of solving the crisis of capital shortage.

In late 1962, Korean policymakers became aware of an economic crisis in which, due to the shortage of foreign capital, they could not continue their original economic development plan. In the early 1960s, US aid further declined from $225,236,000 in 1960 to $154,319,000 in 1961, and to $88,346,000 in 1964 (Kim, Bohyun 2006: 203; Kim, Chung-yum 2006: 150). Although the Korean government needed more foreign capital to build factories and import materials and machines, the foreign exchange reserve radically decreased from $166,793,000 in 1962 to even $93,298,000 (Lee, Kunmi 1996: 540). Former presidential economic secretary Oh Wonchul recalls that "1963 was a gloomy year. We were about to launch the First Five-Year Plan, but we ran out of money, the most important thing. We could not conduct war because we were out of ammunition" (Oh, Wonchul 1995, vol. 1: 220). Korean policymakers thought that they could not continue their original developmental plan. For example, the government could not continue building the Najoo fertilizer plant which it launched in 1958 (Cho, Gab-Je 2015, vol. 5: 199).

To overcome the shortage of capital for economic development, the Korean government desperately searched for foreign capital because, through the currency reform of 1962, they recognized that mobilization of domestic savings would not be a feasible option. However, unlike the developmental strategy of Latin American countries, the Korean government relied on foreign loans, rather than foreign direct investment (FDI), to maintain national control over economic development, while simultaneously earning foreign currency through exports.[8] The former was carried out mainly by EPB, while the latter was found and implemented mainly by MCI.

Notably, however, EOI was not proposed by MCI staff but discovered in the practice of trial and error. Until at least 1961, ISI was dominant even inside MCI. At that time, the urgent issue that MCI recognized was transformation from an economy dependent on foreign aid to an independent economy. In order to achieve this shift, they pursued ISI (MCI 1969). MCI's economic bureaucrats believed that it was impossible to export manufactured products due to such low and backward levels of Korean technology and manufacturing skills. In 1961 when the First Five-Year Economic Development Plan was made, MCI was not

---

[8] According to Wallerstein (1979: 76–83), there are three main strategies for economic development in the developing countries: import-substitution industrialization (ISI), self-reliance breaking away from the world capitalist economy, and outward looking industrialization. The Korean government changed from the existing ISI toward outward looking industrialization in 1963–1964. Nevertheless, its outward looking strategy differs from those of many Latin American countries in the sense that the Korean government gave priority to indirect foreign investment. Considering that the multinational corporations (MNCs) might be disruptive to the nationalistic logic of capital accumulation, the Korean policymakers tried to control foreign presence by favoring foreign loans over FDI because loans do not entail foreign control of the local firms (Lim 1985: 93).

interested in export. According to a memoir of a former MCI Minister, MCI did not consider seriously whether to choose ISI or EOI because "MCI then did not dare to think over the export-led industrialization; our thought simply leaned toward ISI" (Shin, Kookhwan 1994: 93).

However, in the desperate search for solutions to the foreign currency shortage, MCI slowly came to see the feasibility of exports and gained confidence in their practices. The initial two years of the economic development, 1961–3, showed no progress but mostly bad news, including the decline of foreign currency reserve. One positive sign of export growth was in the export of plywood (Lee, Kunmi 1996: 541). The First Five-Year Economic Development Plan of 1961 did not consider manufactured goods. Exports under the first plan focused instead on agriculture and minerals. However, while MCI implemented some export promotion policies, including the linkage of exports and imports, along with export subsidies, agricultural exports declined from the expected 80% to 55%, but manufactured goods increased to 45%. As MCI was confirmed by their practices of export promotion, it gained confidence in exports of manufactured goods. Thus, it revised its export goals of 1966 from $137,000,000 to $250,000,000 (Cole and Nam 1969: 27; Kim, Bohyun 2006: 210; Shin, Kookhwan 1994: 92). Shin Kookhwan, former Minister of MCI, says in his memoir that "as the exports of manufactured goods gave a good sign and a feasibility for economic development, we came to have a real confidence in export promotion policies" (Shin, Kookhwan 1994: 92). The process of turning toward EOI helped to create core leading organization like MCI.

In fact MCI did change its identity in the EOI process. Initially many MCI bureaucrats were interested in maintaining the easy ISI policy, rather than EOI. Many who were connected with private companies importing materials opposed the liberalization of material-imports for exports. However, key MCI economic bureaucrats, including then-Minister Park Choong-hoon and vice-Minister Kim Chung-yum, emphasized the shift from ISI to EOI through daily discussion with bureau directors, as the Minister and vice Minister of MCI were newly recruited in May 1964 (Kim, Chung-yum 2006: 153–154).

In 1964 key policymakers gained confidence in EOI. In November of that year, Korea achieved $100,000,000 in exports, a first in its history. Due to the growth of exports, Korea reached 8.5% in economic growth, much higher than the planned 5% for 1964. Particularly, exports increased at double the expected growth (Lee, Kunmi 1996: 549). Many MCI staff members recall the overwhelming moment, and an MCI section chief remembers the mood over the news of the export achievement of 1964:

Finally we reached the export goal of $120 million at about 10 o'clock on December 31, 1964.... Just 7 months ago we could not but reduce our original economic development plan, and the foreign exchange reserve almost ran out.

But a miracle came to be. We accumulated the statistics of exports and reported it directly to President Park. President Park could not hide his joyfulness and gave all staff his comfort and encouragement. We MCI staff were moved to tears and cried hurrahs in our offices. When we went home almost at curfew time, our eyes all turned red.   (Lee, Kunmi 1996: 547)

Thereafter MCI became the core leading organization for Korea's export-oriented industrialization (EOI). MCI had continuously expanded EOI in the process of competing with other economic ministries, such as EPB, for organizational authority. Even EPB was initially half-hearted in turning toward EOI, because it lacked confidence in such a turnaround (Kim, Hungki 1999: 138–140). Other ministries related to the Military Assistance Program opposed the shift toward EOI because EOI reduced the income through foreign aid (Cole and Lyman 1971: 88–89; Haggard 1990: 71). However, by organizing the monthly National Export Promotion Meeting chaired by President Park in which top bureaucrats, economists, representatives of trade associations, and chief executive officers of large firms participated, MCI could control opposition and drive export promotion as a national priority, in which MCI increased its own authority (Oh, W. 1995: 245–246; Kang, Lee, and Choi 2008: 168–177).

Transformation toward EOI was not by voluntary actions of private firms in the free market, but by the Korean state's intentional strategy. Initially private firms were more interested in imports. For example, one export promotion method was the linkage of imports and exports, which permitted firms to import the allocated products based on their export performance. Private firms earned more money by imports. During the 1960s, exports remained less profitable than production for the domestic market (Kim, Seung Hee 1970: 99; Lim, Youngil 1981: 44–45; Hamilton 1986: 44; Kim Mytelka and Ernst 1998: 90). However, due to many export promotion policies, including tax and financial incentives, the firms slowly became export-oriented. Starting in 1965, many catch phrases including "the export-firstism" or "export is only our survival" appeared, and EOI became firmly the first priority for Korean developmentalism. Then-Minister Park Choong-hoon thought in his memoir that not only the President and staff but also almost all Koreans became confident in the belief that Korea successfully grew by exports (Park, Choonghoon 1988: 81, 86). Real export growth confirmed the belief: Korean exports led the economic growth, with export growing at 26.3% on annual average from 1964 to 1992 (Lee, Kunmi: 1996: 549).

The Textile Industry as Case Study

By briefly examining the textile industry as a case study, this section explores how export-oriented industrialization (EOI) worked in Korea in the 1960s. Before turning toward EOI, the Park Chung Hee military government played an active role in nurturing national industries, including textiles. But this initial stage of state-led developmentalism was oriented toward import substitution. Unlike the neoclassical economist discontinuity thesis of free market of the 1960s and the developmental state of the 1970s, the Park Chung Hee administration had already established its classical form of state-led developmentalism in the 1960s, but by shifting from ISI to EOI, and from balanced to imbalanced and strategically selective policies.

The textile industry was one of Korea's main industries in the 1950s and 1960s, and became a main target for economic development by the Park Chung Hee military government. Textiles received the most benefits from foreign aid as well as from trade protection (Kim, Yung Bong 1977: 35, 48). The military government systemically intervened in the production of textiles, particularly, the chemical textiles. Based on the First Five-Year Economic Development Plan, rather than on market demand, EPB and MCI calculated the domestic demand, and permitted the building of new factories and expansion of existing production by sanctioning the introduction of foreign loans. In the First Five-Year Plan of July 1961, the government planned to build two factories for viscose silk, two factories for acetate fiber, and one factory for nylon F-fiber. With the introduction of foreign loans, the government controlled market entry and firm size to realize the economy of scale (Amsden 1992: 43; Lee, Sangchul 2002: 125; 2003: 322; Kim, Yang-Hwa 2017: 421–422).

Due to the underdevelopment of domestic firms, the government took a leading role in building industries. Anticipating domestic demand, the government planned the total volume of production and how many factories should be built. For instance, as the Korean Polyester company submitted a business proposal in which it planned to introduce commercial loans and production technology from Mitsui and Chemtex, Inc., and to build a factory to produce approximately 10 tons of polyester fiber, EPB reviewed the economic relevancy of the proposal, while MCI investigated the technical issues in the proposal. Although EPB was worried about overproduction in the polyester market through the deliberation process inside the government, MCI permitted the business proposal, noting the conditions on which the firm should export all the products and enlarge its production to compete in international markets (Lee, Sangchul 2002: 123–124). Unlike the free market, the Korean government intentionally aimed at the economy of scale. The Korean government provided payment assurance for the private industrialists' foreign loans and controlled the process of introduction and allocation of foreign loans, thereby selecting appropriate industries and companies strategically.

The Korean state heavily intervened in economic development due to industrialists' shortage of capital. Therefore, once the government chose the strategic industries and firms, it supported and guided them in detail. For example, in the early 1960s, the Korean textiles companies were backward and particularly short on capital. Although the government set self-financing rates as the criteria to select firms for foreign loans, most firms had difficulty in meeting the government self-financing criteria. Even the largest Hunghan Corporation could mobilize only 43% of total finances for building a new nylon factory, and could cover only 76.1% of payment insurance for the foreign loan. The Sunkyung Chemical Textile which would be responsible for building the acetate fiber factory could cover only 13.74% of the security for foreign loans and could borrow them only by the security of the machines and buildings (Lee, Sangchul 2003: 324). Due to the shortage of industrialists' capital, the Korean government also provided capital for building factories, as well as loans for operating the initial production, through the Korean Industrial Bank. Furthermore, the Korean government overviewed the contracts with foreign firms and investigated the functionality of the imported machines.

However, the initial developmentalism was import-substitution industrialization (ISI), rather than EOI, although both were forms of state-led developmentalism. Despite excess capacity of the early 1960s, the Korean textile firms conducted little export activity (Amsden 1989: 65). In particular, the cotton textile industry suffered from the devaluation of Korean currency because the costs of raw cotton imports increased (Mytelka and Ernst 1998: 95). However, starting in 1964, the textile industry changed from a domestic-oriented toward an export-oriented industry. Exports of cotton textiles have increased radically since 1964. For example, the share of exports to total demand in textiles production changed from 4.8% in 1963 to 47.2% in 1973. Such remarkable export growth is not due to private firms' voluntary action in the free market, but to the Korean state's active promotion policies (Kim, Yung Bong 1977: 48; Amsden 1989: 67).

The case of turning the textiles industry from ISI to EOI reveals the typical pattern of classical Korean developmentalism. In the process of promoting exports, the Korean government developed strategically selective industrial policy. Korea addressed two main measures: one was removing difficulties in trade; the other was supporting export firms. In the early stage of its export promotion policy, the import requirement like the linkage policy of export and import was a key method for export promotion because the firms could earn the import permission in proportion to their exports, given the situation in which imports were the most beneficial to firms. If the firms were in the free market without the government's special incentives, they would rarely change to EOI (Kim, Y.-H. 2017: 421–422).

The industrial policy for export promotion was strategic targeting. Oh Wonchul, former presidential economic secretary and key policymaker, describes the strategic policy method as follows:

> Although we wanted to promote exports, we did not help everything, but chose and concentrated on strategic products and elements. This is the point. First, we should not support every business loosely and evenly. We choose business items

appropriate to our advantage and focus our support on them. That's promotion of special industries. In addition, we should not support them all at once but help them one by one. Second, we should not support all the selected firms. Our support depends on whether the selected firm exports or not and how much they export. We help the followers but isolate the non-followers. The target was not business but firms individually. We should not select so many firms, but increase the number of the selected step by step. Third, we should support the followers in the selected business with all our efforts.

(Oh, Wonchul 1995, vol. 1: 233)

Oh Wonchul, as then-director of the industry bureau in MCI, selected the textiles industry as the export strategic industry, and drafted a textile promotion plan in June 1964. The basic plan was to transform the textile industry from domestic-oriented to export-oriented (Oh, Wonchul 1995, vol. 1: 258).

In June 1964, MCI selected 150 firms as potential export firms and concentrated its support on them at the initial stage. After evaluating their export performance, MCI supported the followers. In the second turn, 167 firms were selected and in the third turn, an additional 133 firms were selected for promotion. The implementation of export promotion was very concrete intervention in private business. For example, MCI staff set export goals every month with textile firms. They allocated export targets to each factory. MCI staff supervised and encouraged the achievement of goals. In order to improve productivity, MCI organized field-trips to the best performers and shared information (Oh, Wonchul 1995, vol. 1: 234–235, 256–261).

State-led developmentalism's importance lies both in promotion of under-developed firms and in resetting the direction of industrialization, major changes which individual firms concerned with their own profits hardly make. From the perspective of industrial linkages as a whole, the Korean government, particularly MCI, developed a vision to build a whole national economy through backward integration. MCI developed a plan to expand the scope of industries while targeting the textile industry for promotion. Oh Wonchul says in his memoir about the backward integration:

If the textiles develop like this, the demand on chemical fibers such as nylon, acrylic, and polyester, also increases. We have to localize them because their imports need massive foreign currency. We should promote them. It will be in late 1966 when we start to promotion. If chemical textiles develops, the imports of raw materials increases. As a result, we need the petrochemical industry. We should start it in 1967. An oil refinery to get the raw materials for the petro-chemical industry should be 100,000 barrels at least to be economically relevant. Like this, we made one cycle of our self-sufficient industrialization.

(Oh, Wonchul 1995, vol. 1: 243)

Although MCI targeted some industries for exports, it developed a vision to further develop industries and make a cycle of self-sufficient industrialization. Particularly, this backward integration from the perspective of industrial linkages has been developed not only in the competition with other departments like EPB, as shall be examined later, but also in the process of strategic coordination with private firms.

Backward integration, such as the building of the petrochemical industry, was accomplished not by the voluntary actions in the free market but by the state's intentional policy. Late-late comers like Korea encountered many difficulties in building their petrochemical industry for industrialization. For example, advanced countries like Japan attempted to disturb the process. When the Ulsan methanol factory was established in Korea, Japanese firms reduced the price from $70 per ton to $40 (Oh, Wonchul 1996, vol. 3: 14).

More problematic was that Korean customer firms were not interested in buying local materials but preferred to import, based on their individual cost calculation. For example, Korean textile exporters distrusted the quality, costs, and delivery schedules of domestic chemical fiber manufacturers (Lee, Sangchul 2002: 126). However, the unreasonable implementation of backward integration or localization of materials can impair the competitiveness of textile exporters. Another example is the building of the methanol factory in the mid-1960s. Plywood companies opposed the government plan in order to import methanol. If the new factory could not produce methanol to meet the minimum criteria of the international market, then local consumer firms like plywood firms would lose their competitiveness. The alternative was that the new petrochemical factory would die in the free market (Oh, Wonchul 1996, vol. 3: 14, 18).

Late comers rarely entered the petrochemical industry through private firms' voluntary actions in the free market. To meet the minimum standard prices of the international market, MCI planned to build a large-size petrochemical factory to realize the economy of scale. When MCI planned to build a naphtha factory in 1966, it decided to build a 60,000-ton factory in advance. And for ethylene produced by the factory to compete in the international market, MCI policymakers decided the target price, 3.9 cent per lb, in advance. And then, to meet the target price, the Korean government supported all other costs, such as electricity (3.5 won per KWH), water (2 Korean won per ton), and exempted all taxes for machine imports, land acquisition, and corporate taxes (Oh, Wonchul 1996, vol. 3: 43–48, 63–54). In order to build backward industries like petrochemicals, the Korean government developed an administrative coordination system, to adjust domestic material and accessory costs and double the price system to support exporters, while protecting domestic petrochemicals from imports of foreign materials (Lee, Sangchul 2002: 126–127, 132–133; Kim, Y.-H. 2017: 421–422).

Unlike the neoclassical economists' account, Korea of the 1960s was not a free market system but a state-led developmentalism.[9]

Heavy Chemical Industrialization (HCI) Drive in the 1970s

The Park Chung Hee government in the 1970s achieved a great industrial transformation toward heavy chemical industrialization (HCI), from promotion of light industries like textiles to mobilizing massive capital and funneling it to six strategic industries, namely steel, nonferrous metals, shipbuilding, machine tools, electronics, and chemical industries. The HCI drive included the upgrading of export products as well as building the basic structure of Korean flagship industries, including automobiles, electronics, shipbuilding, and petrochemical industries all in a short period (KIET 2008: 4). Emphasizing the discontinuity with the market-conforming system of the 1960s, neoclassical economists point to the HCI drive as evidence of the failure of the Korean developmental state (Stern, Kim, Perkins, and Yoo 1995). By contrast, the developmental statists focus on the HCI drive of the 1970s for the Korean developmental state, emphasizing the strong state's discipline of business and getting the price wrong for development (Amsden 1989; Haggard 1990; Kim, Hyung-A 2004).

Yet contrary to the neoclassical accounts, Korea of the 1960s was not a liberal market system but state-led developmentalism. Actually the HCI drive more distinctively shows the features of Korean classical developmentalism, including imbalanced concentration on strategically selective industries, export-oriented industrialization, large-scale economy, and input-oriented rapid growth. However, compared with the 1960s, the HCI drive of the 1970s was an extreme variant of state-led developmentalism, and of Korean developmentalism in general, compared with that of the 1960s. Unlike the DS demise thesis, stabilization in the 1980s did not mean the demise of Korean state-led developmentalism but readjustment of its extreme variant to a new environment.

The HCI drive differs from developmentalism of the 1960s in its massive and extreme intervention. From an EPB developmentalist perspective, the HCI drive was an extreme case in which the Heavy and Chemical Industry Promotion Bureau intervened arbitrarily and directly in the building of HCI, unlike the EPB's indirect inducements of the 1960s; in addition, the benefits to the selected industries were gigantic (Kim, Hungki 1999: 262–264). Compared with the

---

[9] The output growth of the Korean textile industry declined from 26.3% per year in 1968–73 to 12% in 1974–9, as the Korean policy priorities shifted from light industry toward the heavy and chemical industries (Mytelka and Ernst 1998: 100–101).

developmentalism of the 1960s, the HCI drive of the 1970s shows a massive mobilization of domestic savings, and an extremely skewed input-oriented developmentalism. For example, total investment in the HCI drive increased three times compared with investments of the 1960s. In the second half of 1970s, the Korean government allocated approximately 53% to 63% of total domestic loans as policy loans at a preferential rate, and approximately 70% of those policy loans went to the six HCI industries. The Korean government poured approximately 64% of total manufacturing investments into these six HCI industries from 1973 to 1981 (Koo and Kim 1992: 136; Yoon, D. 2011: 70–71). The HCI drive increased not only total investments, but also increased domestic savings to cover the capital needs for the HCI project up to 88% of HCI total capital resources. It was total mobilization with significantly tilted investments, particularly to large chaebols. The Korean HCI drive manifested the features typical of Korean developmentalism distinctively, including chaebols' diversification and dominance in the Korean economy.

Why and how has the Korean government changed to an extreme version of developmentalism? Unlike the prevalent accounts of DS theorists, neither domestic institutions of the strong state nor the external threat of North Korea and security issues can tell the whole story. We focus on the competition among economic bureaucrats, such as EPB and MCI within the Korean government, as well as state-business relations in the transformation process.

State-Business Relations in the Transformation to HCI

Korea's HCI drive of the 1970s not only built the current flagship industries including automobiles, shipbuilding, chemicals, and electronics in short period, but also established the chaebol-dominant structure of economy. The Korean HCI is best understood through the interaction of private companies and the state since it was basically conducted by private large corporations, unlike the Taiwan and Latin American models where public corporations implemented HCI (Ko, Youngsun 2007: 52; Noble 2011: 604–605). But Korea's private initiative does not suggest a free market system. On the contrary, Korea's transformation toward HCI was not due to voluntary action of large corporations but to the state's intentional driving policy. This is why most scholars, whether the neoliberals or the DS theorists, focus on the HCI drive of the 1970s as Korean state-led developmentalism. Initially, large corporations opposed or were reluctant to participate in the heavy chemical industries. They later changed their attitude and ardently competed to increase their shares in HCI, so much so that their competition for involvement resulted in overinvestment and the problem of a high-debt-based economy (Park, B.Y. 1980: 198–205).

In the initial stage of the HCI drive, the plan could not be executed because large corporations were reluctant to participate in the project. Businesses thought that HCI was premature in Korea; they were not ready to build heavy chemical industries due to their low levels of technology (FKI 1983: 267–268; Yoon, D. 2011: 72–73). For example, when the government tried to build the machine tool industry complex in Changwon, a southern city in Korea, private firms were reluctant to invest because they believed that the government plan was too audacious and unrealistic. Businessmen had doubts about their ability to mobilize investment capital and to manage the plants due to their underdeveloped technology. In addition, the International Bank for Reconstruction and Development (IBRD) had doubts about the Changwon industrial complex as well as about Korea's capability to develop the machine tool industry. Until 1974, only two large corporations and 25 Small and Medium-sized Enterprises (SMEs) had entered the industrial complex, while most firms waited to see results (Rhee 1994: 71; Choi, D.-k. 2006; Rhyu and Lew 2011).

In response to private firms' reluctance, the HCI's Planning Office employed both compulsory and conciliatory measures to force big corporations to participate, using the so-called "defeating one by one strategy" (Park, B.Y. 1980; Rhee 1994: 65, 71). Through its financial control system, the Korean state threatened to suspend loans to noncompliant firms, while giving compliant firms massive preferential benefits. The Korean state used competition among big corporations, bypassing big business organizations and associations. Through direct state-chaebol relations, they compelled or incentivized them to invest. Due to these measures, large corporations began to invest, starting in late 1975. Firms which took part in the Changwon machine industry complex increased from 27 in 1974 to 38 in 1975, 88 in 1977, and 122 in 1978 (Rhee 1994: 77). Without a broad range of policy measures including preferential policy loans, subsidies, and tax reduction and exemption, few large corporations in Korea would have been willing to bear the risks due to the HCI industries' need for massive investments and a long gestation period for profits.

The situation turned around, due to competition among large corporations, to the extent that the HCI rush among business groups surpassed a government-scheduled target HCI project investment for 1977–81 (Park, B.Y. 1980: 199–205). In the second half of the 1970s, approximately 70% of policy loans went to the HCI sectors. Through the HCI drive, large corporations began to diversify into many industries to better compete for government projects and preferential loans (Amsden 1989: 129). As a corporation grew, it had a better chance to participate in the state's priority projects, obtaining policy loans and other bank credits. Thus, large corporations also were focused on expanding their size and diversifying their businesses "octopus style," as Koreans say.

The chaebols greatly increased their horizontal and vertical integration tremendously during the 1970s. From 1972 to 1979 the average number of firms owned by the 10 largest chaebols increased from 7.5 per chaebol in 1972 to 25.4 in 1979. The number of industries in which they operated grew from an average of 7.7 industries (by 2-digit industrial classification) in 1972 to 17.6 industries in 1979. The share of top 10 chaebols in the GNP increased from 15.1% in 1974 to 48.1% in 1980, and continuously grew to 68.8% in 1987 (Koo and Kim 1992: 136–137).

The HCI drive enabled Korea to jump into capital-intensive and technology-intensive industries within a short period. As Amsden points out, based on the state's support, chaebols could enter into a new industry by transferring their intragroup money and personnel to a new business and compete internationally by using economy of scale and foreign technology (Amsden 1989: 151, 267). However, the HCI drive caused many problems and distortions which needed revision after the 1980s.

For example, the ideas that "size matters," rather than market profitability, produced overexpansion and many insolvent enterprises. The debt-to-equity ratios of Korean export corporations increased significantly from 117.7% in 1966 to 328.4% in 1970, and again to 487.9% in 1980 (Yoon, D. 2011: 147–148). In addition, the significantly skewed investments by the HCI drive deterred SMEs from growing due to shortages of capital resources, which made it difficult to build innovative interfirm relations as Japanese firms had done. Actually, this input-oriented overexpansion by state encouragement and the chaebols' competition became a cause for the economic crisis in the late 1970s. However, it took a longer time to correct the input-oriented overexpansion and diversification by Korean chaebols, which revised apparently only after the 1997 Asian financial crisis, as we will examine later.

Crisis and Competition for Solutions

Why did the Park Chung Hee administration launch the HCI drive? For the cause of Korea's HCI drive, many political-economic scholars point out the external shocks, such as economic and security crises (Lee, Suk-Chae 1991; Horikane 2005; Kim, B.-K. 2011a; Moon and Jun 2011; Noble 2011). In fact, in the late 1960s and early 1970s, Korea fell into complex crises including security threats from North Korea and protectionism from advanced countries. Since 1968, with North Korea's several guerilla invasions and the American Pueblo hijacking incidents, the sense of a national security crisis soared. In addition, US President Nixon proclaimed the Guam doctrine in January 1969, stating that Asian countries were expected to have first responsibility for their own security, and soon announced that the US army would retreat from the Korean peninsula. South Korean visitors to North Korea in 1972 were overwhelmed by the development of North Korean heavy chemical industries. Because they had focused on nurturing the light industries like textiles until then, South Korean key policymakers now began to pay attention to heavy chemical industry promotion (Lee, Sangchul 2002: 128; Kim, Chung-yum 2006: 382–390).

In addition, the Korean economy based on foreign debt fell into economic crisis in the late 1960s. Initially, due to a shortage of capital Korean export-oriented industries relied heavily on foreign loans controlled by the government. At favorable interest rates, Korean export companies used them, backed by government guarantees, and their debt-to-equity ratios significantly increased. In 1969 the Korean economy was a high-debt based, high-growth model. As the IMF began to restrict Korean firms' foreign borrowing, they began to use private loan despite its high costs of borrowing. In addition, advanced countries turned toward protectionism to restrict imports of consumer products like textiles. In the 1960s, textiles were about 40% of Korean exports (Lee, Suk-Chae 1991: 436; Horikane 2005: 380–381). In 1971, about 200 export firms which used foreign loans fell into insolvency, and Korean foreign debt increased to 30% of GNP (Thurbon 2016: 67–68).

However, the crisis itself does not determine the direction of the solution. Considering the crisis of this high-debt-based, high-growth model, not only many progressives including opposition leader Kim Daejung, but also the government's EPB suggested a reform of the existing strategy of high-debt-based overexpansion. In addition, in the late 1960s, large corporations worried about another overexpansion in the HCI drive. They believed that HCI was not familiar enough to them, and that HCI was premature in Korea (Choi, Byung-sun 1991a: 51; Thurbon 2016: 67–68, 70). However, the Park Chung Hee administration chose a yet bigger expansion of the HCI drive to solve the crisis of the debt-based overexpansion. The Park government declared a moratorium on corporate repayments to the private curb-market loan in August 1971, and rescheduled the firms' short-term debts or wrote them off through the Emergency Economic Decree of 1972 to solve the problem of exporters' debts and ordered banks to provide more loans (Kim, B.-K. 2011a: 3; Thurbon 2016: 68–69). The Park administration launched the HCI drive officially in January 1973.

Why and how could the Park administration choose another bigger overexpansion strategy of the HCI drive? It was not just because the Park administration had institutional capability to require domestic banks to mobilize massive savings like the National Investment Fund (NIF), and provide preferential policy loans to selected firms in the heavy chemical industries. More importantly, it is because of the shift of initiatives in the economic policy-making. The growth-first strategy and further expansion even in the oil crisis of the early 1970s were clearly unconventional. Due to the oil shocks, Korea suffered from the decline of exports, its main growth engine, and from inflationary pressure. EPB, most powerful developmental agency inside the Korean government, as well as IMF, recommended stabilization policies, including scaling back investment and reducing foreign debt. However, in competition with EPB, another key organization, MCI, supported the HCI drive as a feasible solution to the crisis, which President Park accepted. Without diverse and competing interpretations and solutions to the crisis, it is hard to understand the direction the situation would take.

Competition among the Economic Bureaucrats

The HCI drive proclaimed in 1973 was a turnaround from the original plan of "stabilization and balance" in the Third Five-Year Plan to the growth-first strategy. This shift in policy direction meant a changes of initiatives in the economic policy-making. The Blue House (Presidential Residence) secretary groups and MCI offering the growth drive strategy seized the initiative in late 1971, whereas EPB became apparently marginalized (Park, B.Y. 1980: 196; Kim, Hungki 1999: 206ff; Kim, Bohyun 2006: 217). According to the EPB's evaluation, the developmentalism of the 1960s marked the EPB's glory days, while HCI of the 1970s saw the decline of its influence because in the 1970s, the EPB's ideas on developmentalism diverged from those of President Park (Kim, Hungki 1999: 115, 211–219; Lee, Manhee 2010: 87).

As American-trained economists entered EPB, its idea changed from the existing strategy of foreign loan-based expansion to stabilization in the late 1960s. By contrast, the MCI's economic bureaucrats considered further upgrading the industrial structure from light to capital-intensive, heavy industries in the late 1960s (Kim, Chung-yum 2006: 172). Park's political ambition aligned him with MCI and Blue House secretary, rather than with the EPB's stabilization advocates (Nam, Duck Woo 1994: 17–18; Lee, Manhee 2010: 87). Unlike most DS theorists who emphasize the cohesiveness inside the developmental state, to differentiate DS from other non-DS countries like India and Latin American countries (Haggard 1990; Wade 1990; Evans 1995; Chibber 2002) there was severe competition for legitimate authority inside even the classical developmental state of Park Chung Hee. Without rivalry and competition, it is hard to understand the evolution of the developmental state. This section examines why and how the Korean developmentalism evolved toward the HCI drive by focusing on competition among economic bureaucrats, particularly between EPB and MCI.

The diverse responses to the economic crisis of the early 1970s and the development of the 1960s were both driven by the EPB and MCI's competition for influence among economic bureaucrats, especially over the biggest issue in Korea's developmentalism of the 1960s, the shortage of financial resources and technology. EPB had the upper hand in economic policy decision making by its capability to mobilize and allocate domestic savings and foreign loans. EPB gained the confidence of President Park by borrowing and allocating foreign loans, and justified its developmentalism with its organizational rationale that the more that foreign loans contribute to development of national industries, the more that "the economic development wholly relies on the foreign loans" (Hwang, Byungtae 2011: 76–77, 79–81). As policymakers came to recognize through the failure of the 1962 currency reform that the mobilization of domestic savings was very difficult, they believed that introduction of foreign loans was the most important support for economic development (Hwang, Byungtae 2011: 105). Even MCI admitted that foreign loans were decisive to Korean economic development, because due to the shortage of financial resources, they could not build a factory. For example, in September 1963, the Korean foreign currency reserve ran to below $100 million, and the government could not pay for the second construction phase of the Ulsan refinery factory (Oh, Wonchul 1995: vol. 1: 65, 109).

In contrast to the EPB's priority on foreign loans, MCI justified its influence by improving exports, beginning in 1964. Although EPB and MCI shared the idea of export-led industrialization, they competed for its policy initiatives, arguing who contributed more to the national development. As Chang Kiyoung, Minister of EPB, institutionalized the Monthly Economic Review Meeting in which President Park participated, Park Choong-hoon, Minister of MCI, organized the Comprehensive Export Promotion Conference every month in which President Park also participated (Bae, Kwanpyo 2012: 248). Both the EPB's Monthly Economic Review Meeting and the MCI's Comprehensive Export Promotion Conference revealed the severe competition for legitimate authority between the two ministries, fighting to attract President Park's trust and to show their organizational influence throughout the 1960s and 1970s.

Furthermore, as EPB encroached upon the jurisdiction of MCI by engaging directly in industrial policies through its introduction and allocation of foreign loans, MCI was in direct competition with EPB for its influence. In the case of building an oil refinery factory in the mid-1960s, EPB tried to earn more investments from Esso, a subsidiary of American Standard Oil, by giving management rights to them. But MCI opposed the EPB idea, suggesting instead their justification of the scale economy and building a nationally owned factory. They had to resolve their conflicts by competitively briefing before President Park (Oh, Wonchul 1995: 47–48; Bae, Kwanpyo 2012: 246–247).

The competitive case of building a fertilizer plant in 1963–5 also shows the different rationales of EPB and MCI in carrying out developmentalism. In a plan to build fertilizer plants, EPB planned to make contracts with the US company Swift for the third fertilizer plant, and with Gulf for the fourth plant, emphasizing stable foreign loans. EPB also did not want Samsung to build a fertilizer plant because it could deter the introduction of US loans. However MCI opposed the plan for two fertilizer plants and suggested a single plant built by Samsung, based on the idea of economy of scale. Again, to resolve the conflicts, EPB and MCI presented their ideas in front of President Park at the EPB office in 1964, and the final decision went to the EPB idea (Oh, Wonchul 1995, vol. 1: 169–170, 171, 175–176; Hwang, Byungtae 2011: 108, 111–112, 125).

Another big match between MCI and EPB was how to build a naphtha cracking plant. In January 1965 when President Park made his New Year inspection tours across ministries, Oh Wonchul, then-director of the industry bureau in MCI, suggested building the petrochemical industry as a backward integration from the perspective of industrial linkages, and the plan for a naphtha plant was included in the Second Five-Year Plan. However, MCI and EPB conflicted again over how and where to build the factory. Based on the priority of introducing foreign loans, EPB supported a plan to build the naphtha factory in Incheon with Union Oil company which promised to provide $76,000,000. But MCI argued that the naphtha factory should be built in the Ulsan industrial complex to easily source raw materials from the Ulsan oil refinery plant. Finally MCI and EPB presented their ideas in front of President Park, and this time the victory was MCI. The EPB director, who was responsible for building factories, reflects on the frequent conflicts inside the state as follows:

> This issue [building the naphtha factory] was his jurisdiction [Oh Wonchul in MCI]. Indeed the entire chemical industry was under the jurisdiction of MCI, but our EPB could not wash our hands of that matter because it was the business of foreign capital. By and large it was habitual practice to have conflicts with MCI in the deliberation of business. For instance, we did not get on well with each other. We always sparred over, say, Park Taejun's soda factory, the third and fourth fertilizer factory, the issue of permission on Samsung's building a fertilizer plant. I believe that they might be dissatisfied that we would overstep their jurisdiction by our authority over foreign capital business.
>
> (Hwang, Byungtae 2011: 128–129)

However, the biggest match was over the heavy chemical industrialization drive. For example, EPB and MCI competed for initiatives in building an integrated steel factory. In 1969 when Kim Hakryul became an EPB minister, he excluded MCI in the building of a comprehensive steel factory (Oh, Wonchul 1999, vol. 7: 152; Park, Younggoo 2008: 83; Bae, Kwanpyo 2012: 254). As fear of security crisis soared in the late 1960s, Korea's key policymakers planned to build four core factories for defense purposes, including foundry pig, alloy steel, heavy machinery, and shipbuilding factories in July 1970. EPB led HCI in the early stage, as seen in the business of four core factories as well as a comprehensive steel factory (Bae, Kwanpyo 2012: 256). To build these factories, EPB focused on foreign loans from advanced countries, and attempted to contact first Japan, and then the United States and Europe. But these efforts failed to make progress. The EPB's failure opened a window of opportunity to MCI. In November 1971, when President Park received a briefing from EPB and expressed disappointment at EPB's failure, MCI offered an alternative solution to combine HCI and defense industries. Then-chief presidential secretary Kim Chung-yum describes the moment vividly as follows:

> President Park, worrying about national security, was so despairing in the car on the way to the Blue House after hearing the EPB briefing. At the moment when I returned to the Blue House and thought over national defense industries, Oh Wonchul, assistant minister of MCI, called me. He said that he had also attended the EPB briefing and he had some idea on how to build defense industries. I said that he had better immediately come up to the Blue House. After I discussed the issue seriously with assistant minister Oh, we concluded as follows: first, a special military factory had better not be built, due to the economic ineffectiveness, except for the already launched M16 rifle factory; second, the private military factories are also irrelevant in the economic sense; third, "all weapons are composed of parts, so we need to just assemble them if we develop heavy chemical industries..." We also emphasized the training of engineers and technicians. I immediately brought Oh to the presidential office. I let him brief our discussion to President Park. The President was so interested in it and raised this or that question even after the brief.... He basically agreed on our idea. Only one thing he worried about was that it would take a long time, about 4–5 years. After considering seriously, he ordered to build heavy chemical and defense industries at the same time with the least money. After we retreated, he called me to come again. When I came back to the office, he said to me that he would take care of the defense and HCI by himself, and ordered to let Oh work in the Blue House. .... That was on November 10, 1971.   (Kim, Chung-yum 2006: 392–394)

In November 1971 the initiatives in economic policy-making in Korea shifted from EPB to the newly formed HCI Promotion Bureau and MCI. In order to drive HCI, the Park administration built new special organizations like the Heavy chemical Industry (HCI) Promotion Committee and the HCI Promotion Bureau. However, the Committee was simply a formal organization, and the real power lay with President and the HCI Promotion Bureau (Kim, Hungki 1999: 218, 261; Park, B.Y. 1980: 195–196). Oh Wonchul became a chief of the HCI Promotion Bureau in the Blue House as well as a chief of second presidential economic secretary. The presidential economic secretary team responsible for HCI was filled with MCI staff by almost 80% (Bae, Kwanpyo 2012: 256). In the process of the HCI drive, MCI and the HCI Promotion Bureau got the initiative, while EPB was marginalized in the economic decision making. An EPB former minister says that "there were many projects which [HCI Bureau] continued implementing even though EPB said no" (the testimony of Choi Changrak in Kim, Hungki 1999: 216).

EPB was not a collection of neoliberal free marketers, but moderate developmentalists emphasizing the comparative advantages in the international market. Nevertheless, the EPB's gradualism differed from the HCI drive of President Park, HCI Bureau, and MCI, although EPB agreed with MCI on the idea that Korea needed to develop heavy chemical industries because the labor-intensive light industries including shoes and textiles would lose to the late developing countries pretty soon (Nam, Duck Woo 2009: 112). EPB argued for the reduction of HCI investments at the time of the first oil shock of 1973, emphasizing the concentrated investments in the high-labor-coefficient and internationally competitive industries (FKI 1983: 552, 548; Lee, Manhee 2010: 91).[10] However, in contrast to the EPB argument, President Park and the HCI team were firm in continuing its drive although with some adjustments. The HCI drive was accelerated again from late 1974. EPB planned again to reduce the investment when it made the Fourth Five-Year Economic Development Plan in 1976, in light of international economic difficulties (Park, B.Y. 1980: 197; Kim, Hungki 1999: 219, 262; Kim, Yonghwan 2002: 157–85). Despite the EPB's raising the alternative of gradualism, the Blue House and MCI were firm in the HCI drive.

However, in the late 1970s, conflicts surfaced again between the economical perspective of EPB and the industrial-technical perspective of the HCI Bureau and MCI. This time the EPB's idea on stabilization gained more attention. In the late 1970s, the international economy fell into a steep recession and the Korean economy faced economic crisis. Korean exports, its growth-engine, became sluggish; the international balance of payments deteriorated, and inflation went up. Furthermore, the excessively skewed investments in the HCI destabilized the Korean economy. Considering the seriousness of economic crisis, President Park also attempted to find a solution. Criticizing that the current HCI drive disregarded investment efficiency and profitability, EPB gave concrete shape to its idea of stabilization and liberalization by presenting "the Comprehensive Economic Stabilization Measures" in April 1979, in which they argued for delay or revocation of the current HCI (Lee, Manhee 1996: 252, 258–65; 2010: 93). Although the EPB's idea on stabilization and liberalization did not materialize in the Park administration, it provided a basic plan in the subsequently established military government beginning in 1980.

---

[10] For the debate between MoF and EPB regarding the establishment of National Investment Fund, see Choi, D.-k. (2006).

5

Transition I

Liberalization in the Chun Doo-hwan Administration

The classical developmentalism of the Park Chung Hee era, particularly the heavy chemical industry (HCI) drive of the 1970s, enabled Korea to take off with its industrialization and build national industries rapidly. However, it caused many problems including excessive input-oriented overinvestments, heavy-handed and highly detailed state control, imbalanced development of large final product producers and small parts suppliers, and chaebols' excessive preoccupation with volume orientation rather than market efficiency. These problems emerged at the same time in the late 1970s. Throughout the 1980s Korean capitalism underwent significant changes in the direction of liberalization, including open trade, privatization of banks, reduction of policy loans, and emphasis on private initiatives in the free market. Yet these liberalization measures do not mean an entire transformation of the developmental state to a neoliberal free market system. On the contrary, the reform deliberation and adjustments of the late 1970s and early 1980s initiated the transformation of the classical developmental state (DS) to a new version of state-led developmentalism, although it took more time to materialize through political practices, including state-business readjustments as well as bureaucrats' redefining of their roles inside the state.

Why and how did Korea continue its state-led developmentalism, even in the process of overcoming the problems which resulted from state-led developmentalism? First, the opposition party and civil progressives, including labor organizations, lacked the capability to develop a persuasive alternative to the post-DS economic development. The alternative was mainly initiated by EPB through debates inside the state. A new version of state-led developmentalism in the 1980s was formed mainly at the EPB's initiative, and readjustments of roles and functions by the other industry-related ministries, including MCI and the Ministry of Finance (MoF), came through political contests.

This chapter explores first to what extent Korea capitalism in the Chun Doo-hwan administration era (1980–7) changed compared with the former DS. Second, we explore why Korea continued its state-led developmentalism by focusing mainly on bureaucratic contests inside the state.

Changes by Competition: The Evolution of the South Korean Developmental State. Hyeong-ki Kwon, Oxford University Press (2021). © Hyeong-ki Kwon. DOI: 10.1093/oso/9780198866060.003.0005

Liberalization of the Korean Developmental State

To overcome the problems of overcapacity and excessive investments resulting from the developmental state of the Park Chung Hee era, the Chun Doo-hwan administration launched liberalization in Korean capitalism, including reduction of policy loans, financial deregulation, and trade openness. Although these measures launched many liberal reforms, they did not destroy the state-led developmentalism. These new measures addressed the problems of the old-style DS excesses, rather than introduce a noninterventionist and neutral state model. Before examining why Korea continued its state-led developmentalism and turned toward a new version of DS, this section explores to what extent the Korean state-led developmentalism changed in the Chun Doo-hwan administration (1980–7).

The Chun Doo-hwan administration was similar to Park Chung Hee's in the sense of a highly authoritarian state of military dictatorship. However, in the sense of economic policy, it presented a significant turnaround. To overcome the economic crises due to the Park administration's overexpansion of HCI investments, the Chun administration pursued a stabilization policy, reducing money supplies and cutting government expenditures to curb inflation. The Chun administration launched the Comprehensive Plan for Stabilization and Structural Reorganization, which was developed by EPB under the Park administration of the late 1970s. It was not simply an adjustment of macroeconomic policies including foreign exchange and reduction of money supply, but more importantly, it was a radical reorganization of the existing developmentalism and industrial policy methods. Criticizing the excessive state intervention in industries, the Chun administration emphasized promotion of a market system, such as private initiatives in the economy, enhancement of market competition, and a wide opening of the domestic market to foreign goods (Koo and Kim 1992: 140). The Chun administration liberalized key policy instruments of the Park Chung Hee era, including state control over finances and many permission rights.

First, the Chun administration deregulated to a large extent the permission rules to control market entry as well as investments in the market, wielded mainly by the Ministry of Commerce and Industry (MCI).[1] This deregulation was implemented through severe conflicts between the Economic Planning Board (EPB) and MCI, which we will examine later. Although reforms on control over market entry and investments, as well as price control, were launched in the Chun administration, they were dismantled seriously by the Roh Tae-woo (1988–92)

---

[1] For MCI, it was a radical change to deregulate their permission rights on market entry and investments. MCI had to find new methods, including R&D incentives, as well as a new developmental strategy and new roles. Personal interview with the chief of R&D Strategy Planning Bureau in the Ministry of Industry (MoI) on June 18, 2018.

administration (Ko, Youngsun 2007: 58–59). Thereafter investment decisions were made, not by the state based on its demand forecast, but by individual firms' calculation in their markets (You, Heeyul 1996; Hahm and Plein 1997; Yoon, Jinhyo 2006: 79, 108).

In addition, the Chun administration began to liberalize financial measures, including liberalization of interest rates, reduction of policy loans, and privatization of banks, although some measures like liberalization of interest rates materialized later in 1996 (OECD 1996: 48; Cho, Yoon Je 2003: 85–86; Ko, Youngsun 2007: 54). In the early 1980s, the Chun administration began to privatize commercial banks including the Hanil Bank in 1981, the Korea First Bank and the Bank of Seoul and Trust Company in 1982, and the Choheung Bank in 1983 (Ko, Youngsun 2007: 54–55). The Chun administration also liberalized interest rates and made the differences between policy loan and general interest rates disappear. Furthermore, the state reduced its scope of industrial policy to focus on corporate restructuring and promotion of promising industries (Lim, Haeran 1998: 87).

However, despite these liberalization measures, including the privatization of banks, the Korean state still maintained powerful instruments with which it could ensure the compliance of private firms (Jung, Joo Young 1991: 186–190; Kong 2002: 107). For example, compared with extreme mobilization and skewed allocation of domestic finances in the HCI drive of the 1970s, the amount of policy loans in the Chun administration decreased. But the process moved slowly, while the Korean state kept its loan volume relatively high, compared with those of other countries, in order to emphasize new industrial policies such as support to small and medium-sized enterprises (SMEs) (Ko, Youngsun 2007: 54).

Even after the privatization of banks, the Korean state still maintained its strategic influence in the allocation of loans through its involvement in executive appointments and asset management of the banks (Kong 2002: 107; Cho, Y.J. 2003: 94). Despite liberalization measures, the Korean state still held many policy instruments including preferential taxes, loan restrictions, reduced but still large policy loans, and government budgets. For example, in the process of industrial rationalization of the mid-1980s, the government used discretionary industry-specific and even firm-specific policy, rather than a nondiscretionary, free market approach, with the policy instruments including loan restriction and preferential loans (Moon, Chung-in 1994: 148; Kim, B-K 2003: 59–61).

The Chun administration developed new industrial policies of selective and strategic developmentalism, focusing on technology-intensive industries such as electronics, information, and telecommunications industries (Lim, Haeran 1998: 90–91). Korea's liberalization measures of the 1980s did not mean the demise of state-led developmentalism, but marked the beginning of a new developmentalism based mainly on the R&D policy, to correct the input-oriented developmentalism of the Park Chung Hee era. Proclaiming the Measure to Rationalize Corporate

Structure in September 1980, the Chun administration pursued a redirection of corporate strategy, from the existing input-oriented volume expansion to specialization in some core businesses. Although this specialization policy did not achieve much success before the Asian financial crisis of 1997, it took a new direction which needed further state-led developmentalism. Since the early 1980s, the Chun administration enacted the Monopoly Regulation and Fair Trade Act, although monopoly regulation aimed basically at controlling large corporations' excessive diversification and overexpansion rather than a simple free market system.[2]

In the 1980s, the new developmentalism emphasized the promotion of technology-intensive industries by R&D policy. Recognizing the changes in international competition in which firms in advanced countries like the United States and Japan were reluctant to transfer their lower-end products to Korean firms, and firms in low-wage countries like China and Southeast Asian countries tended to catch up to Korean firms, Koreans began to focus on the technology-intensive industries as a solution (Lim, Haeran 1998: 92). In the 1980s, large Korean corporations began to increase their R&D activities. However, as Amsden rightly points out, initially the private firms were reluctant to make R&D investments. Not until the late 1980s did companies such as Samsung, the most technology-advanced firm in Korea, begin to invest seriously in major product improvement (Amsden 1994: 98–99). Private firms hesitated to take risks by making large-scale investments in unproven technologies. Korea's transformation toward a technology-intensive economy was not by the free market but by the government's initiation of a R&D-based industrial policy (Lee, Sangchul 2004a: 174–179; Kim, Bohyun 2006: 228).

For example, in the 1980s, the Korean government and large corporations collaborated on numerous R&D projects in the selected industries including semiconductor and IT industries, such as the 16 DRAM memory development project (Amsden 1994: 100). Consequently private firms had to increase their R&D activities in order to get government support.[3] Furthermore, competition among large corporations in Korea slowly changed from traditional competition for market share to competing to build in-house R&D capabilities, which accelerated the transformation toward a technology-intensive economy in Korea (Lim, Youngil 1999: 97).

In order to transform the national economy from the existing input-oriented economy to a technology-intensive economy, the Korean government increased its national R&D investment from US$28.6 million in 1971 to US$2.37 billion in

---

[2] The Chun administration enacted the Fair Trade Law, but the Fair Trade Committee was placed inside EPB, rather than as an independent agency. This meant the Regulation and Fair Trade rule was aimed at the industrial policy (Moon, Chung-in 1994: 148–149).

[3] Personal interview with General Manager at Kamtec (automotive parts maker) on November 10, 2015.

1987. The R&D expenditure rose faster than GNP. The Korean government began to promote corporate R&D activities by offering various programs to induce the private sector to set up formal R&D laboratories. Three main mechanisms through which the government supported corporate sector funding for R&D activities included direct R&D subsidy, preferential financing, and tax incentives. Indeed, in the 1970s, the Korean government had no direct R&D subsidy programs. Only in the 1980s did the government introduce two main schemes for direct funding of private R&D, including the National R&D Projects (NRP) and the Industrial Base Technology Development Projects (IBTDP). The most important mechanism for funding corporate R&D is preferential financing by state-controlled banks and public funds. The total amount of public financing, mostly in the form of preferential loans, accounted for 64% of the total R&D expenditure in manufacturing in 1987, while tax incentives were a major indirect mechanism in making funds available to corporate R&D (Kim, Linsu 1993: 360–374; Jung, Duck-Goo 2006: 95).

Korea's R&D policy was a major industrial policy, not merely a liberal state's general services policy of pure science available to all citizens. According to an empirical analysis on IBTDP, about 61% of all projects were at the prototype stage for commercial products, and another 32.2% were at the stage of mass production. These kinds of R&D projects were almost similar to the subsidies for industrial development. Furthermore, the R&D policy as an industrial policy was very selective and targeted at strategic industries, including the semiconductor and IT industries, as was the case with traditional developmentalism (Lee, Yu, and Bang 2005: 69).

For example, Presidential secretary team of the Chun administration, including the liberalization leader Kim Jae-ik, focused on development of the semiconductor, electronics, and IT industries, even against the opposition of EPB, as we will examine later. They launched many national R&D projects targeting these strategic industries, like the VLSI development project, while providing massive investments through collaboration between private firms' R&D labs and public research institutions like the ETRI. The Chun administration reduced the duty on R&D-related imports and gave tax exemptions to the private firms' R&D (Amsden 1989: 83).

In addition, from the 1980s the Chun administration began to emphasize development of SMEs to correct the structural imbalance of Korean industries by the skewed funneling of financial resources in the HCI drive of the 1970s. The Chun administration ordered commercial banks to provide SMEs with 35–55% of total loans at a minimum. If the state did not intervene in the allocation of credit to SMEs, the privatized banks and newly created nonbank financial institutions would not lend to SMEs. For example, foreign banks operating in Korea, which were always free to lend to whomever they wished, did not lend extensively to SMEs (Amsden and Euh 1993). However, the state's redirection of loans to SMEs was not to correct a social injustice but, from the perspective of developmentalism, to reduce the dependence on parts from Japan (Moon 1994: 148–149).

Many scholars of the DS demise thesis point to the Chun administration's financial liberalization measures as evidence of the demise of the Korean DS by focusing on policy instruments such as state control over finance. However, these liberal measures adjusted the excessive and direct allocation of financial resources, but did not signal the entire retreat of the state and transformation toward a neoliberal, noninterventionist state.

Politics of Transformation

In solving the economic problems including distortion of credit allocation, over-expansion, and inflation resulting from the HCI drive, Koreans criticized the traditional, state-led developmentalism, and adopted many liberalization measures. However, the 1980s liberalization led by EPB was neither a whole retreat of the developmental state nor transformation to a neoliberal, neutral state. Rather, it was a turnaround toward another version of developmental state. How did another state-led developmentalism, rather than movement to a noninterventionist state serve as a solution? Why were the economic bureaucrats not held to account for the economic crises of the late 1970s?

Indeed some economic bureaucrats, such as MCI and MoF staff, were called to account for the crisis, while EPB bureaucrats were relatively free of the criticism. Civil organizations and other progressives such as labor organizations were unable to offer a feasible and persuasive solution. The crisis itself does not indicate the solution, but the contested narratives on the crisis constitute the solutions and point to the direction of change. Unlike many DS theorist accounts of state bureaucrats' cohesiveness and single mindset for developmentalism (Haggard 1990; Wade 1990; Evans 1995; Chibber 2002; Thurbon 2016), economic bureaucrats even in the heyday of Korean developmentalism were not single-minded. Without understanding the discursive conflicts in the crisis, it is hard to figure out the evolution in the state-led development. Furthermore, the outcome of adjustments in the crisis and the turn toward a new version of developmentalism were not simple materialization of the leading EPB idea, but resulted from the politics of competition for influence inside the state, in which losers, like MCI, could redefine their identity, and bring new compromises beyond the original idea of old-style developmentalism. Willingness to change, rather than persist with existing practices, enabled developmentalism to continue.

This section first examines the diverse and competing narratives on the economic crisis of the late 1970s both inside and outside the state, and then explores the political process of competition for influence inside the state.

Economic Crisis and Contested Solutions

In the late 1970s and early 1980s, Korea fell into economic crisis. Exports declined; the international balance of payments deteriorated; inflation skyrocketed at double-digit rates, and large corporations lost profitability but still expanded and diversified (Kim, Yongbok 1996: 132–134; Kang, Kyungsik 2003: 96; Krause 2003: 67). Facing the economic crisis, the Chun administration (1980–7), established by a military coup, could not but execute economic reforms to gain some political legitimacy. The issue was over what kinds of reforms it would make. The Chun administration largely relied on EPB's idea of stabilization and liberalization, reasonable when understood through the cleavage structure of discursive politics in the late 1970s and early 1980s. Economic bureaucrats, particularly in MCI and MoF, were a main target of criticism for the existing state-led developmentalism, while civil organizations, which had a legitimate voice in the crisis, could not offer a persuasive and feasible solution. However, in contrast to MCI and MoF who were responsible for overexpansion, EPB which opposed the HCI drive was relatively free of criticism and continuously offered its alternative to the Park administration's excessive developmentalism, even before the economic crisis surfaced in 1977. This section explores how diverse options were offered and how EPB led the reform in the early 1980s.

Unlike many European corporatist countries, including Sweden and Germany, where trade associations offered persuasive solutions to economic crises and negotiated with business as well as policymakers, progressives in Korea including the civil organizations and trade unions were relatively underdeveloped in the 1980s, and were incapable of offering a persuasive alternative to state-led developmentalism. There was a loose political camp called *Minjoong Yundae* (People's Alliance) in civil society. Although it lacked a cohesive organization among peasants, blue-collar workers, and white-collar workers, it did have vague criticisms of the state's distributive injustice favoring chaebols, and demanded that the state control the growth of chaebols and ensure distributive justice. However, the alliance lacked an alternative strategy for economic development (Koo and Kim 1992: 140).

On the other hand, large corporations in Korea offered a free market alternative to the existing state-led developmentalism. Criticizing the inefficiency of resource allocation by the state's excessive intervention, the Federation of Korean Industries (FKI), a large corporations' association, suggested in December 1979 a private-led market economy as an alternative to the state-led developmentalism. Chaebols gained an important voice in demanding that the existing state should reduce its control in the economy, although they owed much of their earlier prosperity to state subsidies and protection. The FKI's 1981 report "Recommendations on the Basic Directions of Management and Control of the Economy in the 1980s" emphasized the principle of free market economy (Suh, Jaejin 1991:

125–134; Koo and Kim 1992: 140–141; Kim, Eun Mee 1997: 198). Chaebols opposed the EPB-led reform which could result in another form of state control. International economic organizations like the International Monetary Fund (IMF) also supported the free market, arguing that Korea should recover the private-led market system (Kim, Yong-bok 1996: 135).

However, chaebols' alternative of the free market principle was persuasive to neither ordinary people nor economic bureaucrats. EPB and MCI bureaucrats as well as many ordinary people believed that chaebols wanted to continue an old-style input-oriented expansion strategy, rather than pursue market profitability and international competitiveness (Rhee 1994: 137). The chaebols' input-oriented overexpansionism, which would prevail if chaebols' free market was adopted, was regarded as the cause for the economic crisis of the late 1970s and early 1980s, which was seen as the target of reform rather than a goal to be pursued.

Actually, chaebols' demands were relatively complicated, although their first priority seemed to be freedom from state intervention. They wanted to make their own decisions in investments, independent of state intervention, to pursue their input-oriented expansionism, while at the same time they wanted protection from foreign competition and preferential state support. They argued for the abolition of state control over finance, yet they preferred the old-style preferential loans. They supported privatization of banks but they opposed the liberalization of interest rates. By financial liberalization, chaebols wanted to own the second financial institutions or nonbank financial institutions in order to easily mobilize the capital needed for their diversification (Amsden and Euh 1993: 380–381; Kim, Yeonchul 1993: 182–183; Ko, Kyungmin 2000: 71–72; Jun, Changhwan 2004: 112, 124–125; Park, Jihoon 2007: 50–54). Chaebols wanted neoliberal deregulation and flexibility in the labor market, yet they opposed opening domestic markets to foreign capital. Chaebols opposed liberalization of imports from the early 1980s. FKI suggested in its 1983 recommendation to the government that import liberalization and reduction of duties should be held back (Ji, Joohyung 2011: 115).

Large corporations' attempts to continue existing input-oriented expansion strategy were the object of criticism as cause for the economic crisis of the late 1970s. Chaebols' failure to offer an appropriate solution contributed to opening another window of opportunity for economic bureaucrats' new state-led developmentalism. The economic bureaucrats justified a new version of state-led developmentalism by emphasizing market failure in the chaebol-dominant structure. Indeed, although EPB, MoF, and MCI disagreed with how to overcome the economic crisis, they shared the idea of market failure in which chaebols would continue their existing input-oriented expansionism and might endanger the national economy. This shared idea of market failure contributed to the compromise among economic bureaucrats at a new state-led developmentalism, as shall be examined later.

Meanwhile, in contrast to the failure of civil progressives and chaebols to offer a persuasive alternative, EPB led the reform out of the economic crisis of the late 1970s and early 1980s. EPB was relatively free of the direct cause for the economic crisis, while MCI and MoF were deeply involved in the HCI drive of the Park administration. EPB was the single organization to predict and criticize the problems with the HCI drive (Choi, Byung-Sun 1991: 15–16; 1990: 253–254).

The economic bureaucrats of EPB and KDI (Korean Development Institute), including Kim Jae-ik, Kang Kyungsik, and Kim Kihwan,[4] prepared solutions to the economic problems earlier in the late 1970s. After the assassination of Park Chung Hee on October 26, 1979, the political and social situation escalated into serious turmoil. However, the economic bureaucrats around EPB and KDI were immersed in seeking solutions to the problems of the overexpansion policies of the 1970s (Choi, Byung-Sun 1990: 256–257). Furthermore, through the reshuffle of the economic cabinet after the failure of the general election in late 1978, the liberal economists occupied key posts in Korean economic decision-making. EPB became filled by the proponents of stabilization and liberalization (Choi, Byung-Sun 1991: 15–16), meaning that the identity of EPB changed, making it the leading organization of stabilization and liberalization through their practices, from the growth-first strategy based on foreign loans of the 1960s. The EPB's stabilization policy was mixed and inconsistent in the early stage of reform in the late 1970s. To stabilize prices, EPB initially adopted short-term macro policies from an optimistic perspective, including direct price control and stockpiling industrial and agricultural products that were in short supply. However, as they recognized that these measures were ineffective, they searched for more fundamental reforms. They proposed import liberalization as a solution to inflation, rather than the tight monetary policy of the Korean Bank. In addition, they prepared for structural reforms including private initiatives in the economy and liberalization of finance and trade (Choi, Byung-Sun 1991: 258–259; Jun, Changhwan 2004: 106).

However, this new group of US-trained economic bureaucrats in EPB and KDI were not such radical free marketers, abandoning wholly the industrial policy, as did US-trained free market fundamentalists in Mexico and Brazil who abandoned industrial and developmental policies for liberalization. In the process of contesting the developmentalist protectionism and the dependency theory, the US-trained economists of the Latin American countries, particularly Mexico and Brazil, emphasized a laissez-faire neoliberal state, giving up industrial developmentalism and focusing on the openness to foreign direct investment (FDI) (Fairbrother 2007:

---

[4] This was the so-called liberal group of EPB as well as US-trained economists of the Korean Development Institute (KDI). These reformists studied economics at US universities. These US-trained economists, who mostly majored in monetary economics and were influenced by monetarism, led liberalization in Korea (Kim, Y.T. 2000: 171; Baek, Wanki 2003: 179; Sakong 2003: 444; Ji, Joohyung 2011: 486).

269, 292 endnote 17; Heredia 1996: 110–116; Cypher and Wise 2010: 19–21, 29; Babb 2001: 11, 171–180).

In contrast to the free market fundamentalists in Mexico and Brazil, the so-called liberal bureaucrats of EPB in Korea were more liberal developmentalists who did not assume the exclusive relations of liberalization and industrial policy. Korean liberal bureaucrats adopted another version of developmentalism in the course of liberalization. For example, the EPB's 1982 Economic White Paper suggests a new industrial policy, different from the existing policy of the Park Chung Hee era, emphasizing the development of technology, human skills, and private initiatives to improve international competitiveness. What EPB emphasized in the process of liberalization was not giving up industrial policy, but turning the existing volume-oriented policy to high-value-added exports through a new industrial policy (Lee, Manhee 1993: 296). In particular, Kim Jae-ik, leader of the liberalization reform in the late 1970s and 1980s, emphasized promotion of technology-intensive industries, including semiconductor, information, and tele-communications, rather than abandoning the industrial policy for liberalization. He organized the Blue House developmental team which led the development of Korean IT industries thereafter, as we will examine later (Hong, S.G. 1997).[5]

The EPB's White Paper emphasized the need for state coordination to complement the market failure and to actively promote comparative advantages in the international divisions (Lee, Sangchul 2004a: 198). Criticizing the chaebols' argument for the noninterventionist state, the EBP's economic bureaucrats worried that the noninterventionist free market in Korea would continue the chaebols' market dominance and enable them to continue their existing input-oriented overexpansion (Rhee 1994: 103–104). Indeed throughout the 1980s and 1990s, in pointing out the market failure, the Korean economic bureaucrats including the EPB emphasized the state's active involvement in redirecting chaebols' volume expansion strategy to specialization in core business, which became apparent in overcoming the Asian financial crisis of 1997 (Hundt 2009: 103–110). In addition, in promoting the SMEs and parts industries, the Korean liberal bureaucrats of EPB and KDI justified their strategic involvement and support by pointing out the possibility of market failure. To develop parts industries, the Korean government strategically selected parts-specialized firms and supported them through policy loans and tax exemption (Lee, Manhee 1993: 219–320). Korean liberal bureaucrats were more pragmatists rather than followers of dogmatic principles (Suh, Junghwan 2007: 57).

---

[5] According to my personal interview with the former bureau director of the Ministry of Industry, Kang Kyungsik (another leader of liberalization) was also a proponent of the industrial promotion of SMEs and venture capital firms just before the 1997 Asian financial crisis. Personal interview with the former director general for capital goods industry on June 17, 2015.

However, the more concrete version of new developmentalism in Korea had been formed, not by the EPB's unilateral action but by mutual adjustments of competing organizations inside the state, including MCI and EPB, as well as interactions between government and business. For example, the important reform of industrial policy was realized in the enactment of the Industrial Development Law in 1985. This law was established by the MCI's redefinition of their policy after admitting the EPB's criticism, as shall be examined in the next section.

Recomposition of Developmentalism through Competition for Influence

Korea developed a new version of state-led developmentalism by way of mutual adjustments through political contests among diverse economic ministries, including EPB and MCI. Although MCI and MoF shared the EPB idea that the problem of Korean developmentalism resulted from input-oriented volume expansion, MCI and MoF differed in how to develop a technology-intensive economy. Departing from their old-style policies, MCI and MoF competed now for new methods and strategies for developmentalism in order to increase their influence. The process of transformation in Korean state-led developmentalism resulted from competition among ministries inside the state as well as state-business interaction.

The Chun administration's (1980–7) liberalization reform process began in the debates in the Park Chung Hee administration of the late 1970s, in which EPB increased its influence and finally seized its initiative in the Chun administration. Facing the economic crisis of the late 1970s, the small liberal faction in EPB began to analyze the existing economic problems in 1978. For example, Kang Kyungsik issued two major reports titled "Current Problems of the Korean Economy" in March and August 1978, which requested fundamental economic policy changes, including financial liberalization, measures to counter inflation, and import liberalization (Choi, B.S. 1991: 249–257; Rhee 1994: 93–94; Kang, Lee, and Choi 2008: 216).

However, the initial reforms attempted by the young bureaucrats of EPB and KDI failed because President Park, the HCI Promotion Bureau, and MCI still had strong confidence in their growth-first and expansionist strategy. Opposing the EPB idea of financial liberalization, MoF also focused on providing credits to the HCI drive, while recognizing the necessity of a tight monetary policy to curb inflation (Kim, Hungki 1999: 279). In the cabinet reshuffle of late 1978 a change occurred in EPB, from growth-oriented minister Nam Duckwoo to stability-oriented Shin Hyunhwak. Young reform-oriented bureaucrats began to gain more voice, although their voice fell short of persuading President Park who was confident in a growth-first strategy. In response to the EPB's new policy of stabilization, MCI in 1979 suggested a new development plan to select ten strategic industries, including machinery, shipbuilding, electronics, petrochemicals, and automobile industries, and to provide them with massive subsidies. MCI also requested large corporations to make large investments to improve production capability of the HCI (Choi, B.S. 1991: 249–251; 259).

The MCI and HCI Promotion Bureau argued that the already launched HCI should be completed, whereas EPB held that the HCI project should be delayed or stopped and the overinvestments be adjusted. EPB emphasized economic stabilization and a balanced development, whereas MCI, HCI Bureau, and the Presidential Economic Special Aide asserted emphatically the priority of economic growth, unbalanced HCI promotion, and export-driven development (Rhee 1994: 99–103). Although the HCI Investment Committee was established by EPB after the announcement of Comprehensive Measures for Economic Stabilization (CMES), EPB could not implement its idea due to opposition from MCI and the HCI Promotion Bureau.[6] MoF secretly supported the expansion policy, providing special rescue funds for HCI firms by 505,300 million Korean won (Kang, Kyungsik 1987: 39–40; Kim, Jaemyung 1988; Rhee 1994: 114–117).

Following the collapse of the Park Chung Hee government, EPB seized the initiative in economic decision-making. From the Choi Gyu-ha interim government of 1980, when reformist Shin Hyunhwak became prime minister, and former Deputy Minister of EPB Chung Jae-suk became minister of MCI, the EPB stabilization policy became mainstream. In particular, as Chun Doo-hwan's new military forces seized power and the reform-oriented economist Kim Jae-ik became a key economic adviser to Chun, EPB moved quickly with the initiative in economic reform. From May 1981, EPB briefed President Chun Doo-hwan weekly about its economic development ideas (Kim, Hungki 1999: 287). Although MoF opposed it, interest rates were liberalized. Preferential interest rates for exports also increased from 9% to 15% in 1981, something not dreamed of in the Park Chung Hee era. MoF and MCI reluctantly followed the EPB stabilization policy of tight monetarism, assuming that it was only a short-term policy (Rhee 1994: 135–136; Kim, Hungki 1999: 280–282).

Still, the liberalization process in Korea of the 1980s was not unilaterally the EPB's idea, but resulted from mutual adjustments in competition for influence. EPB initially seized the initiative, but later other ministries like MCI and MoF changed their existing ideas and proposed new developmentalism. For example, since the late 1970s EPB led initiatives in reforming industrial policy, suggesting the abandonment of developmentalism, stabilization instead of expansionism,

---

[6] Even through the so-called economic coup in June 1979 when reformists went overseas, the MCI and the HCI Promotion Bureau revoked the EPB stabilization policy by expanding preferential finances to support export firms. See Kim, Jaemyung (1988) and Kang, Kyungsik (1987: 39–40).

market rather than dirigisme, and market-neutral and functional support such as R&D rather than the existing targeting policy (EPB 1981: 183; KDI 1982; Hong, S. G. 1997: 96). However, even though the EPB idea on liberalization was accepted, there were still options in adjustments, from a shift toward a neoliberal free market system to a correction of the classical DS extremism, rather than total abandonment of state-led developmentalism in general. A new version of state-led developmentalism resulted from political choices and mutual adjustments through competition for influence among the relevant ministries.

Suffering from a rapid decline in influence in the liberalization reform process of the early 1980s, MCI made significant efforts to change its identity and developmental strategy through debates inside and outside MCI. In the early 1980s, MCI seriously suffered from its loss of organizational identity and rationale. Its serious efforts to promote national industries and exports became the target of criticism, rather than a cause for its organizational rationale. The former minister of MCI remembers the organization's suffering in the early 1980s:

> In the transformation period of the early 1980s, MCI was driven to a corner. Criticism concentrated on MCI which had made sincere efforts to promote exports since the 1960s and led the goals of $10 billion exports and heavy chemical industrialization in the 1970s....As overinvestments became the target of reform, MCI men, who carried them out, did not have anyone whom they could open their hearts to rely on....Dissatisfaction by other ministries erupted....Blame for the economic hardship was passed on to MCI. While seniors and colleagues who shared all the joys and sorrows left their seats, MCI fell into disorder, and the MCI's hard times when it could not appoint its own staff as vice minister positions continued for a while....MCI was surrounded by enemies on all sides.   (Shin, Kookhwan 1994: 368)

Facing the situation in which their organizational rationale became a target of criticism, MCI initially opposed the reform, and becoming passive in reform by simply continuing the given projects including building the second comprehensive steel factory and the third oil refinery factory (Shin, Kookhwan 1994: 361). As one former MCI staff member says, "MCI did not know how to redefine its role. We thought, 'Shouldn't we just take our hands off because now the private initiative has become a trend?'"[7] MCI lost its own organizational rationale and roles in the early 1980s.

However, MCI desperately searched for its new roles and organizational rationale through internal debate. In particular, as EPB members including Kim Kihwan and Han Ducksoo were newly recruited in main MCI posts, MCI began

---

[7]   Personal interview with former bureau director of MCI on May 29, 2018.

to seriously think over the problems of its existing policies, including the individual firm-targeting policy and protectionism.[8] While the newly recruited EPB members pressed for a radical openness, moderately open groups and protectionists also prevailed inside MCI in the early 1980s. When Kum Jinho became Vice Minister in October 1981 and later was promoted to Minister of MCI in 1983, a tipping point was reached in MCI debate toward openness.[9] However, the MCI's turnaround toward openness did not mean a shift toward a radical neoliberal free market. Rather than abandoning industrial policy, MCI redefined developmentalism. Once MCI accepted the necessity of trade openness, it emphasized new methods of industrial promotion policy to enable Korean exporters to compete by focusing on the qualitative upgrade of exports rather than maintaining the existing input-oriented volume strategy.

This focus on exports allowed MCI to escape its hard times. From the late 1970s, Korean exports declined and the balance of payments deteriorated due to the oil shock. Payments of oil imports alone reached $5600 million in 1980. Economic growth rates fell into minus territory for the first time since the Korean industrialization of the 1960s. In particular, the balance of international payments attracted significant attention in the first half of the 1980s. Korea's gross foreign debts doubled from $26 billion to $46.7 billion in 1985, ranking fourth worldwide, following Brazil, Argentina, and Mexico. In this period, the trade deficit reached $15.7 billion due to the decline of exports. A former MCI minister recalls, "MCI men had to get through seasons of perseverance and wait for a new mood [for export growth and industrial policy]." In the mid-1980s, not only economic ministries including EPB and MoF, but also Korean people in general shared the idea that exports should be promoted as a solution to the economic crisis. Now MCI staff began to think that "this time we reestablish our industrial and export policy" (Shin, Kookhwan 1994: 369). However, although a readiness for export policy rose, MCI did not use an old-style export drive policy because that export drive was not favored due to its overexpansion.[10] MCI was more careful in promoting exports by emphasizing the quality improvement of exports. In addition, MCI began to counterattack EPB and MoF on the sluggishness of exports, while developing new export promotion policies including the upgrade of export industries toward

---

[8] Personal interview with former Vice Minister of the Ministry of Knowledge Economy on April 30, 2013.

[9] Personal interview with former MCI core staff Cho Hwanik on June 19, 2018. Kum Jinho was not only a powerful man who had a family tie with President Roh Taewoo, but also an excellent bureaucrat graduating from Seoul National University. He served as Vice Minister of MCI from October 1981 to October 1983, and then as Minister of MCI from October 1983 to June 1986. He led MCI during the turbulent period and enacted the Industry Promotion Law.

[10] While searching for new industrial policies, MCI not only reflected upon the problems of its traditional policies including the individual business-oriented promotion policy and protectionism, but also researched the Japanese experience. Personal interview with former Vice Minister of the Ministry of Knowledge Economy on April 30, 2013.

high-value-added industries and the localization of parts and materials (Shin, Kookhwan 1994: 377–381).

Now MCI, as well as industry-related organizations including the Economic Secretariats of the Blue House, began to search for new developmental policies to upgrade industrial competitiveness and the export structure, while accepting the idea of stabilization and liberalization proposed by EPB. Considering the advanced countries' protectionism, including the import restrictions of France and Britain on Korean black and white TVs in 1977, and the US import restriction of Korean color TVs in 1978, the Korean government was forced to liberalize its trade in order to further its exports (Odel 1985: 263–286; Hong, S.G.1995: 42–43).

In addition, emphasizing the market failure, including automakers' overcompetition and overinvestment in a small market, MCI crafted new developmental policies instead of totally abandoning industrial policies in liberalization. For example, MCI developed the Industry Rationalization Rule to remedy the overinvestments in the 1980s.[11] Reflecting upon the problems of their own traditional developmentalism based on the input-oriented volume expansion strategy, MCI also began to emphasize a turnaround in industrial policy, not only from a traditional focus on final assembly to localization of parts, but from traditional volume-oriented export to quality-oriented export industry promotion (Lee, Yu, and Bang 2005: 62). In particular, MCI began to promote value-added industries with R&D incentives. For example, MCI and the Presidential Economic Secretariats of the Blue House made efforts to nurture hi-tech industries. MCI and the Blue House team led the process of drafting the Electronics Industry Promotion Plan and support for its high value-added development in the 1980s, as we will discuss later.

In particular, reflecting upon the problems of input-oriented industrial policy and restriction on industrial subsidies under trade liberalization, MCI chose the R&D policy as a breakthrough for its new roles in industrial developmentalism.[12] R&D policy was also compatible with the EPB's idea of function-oriented industrial policy, although the MCI's R&D policy was more strategically selective. A chief of the R&D Strategy Planning Bureau in the Ministry of Industry (MoI) says about the MCI's redefined role through R&D policy: "We found R&D policy as our new role; instead of traditional permission regulation, we found a new policy instrument; thus we established the Industry Base Technology Promotion Project based on the Industry Development Law of 1985; it began with 10 billion Korean won but grew to 3.2 trillion Korean won."[13] Again, the Korean R&D policy aimed

[11] Personal interview with chief of R&D Strategy Planning Bureau in the Ministry of Industry on June 18, 2018.
[12] Personal interview with former bureau director of the MCI on May 29, 2018.
[13] Personal interview with chief of R&D Strategy Planning Bureau in the Ministry of Industry on June 18, 2018.

not at market-neutral general services available to all citizens, but at technology development of strategic industries as a developmental policy.

The shift toward a new version of developmentalism through conflicts among ministries, rather than total abandonment of state-led developmentalism, is apparent in the enactment of the Industry Development Law of 1985. Through this law, MCI revoked the traditional individual business-oriented promotion and volume-oriented expansion policies, opting for a more function-oriented and quality-oriented path and the legal foundation to support it (Suh, Jaejin 1991: 136; Ahn, Gilwon 1989; Kim, Yong-bok 1996: 158–159; 2005: 239). The 1985 industrial policies included industrial rationalization policy which prohibited over-competition and ensured normalization of business and control of market entry for international competitiveness. The industry promotion policy focused on improving technological capability and promoting the parts industries. For the former policy, MCI established corporate restructuring funds, as well as tax and financial incentives as policy instruments. For the latter policy, MCI established R&D funds as policy instruments, including the Industry Development Fund, the Industry Technology Improvement Fund, and the SME Corporate Restructuring Fund, while developing R&D projects including the Industry Base Technology Development Project and the Special R&D Projects to improve technology capabilities. MCI also launched SME policy loans to promote SME parts industries based on the SME Promotion Long-term Plan of 1982–91, announced in April 1982 (MCI 1988: 54; Lee, Sangchul 2004a: 199–200; 215–216).

This Industry Development Law of 1985 was enacted through competition of EPB and MCI to change existing industrial policy. EPB initiated the reform. Kim Jae-ik of EPB in the Chun military government led the policy reform, drafting the Industry Support Law in September 1980, which aimed to abolish the existing individual industry-oriented laws, such as the Machine Industry Promotion Law of 1976, the Shipbuilding Promotion Law of 1967, the Electronics Promotion Law of 1969, and Steel Promotion Law of 1970. Such individual industry-oriented laws were believed to produce overlapping investments and excessive state intervention. EPB offered more general and function-oriented policies such as general R&D support available to all industries. In addition, EPB aimed to take over policy instruments such as taxes, finances, and import restrictions wielded by MCI and MoF (Choi, B.S. 1990: 33; Yoon, D. 2011: 98). Although the EPB's original draft was suspended by MCI and MoF opposition, it initiated serious debate inside the state over what the most efficient industrial policy would be (KDI 1982; KIET 1983; Yoon, D. 2011: 100–101).

In response to the EPB's reform ideas, MCI offered the Industry Promotion Revision Plan of November 1984. While accepting EPB ideas such as abolition of individual promotion laws and private initiatives, MCI suggested new industry promotion policies to develop promising industries and offer a rationalization plan for declining industries. Finally an MCI draft called the Industry Structural

Upgrade Promotion Law was passed into the Industry Development Law of 1986 (Choi, Jongwon 1991; Kim, Yong-bok 2005).

Why did EPB accept the MCI compromise? The EPB's original reform plan mainly aimed at abolishing the existing individual promotion laws, but offered little detail. There was room for new industrial policies.[14] In addition, key leaders of the EPB reform, including Kim Jae-ik, were killed in the terrorist bombing in Burma in October 1983, and were replaced by the gradual reform-oriented technocrats, including Kim Manjae, Chung Inyoung, and Sakong Il (Rhee 1994: 211–213). More importantly, EPB could not implement its own ideas if it disregarded the other ministries' efforts to change (Choi, B.S. 1990: 246; 1987: 20–21). Although EPB took initiative in the reform, it needed to compromise with other relevant ministries when they replaced their old positions with new solutions. For example, while attempting to reform the industrial policy, EPB established a new bureau called the Industry Policy Adjustment Section inside the EPB in June 1984 to take over industrial policy functions. Although the influence of MCI declined in the early 1980s compared to the 1970s, MCI was still the industrial policy ministry. In order to build industry networks for new industrial policies, EPB needed the MCI's collaboration (Yoon, D. 2011: 99–100).

Furthermore, MCI changed its roles and strategy through internal debates, in which it combined EPB liberalization and new developmentalism, while abolishing its traditional protectionism and input-oriented policy (Kim, Yong-bok 2005: 238–239). When MCI recognized that EPB and MoF would propose new industry policy laws, MCI rapidly resolved its internal conflicts (Ahn, Gilwon 1989: 61; Kim, Yong-bok 2005: 241). MCI then led the enactment of the new Industry Promotion Law while adopting the EPB's ideas to form the legal foundations for MCI involvement in the industrial rationalization and promotion of strategic industries.

Similarly, financial activism in Korea continued in the 1980s, even in the significant changes toward liberalization. Financial liberalization in the early 1980s sharply contrasted with the traditional Korean DS based on state control of finance and allocation of credit (Woo 1991: 191–192, 203). In the early 1980s, the Korean government privatized four main commercial banks including Choheung, Korean First Bank, Hanil Bank, and Seoul Trust, owned by MoF, and reduced policy loans and liberalized interest rates, reducing the differences of interest rates between policy loans and market loans (Kim, Yongbok 1996: 143–144; Kim, Eun Mee 1997: 178–179). However, despite this financial liberalization, Korea continued its financial activism rather than succumb to the free market system, thanks to MoF changing its original idea and its compromise with EPB.

---

[14] Personal interview with chief of R&D Strategy Bureau in the Ministry of Industry on June 18, 2018.

Conflicts over financial liberalization came to the surface in May 1980 when the Emergency Committee for National Security (ECNS) was established under Chun's coup. Liberal reformists including Kim Jae-ik argued for radical liberalization of finance including the independence of the Korean Bank, privatization of commercial banks, financial deregulation, and real-name financial transactions, whereas MoF and the Committee of Finance in the ECNS proposed gradual reform rather than direct opposition. MoF could not continue its old-style financial activism because it lacked legitimacy due to the economic crisis resulting from overexpansion. Although MoF showed some resistance, it lacked a clear voice. Furthermore, most social forces including the large corporations supported financial liberalization. In this situation, MoF searched for a new organizational rationale and new role through internal debate, incurred through changes in key staff by EPB since 1982 when Kang Kyungsik became vice minister of MoF.

Debates raged inside MoF between newly recruited EPB members, including Kang Kyungsik, and the original MoF members such as Lee Kyusung, Chung Youngui, Lee Soohyu (Kim, Yongbok 1996: 139; Kim, Hungki 1999: 324; Lee, Jangkyu 2008: 225–231). Debates focused on the need for financial liberalization to solve existing problems including overinvestments and preferential loans to chaebols. MoF could not continue its old-style state control. Once accepting the basic trend of financial liberalization, MoF argued that even though financial liberalization was needed, a wholesale discard of the state's coordinating power could engender new problems such as chaebols' overinvestments and nonperforming loans; the developmental stage required state coordination rather than a radical free market. MoF compromised on measures including privatization of commercial banks but the state maintained its power in the financial market including "consultation in staff recruitments of banks" (Choi, B.S. 1991: 265, 267).

Although EPB initiated the reform, it could not but compromise rather than persisting its original idea if the relevant ministry replaced its old positions with new solutions, as it did with MCI over industrial policy. Even EPB could not implement its own idea if it disregarded other ministries' efforts to change (Choi, B.S. 1991: 20–21; 1990: 246). Furthermore, EPB and MoF shared the idea of market failure, in that chaebols' current input-oriented actions could engender significant problems in the national economy. EPB proposed financial liberalization, as large corporations did, but they differed with chaebols over market failure if the chaebols continued their input-oriented expansion strategy freely. Indeed, financial deregulation in the Chun administration tended to strengthen chaebols' input-oriented overexpansion, rather than reduce the chaebols' influence, by its preferential access to capital. Through financial liberalization, particularly, chaebols could mobilize massive capital by free access to nonbank financial institutions (NBFIs) independent of state control (Hundt 2009: 79).

This market failure justified another version of state-led developmentalism. Opposing the chaebols' argument for state nonintervention and voluntary corporate restructuring in the free market, the EPB liberals in the Chun government emphasized state intervention in order to liberalize the economy (Kang, Kyungsik 1987: 45–48; Rhee 1994: 158–159). Both MoF and MCI could also justify their new methods of state-led developmentalism, based on the shared idea of market failure. Indeed, as many firms' insolvency and corporate restructuring came to light in 1986–88, state intervention in the financial market was justified (Choi, B.S. 1991: 268). Providing massive capital of $2.1 billion into the financial system in 1985–7, the Chun government was deeply involved in corporate restructuring and dealing with bad debts, not for the purpose of building a free market, but for the developmental purpose of changing corporate strategies to specialize in core business and sectoral rationalization (Kim, B.-K. 2003: 55–56; 2004: 84). In the Roh Tae-woo (1988–92) and Kim Young-sam (1993–7) administrations, the Korean state controlled loans for chaebols' specialization in core business.

As a result, Korea could continue its state-led developmentalism even in the process of liberalization, not by persisting in its traditional developmentalism, but by changing it. These changes and continuity came from competition among ministries inside the state, as well as state-business interaction.

6

Transition II

The Roh and Kim Administrations

Even though the Economic Planning Board (EPB) initiated reforms to the traditional developmental state in the Park Chung Hee era, these reforms took time to
materialize the detailed form of new developmentalism. In particular, EPB waged
many contests between the state and large corporations, as well as inside the state,
to change the national economy from the existing input-oriented volume expansionism to a high value-added, technology-intensive economy. Large corporations pressed for input-oriented volume expansionism, while economic
bureaucrats pressed to change private corporations' strategy toward specialization
in core business and a more technology-intensive strategy, rather than
octopus-like diversification. Conflicts between state policymakers and large
corporations slowly produced adjustments through tedious attrition in the
Roh Tae-woo (1988–92) and Kim Young-sam (1993–7) administrations. During
these two administrations, Korean capitalism was a mix of input-oriented continuance and new initiatives in technology-intensive strategies. Nevertheless,
input-oriented expansionism twice drove the Korean economy into major economic crises in the late 1980s and late 1990s. Only with the Asian financial
crisis of 1997 did the Korean economy seriously begin to transform to a
knowledge-intensive economy. Now large corporations could resist the state's
developmental discipline as their autonomous power grew and the state lost
many of its traditional disciplinary methods such as massive mobilization of
credit and its allocation authority.

This chapter examines how industrial politics between the state and the private
firms, as well as within the state, evolved in the Roh and Kim administrations,
and why Korea continued state-led developmentalism by contentious adjustments through industrial politics. First we examine the industrial politics between
state and business, as well as among the ministries within the state during the Roh
and Kim administrations. And prior to exploring the transformation following
the Asian financial crisis of 1997–8, we will examine the electronics industry for a
micro-level analysis of Korea's new developmentalism.

Changes by Competition: The Evolution of the South Korean Developmental State. Hyeong-ki Kwon,
Oxford University Press (2021). © Hyeong-ki Kwon. DOI: 10.1093/oso/9780198866060.003.0006

Contentious Adjustments in State-Business Relations

The second half of the 1980s was a roller coaster for the Korean economy. The Korean economy in 1986–8 enjoyed a boom based on the three lows of oil prices, interest rates, and appreciation of dollars, but the boom sharply turned to an economic crisis in 1989. In the big boom era fueled by the three lows, Korean exports skyrocketed due to high appreciation of the Japanese yen through the Plaza Accord of 1985, and the trade balance turned toward a profit. In order to avoid trade conflicts, the Roh Tae-woo (1988–92) administration pursued further liberalization of trade and finance, as well as internationalization of industries (Yoon, D. 2011: 90–91). However, this special boom delayed corporate restructuring by continuing the existing volume-oriented expansionism.

The boom crashed in the 1989 economic crisis as external conditions of three lows disappeared. International competition became tougher, particularly in the technology-intensive sectors, while the United States and European countries strengthened harsh measures against dumping (Kang, C.S. 2000: 81–85; Kim, B.-K. 2003: 62–63; Hundt 2009: 82). Korea's exports declined, and its trade balance turned from black to red in 1990, while its economic growth rates fell from double digits, 12% on average in 1986–8, to single digits, 6.8% in 1989. Inflation rates rose in Korea from below 3% to 7.1% in 1988 and to 9.3% in 1990. In addition, after democratization in 1987, frequency of labor disputes rose significantly, and real pay climbed at 10.1% in 1987, 15.5% in 1988, and 21.2% in1989, far surpassing the growth rates of labor productivity (Kim, Hungki 1999: 354–355; Yoon, D. 2011: 92).

However, the crisis itself does not reveal its nature and solutions automatically, but needs interpretations. Chaebols and conservative politicians pointed to rapid growth of wages and labor disputes in the process of democratization, while others emphasized large corporations' extravagant, volume-oriented expansionism as a main cause for the crisis. However, as most economists agreed, the economic crisis of the late 1980s resulted from weakness in the Korean economy's existing input-oriented developmentalism (Cumings 1998; Jeong 1997; Johnson 1998; Krueger and Yoo 2002; Jung, D.G. 2006: 538; Park, Taegyeon 1997: 183–185). As real pay grew through democratization, the input-oriented growth strategy based on low wages lost its competitive edge. Particularly, the competition of Southeast Asian countries and China based on low wages became tougher. Meanwhile, chaebols could expand their existing volume-oriented diversification by mobilizing massive capital through access to secondary financial institutions and the boom based on the three lows, while reducing their dependence on the state (Lee, K.K. 2005: 324–325; Ji, Joohyung 2011: 127; Yu, Chulkyu 2004: 78).

Contesting the chaebols' voluntary actions in the market, the Korean government could continue its state-led developmentalism actively interpreting the nature of the economic crisis and offering a new developmentalism. Korean economic bureaucrats could justify their new developmentalism by emphasizing the need to transform the Korean economy from input-oriented to technology-intensive. Hindsight shows that the Korean government's policies in this period had mixed outcomes. They failed to turn volume-oriented expansionism to value-added specialization in core business, while they succeeded in nurturing technology-intensive industries like semiconductor and the information and telecommunications industries. Before examining the promotion of technology-intensive industries as a case study of electronics, we address the contesting politics of state and business over specialization in core business.

Facing the economic crisis of the late 1980s, the Roh Tae-woo administration (1988–92) pursued a new state-led developmentalism in order to turn the existing input-oriented expansionism to technology-intensive development, in contest with chaebols' demands for a neoliberal market system (Cho, S. R. 1996: 202). The Roh administration's new state-led developmentalism in the early 1990s grew from reflection upon the ineffectiveness of new liberal measures, including private firms' autonomous corporate adjustments in the free market, particularly during the three-lows boom.[1] In addition, the new state-led developmentalism in the early 1990s had been formed in contest with large corporations' voluntary actions in the market. Large corporations tended to turn their business to non-manufacturing and speculative businesses such as real estate and stock markets, rather than upgrading productivity, as their profitability declined due to the disappearance of the three lows. For example, capital profit earned through land transactions increased up to 15.6% of GDP in 1987, 31.9% in 1988, and 37.7% in 1989 (Baek, Jongkook 1993: 159; Rhee 1994b: 268).

Since the EPB's Special Conference for National Economic Recovery in December 1989, the Roh Tae-woo administration developed a so-called Core Business Policy (*Jooryuk Upchae Jedo* in Korean) as a new state-led developmentalism, announced in November 1991. The Core Business Policy aimed to restrain unproductive investments like speculation in real estate and turn volume-oriented, octopus-like diversification to specialization in core business. It also aimed to improve corporations' technology-intensive development capability through the Advanced Technology Development Project called the G7 Project in which the state planned to upgrade Korean corporations' technology to seventh in world ranking within 10 years. To do this, the Roh government planned to develop 919

---

[1] According the evaluation of the MCI over the Industry Technology Promotion Project and the Five-Year Plan of Localization of Parts and Materials, they did not result in much success. For example, the localization of parts reached only half of the original goals, 2157 parts of the original goal 4542 products (Ryu and Lee 1993: 42–43).

production technologies together with private corporations and to share the costs 50-50 with them (Ryu and Lee 1993: 49–50; Yoon, D. 2011: 92–95).

Under the Core Business Policy the Roh government first forced large corporations to sell their nonbusiness lands through the so-called 5.8 measure of 1990, and then announced a corporate restructuring plan requiring the 30 largest corporations to select three core businesses. The government allowed loans to each of these core businesses, while restricting loans to other noncore businesses. In April 1991, the government provided 76 firms, which the 20 largest chaebols had selected as core business, with tax exemption for hi-tech facilities and factory automation, as well as permission for massive loans (FKI 1991: 55–56; Ryu and Lee 1993: 47). Although the government's new developmentalism achieved some success in facilitating private corporations to improve their R&D capabilities, the Roh administration's restriction of volume-oriented diversification did not gain much success. Private firms now could develop their response strategies to evade the government's unilateral enforcements.

Actually, large corporations in Korea of the 1980s were interested in volume expansion and increased market share through nonrelated diversification because they could use their monopoly position to both get government support and to use economy of scale. In addition, large corporations wanted to reduce their risks by diversifying their portfolio, rather than improving profitability by focusing on core business.[2] Large corporations were more interested in volume and market share through diversification, although Korean economic bureaucrats commonly believed since the early 1980s that chaebols' nonrelated diversification was a main cause for lowering industrial competitiveness, a practice that needed correcting (Kim, Yong-bok 1996: 175).

Large corporations strongly opposed the Roh administration's Core Business Policy, arguing that it ran counter to the liberal market economy. They held that in the era of openness and liberalization, government intervention was not only needless but also impossible due to the government's lack of information (Sunwoo and Yang 1991: 27). Chaebols thought that the Core Business Policy was a betrayal of the ethos of the developmental alliance. While promoting their ideology of a noninterventionist free market system and propagandizing their contribution to national prosperity, Korean chaebols began to counterattack the government's new developmentalism. In particular, in May 1991, Chung Jooyoung, president of Hyundai conglomerate, began officially to criticize government policies. The Federation of Korean Industries (FKI), the large corporations' association, demanded a liberal free market and a smaller role for the state to reduce its interventionism. In conflicts with government, corporate CEOs like Lee Myungbak of Hyundai entered into politics. Chung Jooyoung, president of Hyundai

---

[2] Personal interview with a managing director at Federation of Korean Industries (FKI) on May 17, 2018.

chaebol, ran for the 1992 Presidential election. Due to the opposition of large corporations, the Roh administration turned toward an appeasement policy, deregulated the land ownership restriction, and shifted its industrial policy toward a traditional growth-oriented approach (Kim, Yong-bok 1996: 149–50, 153; Hundt 2009: 83–84).

The Core Business Policy of the Roh Tae-woo administration failed, by and large. Although the government tried to restrict loans to chaebols' noncore business subsidiaries, these chaebols could still continue their expansion strategy by utilizing their core business as their financing window, through which they could borrow massive loans free of state loan restrictions, and circulate the loans inside their subsidiaries (Lee, Manhee 1993: 347). For example, the 72 core subsidiaries of the 30 largest chaebols borrowed 44.5% (9.46 trillion Korean won) of the total loan (21.2 trillion Korean won) which 531 subsidiaries of the 30 largest chaebols borrowed in 1991. The debt-equity ratios of the 30 largest chaebols increased from 358% in late 1990 to 435% in late 1991 (Noh, Y. 1991: 55; Lee, Manhee 1993: 349–350; Kim, Yongbok 1996: 190). Although the chaebols initially strongly opposed the state's loan restriction and the Core Business Policy, they utilized the loophole to avoid government regulations, while lobbying high-level politicians.[3]

Despite the failure of the Roh administration's Core Business Policy, the subsequent Kim Young-sam government (1993–7) continued its developmental policy, unlike some DS theorist account of Kim administration as a liberal regime (Thurbon 2016). Although with some revision of the policy name of *Shin Kyungjae* (New Economy, in Korean), the Kim Young-sam administration continued the developmentalism with which it restricted large firms from input-oriented expansionism while attempting to induce them toward high value-added and technology-intensive industries.

The reason for continuity in the Core Business Policy, despite a rebranding from *Jooryuk Upchae Jedo* (specialization in core firms) of Roh administration to *Jooryuk Upjong Jedo* (specialization in core business) in the Kim administration, is because economic bureaucrats, including EPB, Ministry of Finance (MoF), and Ministry of Commerce and Industry (MCI), shared the idea that chaebols should be constrained from expanding to nonrelated businesses and encouraged to invest their financial resources in more innovation-oriented and technology-intensive activities in specialized core businesses (Kim, Yongbok 1996: 181). More importantly, economic bureaucrats competed for initiatives in executing this policy. In the Roh administration, MoF led the policy, whereas in the Kim administration

---

[3] According to Professor Yong-Chool Ha's excellent empirical study, chaebols began to learn how to deal with governments as they grew. Initially, large corporations almost totally depended on the economic bureaucrats because they controlled the financial flow. However, they recognized that economic bureaucrats also depended on economic performance, particularly in exports. In addition, they found that it was more effective to bypass bureaucrats and directly lobby powerful politicians or the Blue House individually (Ha 2006: 198–202).

MCI took the initiative, criticizing the ineffectiveness of the MoF's specialization policy (Korea Institute of Social Research 1995: 58–59).

The debate on the Core Business Specialization policy was launched initially in the Roh administration through competition among the Blue House team of Presidential economic secretariats and MCI for initiative. Economic bureaucrats by and large agreed on the idea of the Core Business Specialization, but they contested about how to execute it, whether to focus on core firm or core business for specialization. MCI argued for specialization based on core business, while EPB and MoF proposed to focus on the core firms of each conglomerate. EPB and MoF argued that if they focused on core businesses, it would be difficult to control loans as a key policy instrument. In addition, MoF argued that the chaebols, as targets of the specialization policy, should be reduced from the 30 largest to the 10 largest chaebols. By contrast, MCI held that the financial support for core businesses should be expanded, while the regulation against noncore business should be strengthened. The Roh administration's final decision leaned toward the MoF idea of core firm-based specialization.

As this MoF policy appeared ineffective, MCI attempted in 1993 to establish a supplemental plan to the specialization policy rather than abandon the state-led specialization program. MCI criticized the MoF's core firm-oriented specialization, arguing that it was policy convenient to select firms which needed more money in each chaebol. MCI argued that MoF policy failed to induce chaebols to invest in technology-intensive specialization. As an alternative, MCI offered specialization at core businesses considering technology linkages and fusions.

In 1993 when Kim Young-sam seized power, the Kim government began to adopt MCI policy as a new industrial policy. Unlike the MoF's core firm specialization, the MCI's core business specialization policy encouraged core business-related diversification, while it restricted nonrelated diversification.[4] The MCI policy prioritized core business specialization, while relaxing the regulation on concentration of economic power. MCI aimed to enlarge core business for economy of scale in the selected specialization to compete internationally, and pursued economy of scope by allowing business-related diversification. The MCI policy focused only on promoting firms' competitiveness, not considering the resulting social injustices and policy conveniences (Kim, Y.B. 1996: 200–201; Lee, Jong-hwa 1994: 92). To support chaebols' core business specialization, the Kim administration in January 1994 relaxed the loan restriction to chaebols' selected core businesses and enabled chaebols to use direct finance in foreign and domestic markets. The Kim government also provided industrial sites with special preference to the selected core business of chaebols while encouraging chaebols to participate in state-coordinated technology development projects.[5]

---

[4] Personal interview with then-Minister of MCI on June 11, 2018.   [5] Ibid.

Large corporations initially opposed the MCI-led core business specialization, arguing for nonintervention in the free market system. But as the government strongly pushed the policy, they avoided direct conflicts with the Kim administration, while proposing revised plans and lobbying to increase the number of core businesses to six in each chaebol. As chaebols showed some compliance, the government became more supportive in providing loans (Jung, D.G. 2006: 532; Park, Jihoon 2007: 85–86). However, the Kim administration's inconsistency in policy, as seen in permitting Samsung's 1995 entry into the automobile industry, and chaebols' competition for increasing market share in a few strategic industries, caused failure of the original specialization goal to restrict input-oriented overexpansionism.

The Kim administration's core business specialization policy caused overlapping investments in a few strategic industries, including semiconductor, petrochemicals, and automobile industries, because chaebols preferred these industries, given the government's strategic promotion policy (Park, Taegyeon 1997: 198–200). In the 1990s, chaebols still continued their volume-oriented, nonrelated expansionism, although competition among chaebols, particularly among the largest, slowly shifted to building in-house R&D capabilities (Lim, Youngil 1999: 97). Second-ranked chaebols began to follow the path by which the largest forerunners increased their size in the 1970s and 1980s. For example, using large debts, the Halla conglomerate entered into the shipbuilding industry in 1990 when Chinese firms did, based on low wages and large financial resources. Chaebols' reckless investments for market share, particularly among second-ranked chaebols, based on short-term and foreign debts, caused insolvency among many large conglomerates, including Hanbo and Sammi Special Steel, Kia automobile, and the Halla and Haetae group, which resulted in the Asian financial crisis of 1997 (Park, Taegyeon 1997: 196–197, 200–201).

However, the new state-led developmentalism to change input-oriented industries to technology-intensive, was not a total failure in the 1980s and 1990s. Large corporations began to change toward competition for building in-house R&D capabilities in the 1980s, although they still continued input-oriented and nonrelated diversification (Lim, Youngil 1999: 97). Large corporations were initially hesitant to invest in hi-tech industries and more interested in large-scale assembly of final products with imported technology and parts and low-wage labor. However, as the government encouraged chaebols to invest in technology-intensive industries and improve their R&D capabilities, they began to compete with each other through R&D. In the early 1980s large corporations began to compete for more PhD recruitment in science and engineering. Until 1995, Samsung was a leader in this competition by employing 482 PhDs, while LG, Hyundai, and Deawoo followed by employing 311 PhDs, 225 PhDs, and 203 PhDs respectively (Lim, Youngil 1999: 98).

Why this competition to build in-house R&D capabilities? First, Korean large corporations, through low wages and imported technology, faced much tougher competition from firms in China and Southeast Asia. Furthermore, as Korean large firms climbed the technology ladder in each industry, they found it more difficult to buy and transfer foreign technology from advanced countries, including the United States and Japan. However, these challenges in the international market were not sufficient to turn Korean firms toward more improvement in value-added and R&D activities. They could make more profits with their monopolistic power in the domestic market and were reluctant to invest in high-risk technology-intensive industries.

The shift in government developmental policy prompted Korean large corporations to turn toward high value-added activities. Starting in the early 1980s, the Korean government focused on changing the traditional volume-oriented expansionism of the Park Chung Hee era toward high value-added and technology-intensive development. It announced *Kisool Yipkook* (literally, Establishment of Nation by Technology in Korean) in contrast to *Soochool Yipkook* (literally, Establishment of Nation by Exports in Korean), the catchphrase of the Park Chung Hee era. Under the buzzword *Kisool Yipkook*, the Korean government enacted laws to provide R&D-oriented firms with preferential incentives, including tax benefits, low-cost financing, and various infrastructural services. The Korean government's new developmentalism enabled large firms to turn toward R&D intensive industries by reducing risks and costs.

For example, after Samsung entered the semiconductor business and made unprecedented investments in the early 1980s, it suffered hard times in the chip market recession in 1983–6 when the price of memory chips nose-dived from $2.50 to 20 cents in 1983. Many people worried that Samsung might collapse. However, due to the Korean government's favorable support, Samsung could endure the plunge, while many American chip-makers wound up their business (Lee, Kiyul 1995: 285–289; Lim, Youngil 1999: 102, 113–114; Mathews and Cho 2000: 127–128).

The Roh Tae-woo (1988–92) and Kim Young-sam (1993–7) administrations further expanded their R&D-oriented industrial policy by the new developmentalism. For example, the Roh Tae-woo administration emphasized promotion of technology-intensive industries as a solution to the crisis of the late 1980s. Based on the Industry Development Law of 1986, MCI in the Roh administration developed mid- and long-term industrial development plans, including the Five-Year Production Technology Development Plan of 1990 and the Five-Year Hi-Tech Industry Development Plan in 1989 (Yoon, D. 2011: 122–125). The Kim Young-sam administration also planned to increase R&D expenditures by 24.5% on annual average from 1994 to 1998, and thus set R&D at the level of 4.0% of GDP (Cho, S. R. 1997: 169).

Actually, in November 1991 the Roh administration initiated national R&D projects, such as the Advanced Technology Development Project called the G7 project, in which the government's 1.6 trillion Korean won, as well as the private 2.08 trillion Korean won, were invested, and a research staff of about 100,000 participated from 1992 to 2002 for the purpose of upgrading the technology of Korean industries to seventh worldwide. This R&D project was not general service for pure science, but a developmental policy targeted to promote the next generation of technologies for Korean main industries, including VLSI semiconductor, broadband Integration Service Digital Network (ISDN), and HDTV (Ryu and Lee 1993: 49–50; Yoon, D. 2011: 94–95). Now, in contrast to chaebols' initial hesitation, they competed for in-house R&D capabilities which contributed to their enterprise visibility and a better position to earn government support.

Continuity by Competition Inside the State

Unlike Latin American countries including Mexico, Argentina, and Brazil, where liberalization meant abandonment of state developmental policies, Korea combined its state-led developmentalism with liberalization, including deregulation and trade openness. In the process of liberalization in the 1980s, economic bureaucrats, whether the relatively conservative MCI or the liberal EPB, shared more or less the idea that they needed to further the industrial policy to promote international competitiveness of national industries. They regarded liberalization and trade openness as challenges to a national economy, which developmental policy would overcome (Ryu and Lee 1993: 37; Ko, Kyungmin 2000: 93). By focusing on competition among ministries, we examine how the Korean state could continue its developmentalism even in liberalization.

Facing the late 1980s economic crisis, industrial policy groups including Ministry of Commerce and Industry (MCI), Ministry of Science and Technology (MoST), and Presidential secretariats related to technology gained a voice independent of the liberal-leaning EPB macro economists who argued for reduction in state intervention. With Samsung's success in the DRAM market, industrial policy groups gained more voice around 1988, while EPB lost influence because it opposed the semiconductor developmental project (Hong, S.G. 1997: 105). More remarkably, after 1988, the state-led developmentalism in Korea continued through competition among industry-related ministries, including MCI, MoST, and the newly established Ministry of Information and Communications (MIC).[6]

Around 1988, almost all economic bureaucrats shared the idea that the government should develop the industrial policy to promote hi-tech industries. In the

---

[6] See footnote 4 in Chapter 1.

early 1990s, Koreans reached a social consensus that the most relevant way to overcome economic crisis was to promote knowledge-intensive industries, with the government implementing the technology drive policy (Hong, S.G. 1995: 55; 1997: 105). However, a contest ensued over who would lead this developmental policy, and how to proceed. As promotion of technology-intensive industries grew, the cleavages between the liberal economist EPB and the industry-related MCI and Blue House technology secretariats receded, while new cleavages around technology-related industrial policies surfaced around 1986 (Hong 1995: 52; Hong 1997: 107).

The major conflicts and competition over the initiative to promote technology-intensive industries occurred between MCI (later renamed as MoI) and MoST. Later MIC joined in. Traditionally the MoST was one of the weakest ministries in the Park Chung Hee government, when presidential policy regarding the technology development was decided mainly by EPB and MCI (former MoI), rather than MoST. MoST played only an advisory role for science and technology policies, because science and technology were viewed as economic matters under firm control of EPB and MCI until the early 1980s (Hong 1995: 45, 52; 2004: 122; Hahm and Plein 1997: 77). However, as technology attracted attention in developing Korean industries in the 1980s, MoST began to increase its voice by turning its policy priority from basic science to industry-related technology development. MoST integrated numerous state-run research institutes under its control, which Kim Jae-ik presidential secretariat and the Minister of MoST suggested in 1981 (Hahm and Plein 1997: 68). Furthermore, MoST pushed for independent R&D projects to promote technology-intensive industries starting with the Fifth Five-Year Social and Economic Development Plan (1982–6).

These MoST attempts caused serious conflicts with MCI. In the course of the liberalization debate in the early 1980s, MCI adopted R&D policy to develop hi-tech industries as a new industrial policy. For example, with the Presidential secretariats in the Blue House, MCI led the process of making a long-term plan to develop hi-tech industries, including semiconductor, computer, communication equipment, and electronic components, and enacted the revised Electronics Industry Promotion Law in 1981. However, MoST began to compete with MCI, arguing that science and technology were their traditional domain (Hong, S.G. 1995: 543–45, 2–53).

Competition between MCI and MoST caused many problems, including overlapping of industrial and technology policies. Yet they complemented each other in launching new developmental policies to promote technology-intensive industries, which contributed to state-led developmentalism. Direct evidence of competition for initiatives to promote technology appeared in similar policy plans announced competitively by both MoST and MCI. For example, MCI announced the Five-Year Plan for the Development of Hi-Tech Industries, including microelectronics, mechatronics, new materials, fine chemicals, biotechnology, laser, and avionics industries in 1989. In the same year, MoST announced a similar Five-Year High Technology Development Plan, although it put more emphasis on science and technology rather than targeting selected industries (Hong, H.G. 1997: 107–108). In order to enact the initiative, MCI selected 146 technologies as promotion targets in 1989, and announced a plan to develop 307 parts and components as import substitution and to support them with policy loans. Meanwhile, MoST announced a joint research plan among related ministries, state–run research institutes, industry, and academia to develop 16M and 64M DRAM (Hong, S.G. 1995: 33; 2004: 121).

In the 1980s, another major industry-related ministry emerged in Korea, the Ministry of Information and Communication (MIC). MIC was renamed in 1994, as the Ministry of Communication (MoC) gained more voice and more functions, particularly enacting initiatives to develop the information and communications industries, as well as Korean Information Infrastructure (KII) project in the 2000s. As we will examine in the next section, the MoC (later renamed as the MIC) initially lacked voice in industrial policy, mainly focusing instead on postal services. However, as information and communications technology became more important, it strategically transformed its identity and increased its voice in industrial policy. In particular, by suggesting a new vision of "building the information society" for developmentalism, MoC grew in status from a second-rank ministry mainly dealing with postal services to the lead agency to develop the ICT industries (Ko, Kyungmin 2000: 52–53). For example, in 1989 when MCI and MoST announced new national projects to promote hi-tech industries, MoC also launched a massive national industrial project to build Korea's national information infrastructure (KII). Under the KII project, MoC planned to invest 63 trillion Korean won for the following 11 years.

Competition among industry-related ministries, including MCI (later MoI), MoST and MoC (later MIC), enabled state-led developmentalism to continue across different administrations up to the present in 2019. While they occasionally caused overlap in developmental policies, they also filled a new vacuum of industrial policies by complementing each other through competition. For example, MoST focused on long-term development of basic technology, while MoI and MIC focused on short-term industry-related development (Hong, S.G. 2004: 114). Economic bureaucrats continued their industrial policy consistently across different administrations by changing their strategies, or sometimes rebranding the names of their developmental policies across administrations.

For example, MoST attempted to enact the Science and Technology Basic Law in 1992, but failed due to opposition by related ministries. MoST tried again to enact the law with a revised law called the Special Law for Science and Technology Innovation. As the special law was near expiration, MoST attempted to enact the

Basic Law replacing the Special Law in 2001 (Park, J.T. 2003: 107–108). Strategies and selected industries which MoI, MIC, and MoST competitively proposed for the Next Generation Growth Engine Development Project in the Roh Moo-hyun administration (2003–07) similarly reappeared in the Green Growth Strategy of the Lee Myung-bak administration (2008–12). Developmental projects continued because as ministries failed to make their projects national, they tried again by revision and rebranding in the next administration (Hong, S.G. 2004: 125).

Electronics and Information Industries: A Case Study

Before examining changes and continuity in Korean state-led developmentalism through the Asian financial crisis of 1997–8, this section explores at the industry level how a new version of state-led developmentalism had formed in the 1980s and 1990s. This section reveals that contrary to the dominant belief, Korea did not abandon its developmental policy in the process of liberalization; rather, it continued its state-led developmentalism by changing its traditional input-oriented developmentalism. This section illustrates these changes through competition among economic bureaucrats within the state, as well as adjustments between the state and private companies. Particularly, continuity of state-led developmentalism in the electronics and IT industries was related to emergence of a new industrial ministry, MIC, and its competition with existing industrial agencies in the Korean government.

Korean ICT industries developed through state-led developmentalism, different from the liberal way of the United States. In the 2010s, the information and communication technologies (ICT) worked as a key source for Korean industrial competitiveness. Korea of the 2010s became one of the leading countries in ICT worldwide. For example, the 2010 report by the Berkman Center for Internet and Society (BCIS) evaluated the development of IT in Korea, saying that Korea's broadband networks are half a generation ahead of other countries. In addition, according to the United Nation's 2010 e-Government Survey, as well as the Brookings Institute's several years surveys, Korea ranked first worldwide in e-government development, followed by the United States, Canada, the UK, and the Netherlands (Oh and Larson 2011: 13–14).

Korea's ICT industries attracted many policymakers and scholars, not only by its rapid development but also by its state-led development, different from the liberal free market, as many international empirical studies show. For example, after extensive study of ICT development, ranking Korea as one of the top nations in the ICT Development index, the International Telecommunications Union (ITU) succinctly points out "a strong and targeted policy" as the key cause for Korea's rapid development of ICT industries (ITU 2010: 18). The *New York Times* also reports: "With Korea's aggressive electronics conglomerates leading the world's markets into the next frontiers of high technology, an unlikely commander is heading the charge: the government" (Fackler 2006). The World Bank and ITU, as well as many academic studies, recognize Korean ICT development as "a model case of government-led" development in which the state provided planning and financial support for targeted areas (Kelly, Grayand, and Minges 2003: 67; Suh and Chen 2007: 13: Oh and Larson 2011: 57).

Korean state-led developmentalism in the ICT industries is distinct from the US liberal market system. For example, in building national information infrastructure, the US government did not lead any specific broadband certification procedures or information building projects, but dealt only with regulatory mechanisms, based on voluntary growth in the free market. In the United States, broadband networks grew through separate and decentralized attempts, including the Advanced Research Projects Agency Network (ARPNET) in 1969, the NSF's high-speed networks among supercomputers in the 1980s, and the spread of online technologies in schools and research organizations in the late 1980s. The US National Information Infrastructure (NII) aimed to provide general services available to all citizens by systemically connecting the networks voluntarily grown in society (Shin, D.H. 2008: 1788–1789).

By contrast, Korean broadband Internet networks did not voluntarily grow in the market, but were constructed by the government which strategically intended to develop ICT industries as a new growth engine. The Korean government actively developed a set of national policies, such as the Korean Information Infrastructure Project (KII), through which the Korean government in 1993 strategically launched broadband Internet networks. Korean government had already planned the National Basic Information System in 1984. Korea's national information infrastructure was not demand-based in the market but a supply-push enterprise driven by state-led developmentalism. In contrast, the US NII evolved by a decentralized, liberal, and hands-off approach (Lee and Chan-Olmosted 2004: 672; Shin and Kweon 2011: 381). In particular, since the 1997 Asian financial crisis, the Kim Dae-jung administration (1998–2002) used broadband Internet as a new opportunity to recover economic growth, and aggressively expanded its projects for ICT promotion. The Roh Moo-hyun administration (2003–07) also launched national projects like IT839, designed to give new momentum to economic growth after broadband (Shin, D.H. 2008: 1788).

Korean state-led developmentalism for ICT industries continued across different administrations, not because of any cohesive mindset within the state, but because of competition among economy-related ministries, particularly MIC and MoI. For example, MIC introduced numerous projects continuously. MIC proposed a plan in 2003 to put robots in every Korean household and to set the country ahead in next-generation technologies such as cellphones and wireless broadband, following its national projects in TDX development and 4M DRAM collaborative development in the 1980s. It also proposed national projects for broadband Internet KII in the 1990s (Fackler 2006). Up to the current year of 2019, MoI and MIC (now renamed as the Ministry of Science and ICT) compete for influence by proposing new projects for development, featuring them as national priority enterprises. With each new administration they compete for national attention by proposing new visions of development. They competitively develop new rationales to increase their voice and their organizational power. Sometimes, their organizational survival depends on the success of their projects, as seen in the dissolution of MIC in the Lee Myung-bak administration (2008–12) and rejuvenation in subsequent administrations.

Before exploring state-led developmentalism further, this section looks first at how MIC emerged as an ICT-leading ministry in the early 1980s. Unlike the institutionalist account of historical legacy or the repetition of the developmental state and mindset, new developmentalism in Korea emerged with formation of new leading agencies in competition with other state ministries. State-led developmentalism in Korean IT industries began with formation of a new leading organization within the state.

Development of Korean ICT industries began in the early 1980s when traditional development of total mobilization under the HCI drive of the 1970s was criticized by liberal EPB staff including Kim Jae-ik. However, these Korean liberals were not such market fundamentalists as the US-trained economists in the Latin American countries who abandoned industrial policy, arguing for a noninterventionist free market system. Criticizing input- and volume-oriented expansionism of the 1970s, Kim Jae-ik argued for the development of more value-added and technology-intensive industries. Kim Jae-ik, a so-called EPB liberal, thought over how to develop technology-intensive industries, particularly electronics, with the technology staff of Presidential Economic Secretariats in the Blue House, including Oh Myung and Hong Sungwon. Actually, in the early 1980s there were two streams in the Presidential Economic Secretariats: one being proponents of active promotion of technology-intensive industries, the other being proponents of macroeconomic stabilization and liberalization. The former stream, supported by President Chun, formed alliances with outside industry-related ministries, including MCI, MoC, and MoST (Hong, S.G. 1997: 97). Indeed, in 1980 the Blue House technology-oriented secretariat team constituted the Task Force for Development of Electronics Industry with a staff of 20 coming from MCI, MoC, MoST, and Research Institutes and Academic Specialists (Lee, Kiyul 1995: 12–15; Ko, Kyungmin 2000: 85–86; Jung, H.S. 2003: 126–127; Ko and Lee 2013: 221–222). This taskforce made a blueprint called the Basic Plan for Promotion of Electronics Industry in 1981, which was officially announced as the Electronics Industry Promotion Plan in March 1982. The plan provided a basic blueprint for subsequent development of national electronics promotion projects, selecting the three strategic industries of electronic exchangers, semiconductors, and computers.

The process to build a blueprint to promote the electronics industry in the early 1980s meant forming a leading force. The main group which led the development of Korean electronics and IT industries in the 1980s was the Presidential secretariat team of the Blue House, MoC, and Korean Telecommunication (KT). The Blue House team provided overall vision and mobilized political support for the projects; MoC developed concrete policies and was involved in development of communication and electronics parts; KT worked as an executor to implement industrial policies (Lee, Kiyul 1995: 394–395).

This formation of the leading organizations for the ICT industries in Korea began the changes in the identity of MoC in May 1981 when Oh Myung moved from the Presidential secretariat to vice minister of MoC. Thereafter he led the transformation of MoC as well as the development of Korean ICT as vice minister of MoC for six years and two months, and then minister of MoC for one year and five months, across different administrations (Lee, Kiyul 1995: 394). After Oh Myung took his new post as Vice Minister of MoC, he made serious efforts to change the identity of MoC, having discussion meetings with staff twice a week, discussing "what is the information society, why should we promote electronics, and what roles should our MoC carry out" (Lee, Kiyul 1995: 47). Before Oh Myung came to MoC, MoC had not considered economic and industry-related affairs, focused as it was on postal services. However, MoC changed its identity from powerless postal workers to powerful leaders stepping forward to build the future information society. They became confident in their emerging roles and new visions for MoC to lead the building of Korea's information society.

In 1995, approximately 15 years later, MoC became reorganized into the Ministry of Information and Communication (MIC), and became one of the most powerful ministries in Korea. In developing their own industrial projects in the 1980s and 1990s, MIC developed many organizational affiliates such as the Electronics and Telecommunication Research Institute (ETRI), Korea Agency for Digital Opportunity and Promotion (KADO), the National Computerization Agency, the Korean Information Society Development Institute, (KISDI), the Korea Communication Commission (KCC), and the Information Communication Training Center (ICTC). The agency also had a massive budget and funds—for example, a nearly $1billion budget to promote new technologies in 2006 (Fackler 2006).

However, the ideas and policies of MoC and the Presidential technology-oriented secretariats were materialized in contest with other groups like EPB economists. Although they made a plan to develop strategic hi-tech industries, such as the electronics, in the early 1980s, MoC and Blue House technology teams could not implement such massive input-oriented expansion as the total mobilization of the Park Chung Hee era, due to criticism of the liberal EPB group. The Blue House team chose electronics as a strategic target industry because in accepting the EPB stabilization idea, they thought that electronics, particularly industry electronics rather than home electronics, mattered for technology-intensive industrialization as an alternative to existing input-oriented development (Lee, Kiyul 1995: 12, 282; Jung, H.S. 2003: 127–129; Ko and Lee 2013: 219).

However, industrial policy conflicts did not disappear. For example, EPB opposed electronic exchanger (TDX) and semiconductor development projects, based on the idea of the comparative advantages in the international market, while the Blue House team and MoC argued for them based on the idea of strategic concentration for efficient promotion. Although government support was small compared with that of the Park Chung Hee era, the Blue House team and MoC promoted the development of semiconductors and TDX by various tax breaks and assistance of R&D activities. In addition, they established the Korea Advanced Institute of Science and Technology in Daeduk Research Park to nurture work teams for the development of electronics. The KDB policy bank provided private firms with many loans for R&D which enabled numerous venture capital projects to be launched (EIAK 1989: 190–195; Hong, S.G. 1997: 98–99).

However, in the competition between the so-called liberal EPB and industry-promotion groups including MCI, MoST, MoC, and the Presidential Secretariat team, the latter industry-promotion groups gained ascendancy around 1987. EPB initially gained ascendancy in the debate on development of semiconductors. In the mid-1980s when the semiconductor market fell into deep recession and the price of Samsung semiconductors sharply dropped from $3.5 to 20 cents in 1984, the technology-oriented teams including MCI, MoC, and the Blue House secretariats, were driven into a corner, whereas EPB opposing the development plan gained ascendancy. However, despite the political crisis of the technology teams, they persuaded President Chun and enabled further support for development of 256K DRAM. As the price of semiconductors began to rebound in 1987, the technology team gained more voice, while EPB opposition disappeared (Lee, Kiyul 1995: 285–289).

Another reason for ascendancy of the technology-oriented developmental groups was Korea's economic crisis. As wages skyrocketed through democratization in 1987 and pressure from advanced countries for trade openness significantly rose, the export competitiveness of Korean industries began to sharply decline. Against the background of this economic crisis, the industry-promotion group who emphasized state support for hi-tech industries gained more voice (Hong, S.G. 1997: 105). In addition, Samsung's apparent success of DRAM in the semiconductor market not only caused a sensation among private industrialists, but increased the voice of industry-promotion groups including the Blue House team and MoC. Actually, based on this success, Kang Jinku, chairman of Samsung Electronics and Telecommunications, requested President Chun directly to

support the development of IM/4M DRAMs, and in response, the Chun administration created research consortia, led by the state research institute ETRI, with
private semiconductor firms and universities (Lee, Kiyul 1995: 294; Mathews and
Cho 2000: 125–129).

In the late 1980s, there was consensus among economic bureaucrats regarding
state support of hi-tech development, but now they competed over who would
lead the industrial policy and how to develop it (Lee, Kiyul 1995: 291–292; Hong,
S.G. 1997: 105; Oh and Larson 2011: 39). For example, in 1985 when the Blue
House secretariat suggested a collaborative consortium with private firms for 4M
DRAM development, economic ministries competed over who should lead the
project. MCI claimed that it should lead as industrial policy ministry, opposing
the MoC's participation in the project. By contrast, MoST tried to lead the project
based on its alliance with MoC which provided basic funding for to the project.
Regarding who should coordinate the project, MCI suggested its ancillary institute Semiconductor Research Association, while MoST proposed ETRI which
was under its control. As a result, the 4M DRAM development project was under
the joint auspices of MoC, MoST, and MCI, while MoC provided the development funds (Lee, Kiyul 1995: 291–295).

MoC ascended in its status by leading the promotion of electronics industries,
including semiconductor and communication devices in the 1980s, when MCI
lost much influence and could not wholly focus on the electronics industries.[7]
MoST also gained more voice in industrial policy by developing a Special Research
Development Project to support subsidies for the national research projects going
back to 1982 and established the Electronic Telecommunication Research
Institute (ETRI) in 1985, to coordinate research consortia with private firms.

In competition with MoC and MoST, MCI proposed a Comprehensive
Semiconductor Development Plan in 1985 in which it planned to establish a VLSI
research association and promote the export of semiconductors to $3 billion
(MCI 1985; Kim, H.K. 1991: 433–434). In addition, in the late 1980s, MCI competitively proposed a Five-Year Plan for the Development of Hi-Tech Industries
selecting 146 technologies to develop the competitiveness of Korean industries.
Also in 1989, MoST proposed a similar plan called the Five-Year High Technology
Development Plan, while MoC launched a massive development project called
the KII project (Hong, S.G. 1997: 108; Mathews and Cho 2000: 147–148, 155 endnote 80). A former MoI high-ranking staff member says about the conflicts inside
the government:

> There were so many conflicts. Now they became the Ministry of Future Planning,
> but then named MoC (later MIC). They had so many conflicts with MoI. The

---

[7] Personal interview with former director of the MCI on June 19, 2018; personal interview with
former bureau director of the MCI on May 29, 2018.

ultimate issue was who would take over the future industries, for instance, semiconductor. Related with it, there were so many things to deal with, like its trade and patents, and so on.... We did always fight! MoI argued that "we should take over IT hardware." Then, they [MoC] argued that the hardware was also related to IT. I think the conflicts were most severe in the Kim Young-sam government. President Kim Dae-jung stood up for them. But if I think it over now, the conflicts significantly helped our economy to grow.[8]

Competition among economic bureaucrats within the state not only caused problems, such as duplication of national investments, but also enabled the state to expand its developmentalism by complementing the policies while coordinating private firms for the entire national economy. As the policy vacuum for promotion of hi-tech industries occurred due to traditional input-oriented developmentalism, MCI, MoST and MoC rapidly filled it with their new developmental policies in competition for initiatives. In particular, the need for promotion of new technologies continuously emerged, as new industries and technology developed—for example, electronic exchangers, semiconductors, IT, and then new applications of robotics and IT, and so on.

More importantly, the state still has an important role in promoting hi-tech industries in the national economy in the case of market failure, say in building the industrial ecosystem and infrastructure, in which private firms have difficulty in forming the collective goods. In Korea of the 1980s and 1990s, private firms were reluctant to transform their existing volume-oriented expansionism to technology-intensive specialization. The state's developmental policies and its support enabled private corporations to enter into new hi-tech industries and to improve their R&D capabilities.

For example, in the early 1980s when the Blue House technology team and MoC planned to develop a digital electronic exchanger called TDX, private firms including Goldstar (former LG) and Dongyang were against the idea because they were more interested in earning easy profits by introducing foreign analog exchangers like Siemens's EMD. However, the state research institute ETRI succeeded in developing a Korean digital exchanger called TDX by creating a consortium for development in which large private firms were enticed to participate. The private firms changed their position and took part in the development as the government supported the initiative with a $24 million R&D fund, the largest to date in Korea. The public firm Korea Telecom, under the auspice of MoC, provided the funds required for the project and managed the development project (Lee, Kiyul 1995: 127–128, 155; Oh and Larson 2011: 31–33).

---

[8] Personal interview with former director of the MoI on June 19, 2018.

Korean private firms were also indifferent to government ideas regarding the building of a national information infrastructure as well as the development of semiconductors. In particular, large electronic firms including Samsung, Goldstar (former LG) and Daewoo were reluctant to enter into semiconductor development because the memory semiconductor business needed massive investments to establish the facilities, and was highly risky due to the short technology innovation cycle (Lee, Kiyul 1995: 185, 198, 265, 284–285; Mathews and Cho 2000: 119–121).

In May 1982, the president of Samsung, Lee Byungchul, concluded his year-long investigation of the semiconductor business certain that they could enter into the business only if the government would actively support it (Lee, Kiyul 1995: 265). As the Blue House technology team was driven to a corner by EPB criticism against the promotion of semiconductors and their private firms' indifference in the business, the Blue House team gave a firm signal of support, while using the competition among chaebols by introducing Hyundai to the semiconductor business. As Hyundai prepared to enter the semiconductor business in March 1983, Samsung rushed to massively invest. The Korean government reduced the risks of huge investments in the semiconductor business by arranging finances, guaranteeing loans, and providing infrastructure and market. The Korean government made a total public investment of $400 million, 40% of which was financed by the National Investment Fund, and the rest supported by the Electronics Industry Promotion Fund. Due to the Korean state's prodding and promise of support, private firms including Samsung, Hyundai, and Goldstar prepared to enter into the mass production of chips at the VLSI technology level (Lee, Kiyul 1995: 264–265, 285; Mathews and Cho 2000: 119–121).

In addition to the development of TDX and semiconductor business in the 1980s, the development of Code Division Multiple Access (CDMA) in cellular phones, a method of digital wireless transmission in the 1990s, was also a case of state-led development. Private firms opposed the idea of development of CDMA because they preferred to assemble the imported parts and technology based on their individual and short-term calculation for making profits. By contrast, the Korean government, particularly MoC, was interested in developing CDMA from the perspective of the entire national economy and accumulation of national technology. Through a national project to invest 100 billion Korean won, the Korean government could be first in the world to develop CDMA technology (Lee, H.D. 2012: 143).[9]

---

[9] There was also competition between MoC and MCI over the development of CDMA. MCI proposed a plan to introduce TDMA because it was a global standard. By contrast, opposing the MCI attempt, MoC argued that CDMA was the technologically superior and more flexible in its future applications. Due to the Blue House support for CDMA, the MoC's idea of the development of CDMA became a national project (Oh and Larson 2011: 95; Lee, H.D. 2012: 141–148).

Yet state-led developmentalism to promote the semiconductor industry was different from old-style Korean developmentalism of the Park Chung Hee era. In contrast to the heavy-handed state guidance of the 1970s HCI drive, state-led developmentalism in the 1980s emphasized private initiatives in which the state worked as a project instigator and coordinator. Although the Chun administration provided $350 million in low-interest credit through policy loans, it worked as a pump to prime private firms to make the main investments by $1.2 billion in 1983–6. Private firms' independent mobilization of massive capital, through foreign capital markets and nonbank institutions, meant the end of the Korean state's direct control over financing of Korean industrial expansion. Now, investment initiatives lay in the hands of private firms (Mathews and Cho 2000: 125–126).

In addition, although the state research institute ETRI coordinated the consortium for the development of IM DRAM, the real research was carried out mainly by private firms' research teams. As the consortia for the development of DRAMs proceeded, the role of the state came to be reduced, while private firms accumulated more technological capabilities. The Korean government research institute KIET developed no more than the 64K memory chip capacity, while the detailed research and development went to private firms. When MoST initiated the consortium for development of 16M and 64M DRAM, the lion's share of research was in the hands of private firms because the research capabilities of private firms outpaced those of government research institutes. Unlike earlier consortia, Korean joint consortia for the development of DRAM technology shifted from mission-oriented approach to more diffusion-oriented with provision of externalities, such as materials and equipment (Kim, H.K. 1991: 443–444; Mytelka and Ernst 1998: 121–122; Mathews and Cho 2000: 146). This is in contrast to the Taiwanese model of public research institutes' spinning-off or transferring their research outcomes to private firms.

Despite the changing roles in state-led capitalism, the Korean state could continue its developmentalism in the 1980s and the 1990s by changing its strategy and methods, from the volume-oriented expansionism of the traditional developmental state to a knowledge-intensive economy. This continuity of developmentalism by changes in state roles and strategies was realized through competition among industry-related ministries, including MCI, MoST, and MoC. They competitively proposed new developmental visions, while commonly emphasizing the government's active role in development of hi-tech industries as an alternative to the existing volume-oriented expansionism. As we will see, even in the 2000s MIC and MoI competed over new industrial policies, including improvement of industrial competitiveness through ICT technology as well as development of new growth engine industries.

7

Asian Financial Crisis and Transformation of Korean Capitalism

The Asian financial crisis in late 1997 prompted serious reflection upon the problems of Korea's input-oriented developmentalism. Although large corporations slowly adopted the technology-intensive industrialization, they maintained volume-oriented diversification. For example, Samsung finally entered into the automobile industry in 1996, which placed financial burdens on the entire conglomerate. In particular, second-ranked large corporations including Hanbo, Halla, and Sammi, competed for size based on massive debts, rather than improving their market profitability and efficiency (Park, Taegyeon 1997: 195–197). This high debt-based, volume-oriented expansionism engendered the chain bankruptcies of chaebols starting in January 1997 and resulted in the crisis in late 1997 (Park, Taegyeon 1997: 138–139; Shin Dong-A March 1997; Mathew 1998: 750–751; Ji, Joohyung 2011: 152–153). Chaebols' moral hazard and the ineffectiveness of state intervention were mainly pointed out as causes of the economic crisis. Due to the Korean government's protection and nurturing, chaebols could horizontally diversify and expand, which resulted in a debt-equity ratio of 519% on average held by the 20 largest chaebols in 1997. It is frequently mentioned that the state's excessive intervention in the economy caused not only corruption and crony capitalism, but also moral hazard among private corporations which competed for size and visibility, disregarding their profitability (Dong-A Ilbo Special Report Team 1999 vol. 2: 222; Hayashi 2010: 59; Kwon, O. 2010: 59; Kuk, Minho 2011: 136).

However, to solve the economic crisis of 1997, Korea did not abandon state-led developmentalism. Unlike the account of the many theorists of the developmental state (DS) demise, Korea developed another version of state-led developmentalism, emphasizing the promotion of strategic hi-tech venture firms and SME parts industries. How could the Korean government continue its state-led developmentalism even when state interventionism was pointed out as a main culprit for the economic crisis?

State-led capitalism continued because of the discursive politics in the diagnoses and solutions to the crisis. Facing an economic crisis in Korea of 1997, economic efficiency was emphasized, rather than social justice as proposed by progressives in the civil society. To improve economic efficiency, input-oriented expansionism became a main target of reform, and among the feasible options to transform from input-oriented expansionism to knowledge-intensive industrialization, the state's

Changes by Competition: The Evolution of the South Korean Developmental State. Hyeong-ki Kwon,
Oxford University Press (2021). © Hyeong-ki Kwon. DOI: 10.1093/oso/9780198866060.003.0007

strict regulation of chaebols looked more persuasive than chaebols' voluntary action in the free market. Korean bureaucrats could continue their state-led developmentalism by focusing on chaebols' high debt-based, volume-oriented expansionism as a main cause for the crisis, and competitively offer solutions to the crisis with diverse methods to improve economic efficiency, while strictly imposing debt regulations on large corporations and promoting hi-tech industries.

This chapter first examines the competing diagnoses and solutions to the economic crisis of 1997, and then explores how, through politics between the state and large corporations, the existing volume-oriented expansionism changed toward a knowledge-intensive strategy. Finally, this chapter examines how competition among economic ministries, including the Ministry of Industry (MoI) and the Ministry of Information and Communications (MIC) drove the evolution of Korean industrial policy.

Competition of Diagnoses and Solutions to the Economic Crisis

As the economic crisis broke out in late 1997, economic experts and policymakers both inside and outside Korea pointed out the ineffectiveness of the developmental state (DS). While some critics pointed to the fundamental ineffectiveness of the DS, and others held that the DS performed better in its early stage but was no longer effective in the globalized world, they all agreed that the DS was a target of reform (Cheng and Lin 1999; Hayashi 2010: 59; Kuk, Minho 2011: 136). In particular, Korean bureaucrats were seen as the main culprits of the economic crisis, considering that the existing interventionist state nurtured chaebols' volume-oriented, high debt-based expansionism. For example, MIT economic professor Rüdiger Dornbusch argued in a conference held in May 1998 that Korea should expel the bureaucrats first in order to successfully reform its economy, because they were key obstacles to reform. Alan Greenspan also pointed to Korean bureaucrats as the culprits of the economic crisis, while suggesting deregulation as a solution to the crisis (Park, Taegyeon 1997: 20–21). The International Monetary Fund (IMF) also demanded market-oriented reform based on a Washington Consensus as a condition to provide massive loans to solve the Korean debt crisis. Furthermore, the newly established Kim Dae-jung administration (1998–2002) recruited liberal economists, including professors Kim Taedong and Lee Jinsoon, in key economic decision-making posts, and initially emphasized "free market and balanced development" while criticizing the growth-first strategy of the Park Chung Hee-style developmentalism.[1]

---

[1] Kim Taedong and Lee Jinsoon were in a school of Hakhyun (Professor Byun Hungyoon' pen name), and their group was called *Jung Kyung Hoe*, which means the Kim Dae-jung Economist Meeting, literally, in Korean (Kim et al. 2003: 57–59; Suh, Junghwan 2007: 57).

However the liberal recruits lost their voice and retreated in the competition with economic bureaucrats, including Lee Hunjae and Jin Nyum, because President Kim Dae-jung endorsed the bureaucrats' realistic options rather than abstract principles of market economy (Kim et al. 2003: 57–59). Although the Kim Daejung administration put Kang Kyungsik, former Vice Prime Minister, and Kim Inho, former Presidential First Economic Secretariat, under court custody to bring them to account for the crisis, the main economic bureaucrats gained more voice in the process of recovering the economy (Kim et al. 2003: 54). This section explores how the Korean government could continue its state-led developmentalism despite the crisis which resulted from state-led developmentalism.

First, progressive forces in civil society, including trade unions and civil associations like the Citizens' Coalition for Economic Justice, gained a legitimate voice in criticizing the bureaucrats and chaebols for causing the economic crisis, but they failed to develop a persuasive solution for economic recovery and further growth (Yoon, S.W. 2016: 9–10). Trade unions, including the Korean Confederation of Trade Unions (KCTU) and the Federation of Korean Trade Unions (FKTU), demanded confiscation of chaebols' property as a condition for their participation in the Korean Tripartite Commission (Lee, Y.R. 1999: 49–50).

Although they suggested dissolution of chaebols, criticizing their moral hazard and overexpansionism as a key cause for the economic crisis, it looked unrealistic to achieve economic growth without chaebols, which occupied approximately 70% of national economy in 1998. Economic efficiency was preferred as a solution to the crisis, rather than social welfare and economic justice.[2] Exports attracted attention again as a solution to the crisis. It was broadly believed that chaebols' contribution was needed to improve exports and economic growth. For many Koreans who put more priority on economic growth, chaebols were not objects of dissolution, but objects of reform.

On the other hand, the free market might be a feasible option as an alternative to the existing developmental state. Actually, the IMF requested the Kim Daejung administration to implement neoliberal reform based on the Washington Consensus as a condition for its bailout. The US government and the IMF requested the Korean government to reform its debt-oriented expansionism by market principles. Believing that the Korean government's preferential support to chaebols engendered their debt-based expansionism, they argued that a noninterventionist state and free market would be a solution to the crisis. Actually, William Daley, US Secretary of Commerce, emphasized in his visit to Korea in February 1998 that the United States was investigating whether the Korean

---

[2] Many empirical surveys reveal that Koreans put more priority on economic growth than democracy or nonmaterialistic values because they experienced improvement of their national and social status through national economic growth. See World Value Survey (2005); Kang, Woojin (2015: 36); Park and Kang (2012: 76–91); Yoon, S.W. (2016: 10–11).

government would provide subsidies for exports and production. Lawrence H. Summers, the US Treasury Secretary, also clearly announced in his visit to Korea in February 1999 that the United States was watching to see whether the Korean government would give subsidies to corporations in the corporate restructuring process of steel and semiconductor industries. As a condition of IMF bailout to Korea in 1999, the US government emphasized that IMF bailout money should not be given to Korea's major industries including the steel, semiconductor, and automobile industries (Lee, Y.R. 1999: 148).

The liberal free market had been proposed by large corporations in Korea since the 1980s. However, the financial deregulation and liberalization in Roh Tae-woo (1988–92) and Kim Young-sam (1993–7) administrations, including liberalization of interest rates, banks' autonomous management, and foreign exchange and investments, all contributed to chaebols' volume-oriented expansion which resulted in the 1997 economic crisis. In particular, the Kim Young-sam administration introduced liberalization of short-term foreign loans in 1993–5, and changed 24 investment financial corporations to comprehensive nonbank financial investment institutes, which helped chaebols to compete globally (Hart-Landsberg and Burkett 2001: 411; Ji, Joohyung 2011: 139–143). However, this rapid financial liberalization left the Korean economy vulnerable to unmanaged openness, and contributed to the chaebols' traditional volume-oriented expansionism leading up to the crisis. Many Koreans perceived that the voluntary action in the free market contributed to the chaebols' reckless and octopus-like expansionism, rather than improving the competitiveness of national industries. Hence the Korean people and the government requested chaebols to undergo fundamental reform (Kim, C.S. 1998: 41–42).

Economic bureaucrats in the Korean government regained their legitimate voice by bringing the need of chaebol reform to national attention. The Ministry of Finance and Economy (MoFE)[3] survived intact, despite a serious attempt to break it up (Shim and Lee 1998: 19). Facing the economic crisis of 1998, the Kim Dae-jung administration had several options as a solution. First was the free market proposed by the United States and IMF, as well as the liberal group *Jung Kyung Hoe* within the state; second was the existing input-oriented expansion and export-led growth proposed by Kim Woojung, chairman of the FKI and Deawoo chaebol; the third option, proposed by economic bureaucrats, was changing the existing input-oriented economy to knowledge-intensive by reforming chaebols. Economic bureaucrats' solutions to help the economy recover, including reform of chaebols and improving national industries' competitiveness, gained influence with the United States and IMF, as well as among most Koreans.

---

[3] The Ministry of Finance and Economy was established in 1994 by merging the Economic Planning Board (EPB) and the Ministry of Finance (MoF). It was renamed the Ministry of Economy and Finance in 2008.

However, the Korean bureaucrats' solutions differ from the neoliberal free market proposed by the IMF and the US. The corporate reform by the Kim Dae-jung administration was not transformation toward a noninterventionist free market system. On the contrary, Korean bureaucrats proposed active involvement in transforming chaebols from the existing input-oriented expansionism to knowledge-intensive specialization in core business. In the Kim Dae-jung administration, the state did not retreat but reorganized its developmentalism. The Korean state had significant leeway to reform its economy independent of the IMF's conditional requests (Lee, Byungchun 2001; Lee et al. 2002).

For example, unlike the IMF request for free market principles, including government nonintervention, no use of public funds for bailout subsidies, and voluntary adjustments of private firms, the Kim Dae-jung administration was deeply involved in corporate restructuring (Yoon, D.Y. 2011: 181–182). To change large corporations' volume-oriented strategy, the Kim administration imposed a ceiling of debt-equity ratio of 200% on chaebols while forcing them to make so-called big deals for specialization in core businesses, despite opposition of the liberal *Jung Kyung Hoe*, including Kim Taedong, Presidential Economic Secretariat (Kim et al. 2003: 228). The big deals of swapping business among large corporations was not free market but the government's intentional industrial policy to change the existing volume-oriented diversification to knowledge-intensive specialization.

The basic big deal idea was that industrial policy would concentrate government support on first-ranked firms in a specific business in order to improve the competitiveness of Korean industries (Kim et al. 2003: 228). Unlike the US free market idea which focused on the liberalization of capital markets, the Korean government's solution to the economic crisis was industrial policy to improve competitiveness of national industries and increase exports (Lee, Y.R. 1999: 50–51). The free market system proposed by the United States and IMF was not such an effective option for many Koreans or the bureaucrats, who doubted that the US and IMF free market measures would contribute to "disarming" Korean industries in international competition (Lee, Y.R. 1999: 149). To improve Korean industries' export competitiveness as a solution for national recovery, many Koreans and bureaucrats believed that chaebols should not be dissolved but should be reformed. As a result, Korean economic bureaucrats could continue this state-led developmentalism by offering a relatively persuasive solution to the economic crisis by focusing on chaebol reform and changes in developmental strategies from existing input-oriented to knowledge-intensive.

State-Business Politics for Changing the Developmental Strategy

By exploring the conflict-laden politics between the state and business, this section examines why and how Korean large corporations changed their existing volume-oriented diversification toward knowledge-intensive specialization. The Kim administration proposed export growth as a key solution to resolve the national debt crisis of 1998 by addressing the shortage of foreign exchange. The Kim administration's solution differed from the chaebols', particularly Daewoo Kim Woojung, by changing the existing volume-oriented expansionism to a new knowledge-intensive economy to improve export competitiveness. A conflict-laden process ensued.

Not only progressives in civil society, including the Citizens' Coalition for Economic Justice, and trade unions, including KCTU and FKTU, but many Koreans opposed the chaebols' dominance in the Korean economy. However, although the public support for corporate restructuring of chaebols provided economic bureaucrats with impetus to reform chaebols, they did not follow the progressives' requests. They thought that chaebols were not the target of dissolution, but the object of reform, considering their dominant role in the Korean national economy. Kang Bongkyun, then-Minister of Finance and Economy, succinctly says about the direction of reform:

> That's because we cannot have competitiveness with the old-style inefficient and high debt-based structure. The technology development capability has been encroached because the profits of the good-performing subsidiaries in a chaebol group have been transferred to the bad performers.... Our government should make a reform to correct this. It neither means that chaebols disappear, nor that SMEs and venture firms take over all the roles in our economy. Instead, it does mean that chaebols should lead our economy with SMEs and venture firms collaboratively in a changed environment.[4]

The Kim Dae-jung administration aimed to reform chaebols' volume-oriented expansionism and build collaborative interfirm relations with SMES for a knowledge-intensive economy. Korean bureaucrats believed that this transformation would not happen by chaebols' voluntary actions in the free market but through the government's new developmentalism due to market failure (Hundt 2009: 93–94).

Unlike the IMF accord on market principles agreed upon in May 1998, including government nonintervention, private firms' voluntary adjustments, and no use of public funds for bailout, the Kim Dae-jung administration designed and executed so-called big deals among chaebols for specialization in core business. It selected the 10 largest businesses as a target of reform, namely automobiles, semiconductors, petrochemicals, steel, shipbuilding, liquid crystal display (LCD), electric generator equipment, aircraft, railroad cars, and computers (Lee,

---

[4] Requoted in Kwon, Y. (2000: 68).

Y.R. 1999: 97, 104). Actually, economic bureaucrats developed the idea of technology-intensive specialization starting in the 1980s. The Kim Dae-jung administration's so-called big deal of swapping chaebol businesses was based on the Kim Young-sam administration's Specialization in Core Business program as a *Shin Sanup Jungchaek* (literally, new industrial policy, in Korean), according to a key stakeholder in the Kim Dae-jung administration (Hangyure, February 2, 1998).

However, unlike the traditional method of government direct commands, the Kim Dae-jung administration took an appearance of voluntary adjustments in the market. Formally, private banks as creditors, rather than the government, dealt with the corporate restructuring (Kim, K.W. 2001: 110). But, after liquidating the insolvent banks with massive public funds, the Kim Dae-jung government gave the banks guidelines to deal with corporate restructuring while selecting the target firms and sometimes directly enforcing the merger, because it had control over private banks even after their privatization (Kim, K.W. 2001: 120; Kim et al. 2003: 94–110).

The MoFE and Financial Supervisory Commission (FSC) could be involved in the changes of bank CEOs, as they were in the Commercial Bank (CBK), Chohueng, Hanil, Pyunghwa, Kangwon, and Choongbuk banks in July 1998. FSC had permission to make banks merge and die. FSC also had power to investigate the banks. Furthermore, the MoFE and FSC had financial incentives through public funds to support the banks and corporations (Kim et al. 2003: 94–117). In addition, independent of IMF, the Kim administration made a new rule of a 200% ceiling to the debt-equity ratio, by which private banks could enforce upon the chaebols an approximately 500% ratio of debt to meet the debt-equity ratio of 200% within one year. Although setting the banks as creditors in dealing with large corporations, the government designed the plan of corporate restructuring and enticed chaebols with carrots including financial and tax incentives and market entry permission, as well as sticks including restriction on new loans, prosecutors' investigations, and financial investigation over intragroup transactions (Lee, Y.R. 1999: 72–74, 94, 150; Kim et al. 2003: 230, 250–251; Lew and Wang 2007).

In response to attempts to dissolve or reform chaebols, Korean large corporations initially resisted the government's reform measures, arguing for the free market principle. For example, chaebols opposed the government's principles for corporate restructuring[5] not only because they violated their business freedom,

---

[5] Kim Dae-jung's administration proposed "five + three" principles for the reform of chaebols. Initially the Kim administration suggested five principles, including transparency of management, dissolution of cross payment guarantee, financial structural improvement, specialization in core business, and the group president's management responsibility. After that, in August 1999, it added three principles, including the separation of industrial and financial capitals, prohibition of cross shareholding and unfair insider trading, as well as prohibition of irregular succession and bequeath (Choi, Jungpyo 1999: 159–161).

but because they would cause businesses to contract (FKI 1998; Lee, Y.R. 1999: 51–52; Kim et al. 2003: 41–42; Ji, Joohyung 2011: 258, 278). Furthermore, they tried to turn responsibility for the crisis toward the government and financial institutes, although they accepted their accusation of moral hazard.[6] By criticizing the government, they tried to turn public attention from reform of chaebols to reform of the public sector (Kuk, Minho 2011: 153).

Chaebols tried to recover their legitimacy by making proactive efforts to overcome the crisis through exports and to offer economic reform plans. For example, the 1998 National Recovery Plan by the Export Growth spelled out their plan to overcome the national debt by exporting $50 billion. Kim Woojung, chairman of Daewoo and then-president of the Federation of Korean Industries (FKI) association of large corporations, presented the plan to President Kim Dae-jung in March 1998. To demonstrate real efforts to increase exports, the FKI constituted the Collaborative Meeting for Export Growth in June 1998 and held the Export Support Committee bimonthly meeting with MoI, starting in July 1998 (FKI 2011: 596, 599–600).

However, for one year following the 1997 crisis, chaebols continued their volume-oriented diversification while strongly opposing the government's plan. As Kim Woojung of Daewoo showed, they emphasized export growth as a method to overcome the national debt crisis, and requested the government to support massive export subsidies for growth of exports, all a continuation of their traditional volume-oriented expansionism. Although chaebols made some public gestures of cooperation, they did not hold back their disagreement and disdain for the economic bureaucrats' policy. One newly appointed CEO of a top chaebol affiliate said in 1998 that his strategy for the firm would remain "business as usual," and that many chaebols endorsed the view because "they fervently believed the old strategies made their companies successful, and so could still work" (Shim and Lee 1998: 19). Chaebols thought that if they could resist the reform attempt until late 1999, the government would give it up (Jo, Chulhwan 1999: 34–35).

Despite their initial resistance to corporate reform, Korean chaebols changed their existing high debt-based, volume-oriented diversification to knowledge-intensive specialization in core business within three years, as the economic bureaucrats requested (Ji, Joohyung 2011: 333). According to an empirical study of 125 firms owned by Korea's 30 largest chaebols in 2001, large conglomerates abandoned their existing "high-cost and low profitable system," reduced their expansionist investments, and focused on innovation through significant restructuring. In addition, they sold their nonperforming subsidiaries in order to meet the government's 200% debt-equity ratio, while specializing in core businesses. For example, the disposal of assets by the 30 largest chaebols doubled from 23.1

---

[6] Personal interview with former president of FKI on June 13, 2018.

Table 7.1. Restructuring Results of the Top Four Conglomerates in Korea (unit: %, trillion won, USD billion, number)

	Samsung		Hyundai		LG		SK	
	1997	1999	1997	1999	1997	1999	1997	1999
Debt/equity ratio	366	166.3	572	181	508	184.2	466	161.0
Scale of debt	49.6	23.4	61.3	52.6	42.9	26.3	23.8	22.3
Cross-guaranteed debt	22.8	0	31.7	0	84.9	0	51.1	0
Asset sell-off	–	5.32	–	5.25	–	4.84	–	2.94
Increase of equity capital	–	6.5	–	15.6	–	4.84	–	2.94
Foreign capital attraction (USD bil.)	–	2.74	–	3.18	–	3.65	–	1.25
Number of affiliates	61	45	62	35	52	43	45	39

Source: Kim, K.W. 2001: 104–105.

trillion Korean won in 1995–7 to 66.9 trillion won in 1998–2000 (Park, Sangsoo 2001: 5–8). Korean large conglomerates also reduced external debts while increasing internal funds. For example, Korean large corporations relied on external debts by 75% of their facility investment before the crisis, but in 2000s their facility investment relied on internal funds by approximately 80% (Kim, Yongki 2004: 144–145; Ji, Joohyung 2011: 336–338).

As Table 7.1 shows, the four largest chaebols in Korea made significant efforts to reform their corporate strategy by selling off their assets and specializing in core businesses, although the Daewoo group went bankrupt in late 1999, due to their passive efforts in restructuring (Kim, K.W. 2001: 105). The average debt-equity ratio of the four largest chaebols declined from 352% at the end of 1998 to 174% at the end of 1999. Their total debt scale dropped from 177.6 trillion Korean won at the end of 1997 to 38 trillion Korean won. The amount of cross-guaranteed debt, which was approximately 190 trillion Korean won at the end of March 1998, was completely removed by the end of March 2000. Finally, the average number of affiliates in the four conglomerates declined from 55 at the end of April 1998 to 41 at the end of 1999 (Kim, K.W. 2001: 105).

During this time Korean large corporations shifted toward knowledge-intensive specialization in their core business while giving up their volume-oriented strategy. Korean firms have set the strategy of "choose and concentrate" as the basic principle of their restructuring. For example, the number of affiliates of the largest 30 chaebols decreased from 821 in April 1997 to 544 in April 2000. While slimming down their business, they began to focus on new technology-intensive industries such as telecommunications. For example, trimming down

237 affiliates, the 30 largest chaebols established 53 new firms in Internet and IT-related businesses, 7 venture firms, and 9 cable broadcasting businesses (Kim, K.W. 2001: 87–88).

In addition, Korean firms reduced investment for gross fixed capital, including land, buildings, and machine facilities, from 12.6% on annual average in 1981–90 to 2.7% in 2000–08 (Ji, Joohyung 2011: 434–436). In contrast, Korean firms increased their R&D investments. Although R&D investment was stagnant in 1998 and 1999 because companies reduced spending to secure liquidity and to improve capital structure, they began to increase their R&D investment in 2000. The growth rate of large corporations' R&D investment in 2000 was 16.1%, while that of SMEs was 30.6%. The growth rate of R&D staff in large companies was 6.9% in 2000, while that of SMEs was 25.8%. The number of researchers with a PhD increased at a rate of 46.1% in 1999 and 38.2% in 2000 (Kim, K.W. 2001: 89–90). Korean firms shifted toward a knowledge-based economy by specializing in core business and improving their R&D staffing and capabilities.

Why did Korean firms change their growth strategy through the Asian financial crisis of 1997? It was due to the Korean state's firm and active developmentalism, rather than voluntary action in the free market. As seen in the chaebols' resistance to the government's corporate reforms, particularly Daewoo's continuity of input-oriented expansionism, Korean firms preferred to continue their existing strategy rather than change toward specialization in core business through innovation.[7]

Korean firms may have changed their strategy due to changes in relative power. Large corporations lost leverage in the economic crisis, while government regained its power. As media and public opinion accused chaebols of causing the national economic crisis, even pro-chaebol factions inside the government became weak, making opposition to corporate reform difficult (Ji, Joohyung 2011: 258). As a senior manager of FKI says in a personal interview, for chaebols "there was nothing they could do except expiate for their sins for the economic crisis."[8]

In contrast to chaebols' loss of power, Kim Dae-jung's administration gained power to coordinate in light of the national crisis. The Roh Tae-woo (1988–92) and Kim Young-sam (1993–7) administrations also attempted to change the chaebols' input-oriented development toward knowledge-intensive, but they failed because they lost their traditional policy instruments such as direct control over credit allocation in the process of liberalization and deregulation. However, facing the national crisis, the Korean state gained more autonomy and made new instruments such as regulation of debt-equity ratios. Particularly, the Kim Dae-jung administration received national support for chaebol reform (Kim, C.S. 1998: 42; Cherry 2005: 329, 348; Lew and Wang 2007: 66; Stubbs 2011:

[7] Personal interview with an executive director of FKI on May 17, 2018.
[8] Personal interview with an executive director of FKI on May 17, 2018.

156–157). An executive director of FKI, Korean large firms' association, says about the government's role in limiting chaebols:

> Frankly speaking, wasn't the Asian financial crisis of 1997 a turning point for our industrial structure? The problems, such as octopus-like diversification and speculation in real estate had been accumulating and burst into crisis. Now is not the time to fix the blame. But even though I cannot remember the exact number, I know about 13 or 14 chaebols of the 30 largest chaebols fell down then....The survivors became different...They have their own colors, don't they? For example, Samsung has electronics and finance; Hyundai automobiles; SK telecom and energy and so on....It is not a natural result but the government prohibited them, say Daewoo, from incurring further debts. The government precluded the choice [of debt-based expansionism], and encouraged them to choose R&D.[9]

The government's strict regulation of chaebols' choices facilitated their change. Unlike the traditional Korean government's practice that did not let large corporations fell down, the Kim Dae-jung administration sent a clear signal to chaebols that they would go down if they did not reform.

In contrast to economic bureaucrats' unified voice for specialization in core business, large corporations lacked a unified voice. They struggled as they responded individually to the government's initiative. For example, Kim Woojung, chairman of Daewoo group and then-president of FKI, agreed with the Minister of Labor on the idea of delaying massive layoffs, criticizing Hyundai at a conference held on Jeju Island in July 1998. Kim Woojung announced that Daewoo would actively participate in big deals soon, while other chaebols remained reluctant to participate. Kim Woojung wanted to continue his expansionism with a good relationship with the Kim Dae-jung administration.

More importantly, chaebols changed their strategy because they got clear lessons from other chaebols' choices and the state's reactions. The different outcomes which representative chaebols, including Samsung and Daewoo, underwent sent a clear message to other chaebols. The second-largest chaebol, Daewoo, ultimately fell while pursuing its debt-based expansionism. By contrast, Samsung became a world-leading company by changing rapidly toward a knowledge-intensive strategy (Jo, Youngho 2000: 190).

For Korean economic bureaucrats, Daewoo became "the litmus test for the reform agenda" (Hundt 2009 100–101). Most chaebols tried to show that they were making efforts to reform, even though they gave lip service to bureaucrats whose goal was to reduce debt-equity ratios below 200%. Daewoo increased its levels of debt by about 30% in 1998, and publicly announced its expansionism,

---

[9] Personal interview with director of FKI on May 4, 2018.

based on the relatively good relationship early on between President Kim Dae-jung and Daewoo chairman Kim Woojung (Yoon, Youngho 1999: 268–272; Ravenhill 2001: 3; Hundt 2009: 100–101). Economic bureaucrats took serious measures to prohibit Daewoo from borrowing loans and making further financial injections. Although Daewoo began to restructure in late 1999, the action was too late. Daewoo once was the second-largest conglomerate in Korea, surpassing Samsung, through its debt-based expansionism. Yet it went virtually bankrupt in July 1999 while resisting corporate reform and continuing its volume-oriented expansionism (Jo, Youngho 2000: 190; Kim, K.W. 2001: 105). Other chaebols learned a lesson from Daewoo's failure.

By contrast, Samsung rapidly changed its existing expansionism to specialization in core business, in response to government policy. Unlike Daewoo, Samsung did not have a good relationship initially with the Kim Dae-jung administration, because economic bureaucrats and public opinion in Korea saw Samsung's unreasonable entry into the automobile industry in 1995 as a typical pattern of chaebol expansionism, a cause for the economic crisis and a main target for reform (Jo, Youngho 2000: 190; Hundt 2009: 103). As Samsung tried to take over KIA automobile company even in the crisis, economic bureaucrats again were critical of the move as typical of chaebol expansionism. When Samsung gave up its nonperforming and noncore businesses, including automobiles, and concentrated on several core businesses like electronics and finance and upgrading their R&D capability, the Korean government provided handsome rewards, including permission to publicly list its life insurance unit (Jo, Youngho 2000: 194; Hundt 2009: 105;). Through its own efforts to change and the government's support, Samsung became a world-leading company just three years after the crisis, with 12 products taking the largest share in the world market. These included DRAM at 20.7% of the world market in 2000; SRAM at 21.6%; TFT-LCD at 18.3%; and an oil drilling ship at 60% (Jo, Youngho 2000: 192).

Continuity by Competition Inside the State

Many liberal economists, as well as some traditional DS theorists including Chang and Evans (2005), Mo (2009) and Kim, E.M. (2014), hold that the Korean developmental state came to end after the Asian financial crisis of 1997 because of their focus on state deregulation of finance. However, as Thurbon (2016) reveals, the Korean state expanded its financial activism with policy loans even in the course of financial liberalization. The Korean government adopted financial liberalization measures including removal of capital controls and opening to foreign investors, even while it expanded financial activism through expanding state-owned policy financial institutions such as the Korean Development Bank (KDB) and Korean Export Import Bank (KEXIM). It also nationalized some local banks in order to promote national industries, including venture firms (Thurbon 2016: 89–90). However, unlike the prevalent path-dependent accounts of many institutionalists including Fields (2014) and Thurbon (2016), continuity of Korean state-led developmentalism was due to changes toward a new version of developmentalism to emphasize the promotion of knowledge-intensive industries. Furthermore, the continuity by changes was materialized not by rejuvenation of the cohesive developmental mindset but through competition of key state bureaucrats and competition with social actors. This section explores how competition within the government could continue the path of developmentalism.

Economic bureaucrats could continue developmentalism through competition with newly recruited liberal members of the *Jung Kyung Hoe* (JKH). JKH included liberal economists such as Kim Taedong, Lee Jinsoon, Yun Wonbae, and Lee Sun, all students of Professor Byun Hyung-yun. They were called the Hakhyun school. Similar to President Kim Daejung's idea in his book *Daejung Kyungjaeron* (Daejung Economics), they proposed a parallel development of free market and balanced development, opposing the traditional growth-first developmentalism. After Kim Dae-jung seized power, they occupied key economic decision making posts in the Kim administration (Yoon, Youngho 1999b; Kim et al. 2003: 54–56; Ji, Joohyung 2011: 242).

However, these liberal economists could not remain in the Kim administration due to competition with economic bureaucrats including Lee Kyusung, Lee Hunjae, and Jin Nyum. They retreated from their powerful posts within a year and a half (Suh, Junghwan 2007, 2010). Facing the actual problems of national debt, company insolvencies, and massive unemployment, they failed to propose realistic solutions. For example, Kim Taedong, a key member of the liberal JKH and Presidential First Economic Secretariat, opposed artificial reduction of interest rates, arguing that interest rates should be determined by the free market. Liberal economists including Kim Taedong and Yu Jongkun (Presidential Economic Advisor) also opposed the big deal plan and corporate restructuring through the state's control of banks, arguing that it was old-style developmentalism (Yoon, Youngho 1999b; Kim et al. 2003: 57–61, 84).

Although President Kim also had such liberal ideas initially, he began to prefer more realistic and detailed prescriptions proposed by the economic bureaucrats, rather than the abstract free market principles proposed by the liberal economists. President Kim Dae-jung's original idea in his book *Daejung Kyungjaeron* was more oriented toward a liberal market economy rather than state-led developmentalism found in the ideas of the JKH group economists. Proposing the parallel development of democracy and free market as an alternative to state-led developmentalism, Kim Dae-jung originally argued for a liberal free market system in which state interventionism should recede and chaebols should be dissolved for development in the free market.

However, searching for solutions to the economic crisis, President Kim leaned toward the bureaucrats' ideas on reforming chaebols toward specialization in core business and development of knowledge-intensive industries (Kim, Youngbum 2003: 411–412; Jun-Hong, K. 2009; Yoon, S.W. 2016: 26–27). Economic bureaucrats emphasized market failure in the crisis, proposing realistic solutions instead. Kang Bongkyun, former Minister of Finance and Economy, argued that if private firms could not operate the market smoothly, then the government should lead the reform. Lee Kyusung, former Minister of Finance and Economy also emphasized that the market did not work in the crisis (Kim, Hongki 1998: 176; Kwon, Youngki 2000: 77; Hundt 2009: 107).

Voluntary actions in the free market, as well as dissolution of chaebols, were not a realistic option in the crisis. Competing with liberal economists' free market within the state, and with progressives' chaebol dissolution, economic bureaucrats developed a new version of developmentalism as a solution to the crisis. Before seizing power, President Kim Dae-jung opposed the growth-first strategy and export-led developmentalism in his book *Daejung Kyungjaeron*. However, he abandoned his original liberal idea as he faced the economic crisis. He adopted export growth as a key means to overcome the national debt crisis, and leaned toward the industrial policy proposed by economic bureaucrats to improve the export competitiveness of national industries.

The Kim Dae-jung administration developed new developmental strategies, including promotion of hi-tech ventures and nurturing parts suppliers. These developmental policies, which included promotion of venture firms and the Special Law for Promotion of Parts and Materials, did not come from the path-dependent repetition of developmentalism but from new policies developed through competition among industry-related ministries including MIC and MoI. Although they agreed with government's active roles in overcoming the crisis and promoting the export competitiveness of national industries, they competed for initiatives to lead the developmentalism. Winning ministries gained power and budgets, while losing organizations sometimes risked their own survival. Through competition for influence, economic ministries tried to justify their new visions and rationale as a national priority through which they complemented Korean state-developmentalism.

For example, while losing its organizational influence and power, MoI desperately searched for new industrial visions and proposed promotion of parts and materials industries for an innovation-oriented industrial ecosystem. When the Kim Dae-jung administration was formed, MoI was one of the most losing ministries through restructuring of government organizations. In the restructuring process, the SME section of industrial policy was separated from MoI. Furthermore, through competition with the Ministry of Foreign Affairs to attract foreign investments, the trade division of MoI should be transferred to the

Trade Negotiation Center under the Ministry of Foreign Affairs. What remained in MoI were parts of traditional industries and energy.

However, in July 1998, Japanese economic journalist Ohmae Kenichi criticized the Kim Dae-jung government in Japan's biweekly journal *SAPIO*, stating that the Korean economy would not progress further due to its dependence on Japan's parts industries. Nationalism inside and outside the Korean government burst into flames, and MoI got its chance to put forth a new developmental vision. Ohmae Kenichi argued in the journal that the Korean economy could no longer develop because it was not a self-sufficient economy. It depended on foreign countries, particularly Japan, for its parts; Korean exports relied on appreciation of foreign exchange, rather than on its own technology and parts. While Ohmae Kenichi's criticism of the Korean economy provoked nationwide outrage, Koreans, particularly industrial experts, could not but recognize some accuracies in his criticism, including Korea's dependence on Japanese parts.

MoI had already recognized the relative underdevelopment of Korean parts and materials industries and their dependence on foreign countries, particularly Japan, due to Korea's imbalanced developmental strategy. MoI had made efforts to promote SME parts suppliers since the 1980s, but they found little success in parts localization. For example, as Korea exported more automobiles as a final product, their exports brought similar growth in imports of parts from Japan until the mid-1990s (Kwon with Kim 2017). MoI had already had some ideas to promote parts industries even before Ohmae Kenichi's criticism. A key drafter of the Special Law for Promotion of Parts and Materials in MoI says about its enactment process in a personal interview:

> The beginning of the policy for promotion of parts and materials is not 1999 or 2000, but goes back to 1996. The reason we could enact the Special Law was that we had already had some ideas.... Until then, we had some misunderstanding. We thought that if exports increased, our trade balance would turn to surplus. But our trade deficit was getting larger.... Initially, we thought that the trade deficit was a temporary phenomenon. But in the late period of the Kim Young-sam administration, when Lim Changyul came to the Minister post of MoI,...we changed our idea.... That was why we made the Special Law for Venture Firms at that time. I was the person in charge of it.... Actually the original name of the Special Law for Ventures was not the current one, but "the Special Law for Promotion of New Technology and Knowledge-intensive SMEs." Not for the purpose of distributive justice, but for the purpose of changing the industrial structure, we made it. ....But later, the Ministry of Labor in the Kim Dae-jung administration changed the nature of the Special Law for Venture Firms into a law for employment.... I thought then, something wrong was going on.... Meanwhile, Ohmae Kenichi, the Japanese scholar, provoked us, saying "Korea could never catch up to Japan; Korea is a country where they cannot

develop their own parts." All of us were infuriated.... At that point, the issue of our parts industries came to attract national attention, and we made a new law, the Special Law for Parts and Materials.[10]

MoI had already recognized the problem of the existing final assembly-oriented, imbalanced development before the Asian financial crisis. However, they could not easily enact the law, based on their own idea to change the industrial structure to nurture parts suppliers and develop innovation-oriented interfirm networks for the purpose of building a knowledge-intensive national economy. They had to materialize their idea through competition with other industry-related ministries. Even though they made the Special Law for Venture, MoI lost its initiative and could not execute its own idea. Now as Japanese journalist Ohmae Kenichi aroused national sentiments in Korea and the issue of Korean parts industries began to attract nationwide attention, MoI got a chance to materialize its ideas as the enactment of the Special Law for Promotion of Parts and Materials.

Even in the process of enacting the Special Law for Parts and Materials, there was significant rivalry and opposition inside the state. Both MIC and MoST opposed the MoI's initiative in developing parts industries because MIC worried that it would lose its initiative in developing the IT-related parts industries, considering that the strategic parts industries were parts of the IT and automobile industries.[11] MoFE also opposed the MoI idea, worrying that the industrial policy to promote parts industries was a traditional targeting policy, which might cause trade disputes.[12] In particular, offering an idea of global outsourcing, MoFE opposed the MoI idea on developing national parts industries. For example, counterattacking Ohmae Kenichi's argument of Korea's dependence on Japan, Park Jaeha, a key staff member of MoFE, argued that due to changes of the economic paradigm in the twenty-first century, Korean products could become the world's best by combining best parts at price and quality across national economies, rather than developing Korean parts following Ohmae Kenichi's advice (Park Jaeha's refute article in Wulgan Chosun, Sept. 1999).

However, against the background of infuriated nationalism, the Blue House and Prime Minister supported the MoI's initiative to enact the Special Law for Parts and Materials.[13] To persuade other ministries, MoI studied and proposed new ideas. For example, to counter the MoFE's worry of trade dispute, MoI staff

---

[10] Personal interview with a former senior official for Capital Goods Industry in MoI on June 17, 2015.

[11] Personal interview with a key drafter of the Special Law for Parts and Materials, a former senior official for Industrial Planning in MoI, on May 26, 2015; Personal interview with a former senior official for Capital Goods Industry in MoI on June 17, 2015.

[12] Personal interview with a former senior official at the Ministry of Knowledge Economy (MoI's other name) on June 22, 2015.

[13] Personal interview with a former senior official at the Ministry of Knowledge Economy on June 22, 2015.

studied trade rules and argued that parts industries are not a specific industry and would not cause a trade dispute.[14] In the process of enacting the Special Law for Parts and Materials, MoI developed a more detailed idea for a new version of developmental policy. Another key drafter of the Special Law, a former senior official at the Ministry of Knowledge Economy, states the meaning of the Special Law clearly in a personal interview:

> Yes, the Special Law is not simply a policy for SMEs. It was a policy to change the framework of our industrial policy. We thought that only the final assembly-oriented industries had their limitation. We should develop our intermediate industries. As the international division of labor deepened, we could not compete only with our assembly-oriented corporations. Instead, we should go to the *competition between systems*. In other words, international competition depends on how to build a competent industrial ecosystem by combining final assemblers and parts suppliers. The law might look to a policy to promote parts only, but it was also a policy to improve the final assemblers' competitiveness through a collaborative industrial ecosystem. (Emphasis added)[15]

In the process of enacting the Special Law for Parts and Materials, MoI put forth a new developmentalism to focus on the industrial ecosystem for knowledge-intensive industries, departing from the traditional scale economy which focused exclusively on large assemblers, and from simple localization of parts as import substitution to reduce trade deficits. With the Special Law for Parts and Materials, MoI began to develop an idea of system-based competition, in which the sources of national competitiveness do not rely simply on individual assemblers' large scale or production quality, but on the industrial ecosystem, like the collaborative relations of parts suppliers, assemblers, and R&D and financial centers.

Meanwhile in competition for influence, MIC also drafted its own developmental policy, particularly arguing that IT-related industries were within their core jurisdiction. For example, in the early 1990s when MIC attempted to initiate the Korean Information Infrastructure (KII) as a national project, EPB opposed the plan because the project needed massive public funding. However, the more important competition was between MIC and MoI over who would take charge of the IT industry. Communications had been regulated by MIC, while industrial policies were traditionally under the authority of MoI. MoI opposed the MIC initiative, arguing that all the equipment for the KII project was under the jurisdiction of MoI. However, as MIC justified the KII project as a key growth engine in a plan for national economic development, MIC took initiative in building the KII,

---

[14] Personal interview with a key drafter of the Special Law, a former senior official at the Office of Industrial Planning in the MoI on May 26, 2015.

[15] Personal interview with former Vice Minister of Knowledge Economy on June 22, 2015.

while taking over the IT-related functions and organizations from other ministries including MoI and MoST. MoI still insisted on its established authority to carry out national industrial policy over IT-related equipment (Jeong and King 1996: 129–132; Lee, Kwang-Suk 2009: 572). Competition between MIC and MoI over IT-related industries continued beyond the end of the Kim Dae-jung administration (1998–2002).

Competition among ministries inside the Korean government caused many problems including double investments in the IT industry and building similar trade associations for each ministry. For example, to promote the IT venture firms, MIC and MoI supported the same selected firm over and over (Shin Dong-A, July 2001). However, through competition with other ministries, Korean economic bureaucrats advanced their developmentalism by articulating and searching for new policies and new rationale in terms of national development.

Competition among economic bureaucrats was not carried out, though, to the extent of mutual destruction. Despite the competition and conflicts of economic ministries within the Korean government, they could not but concede and cooperate for the national cause of advancing the competitiveness of national industries. For example, as the United States and Japan proposed national information infrastructure programs, Korean bureaucrats refocused their attention on information technology after a lapse in the late 1980s and early 1990s because they feared a loss of competitiveness of Korean industries (Jeong and King 1996: 129–133).

Similarly, in the Kim Dae-jung administration, economic ministries including MIC, MoI, and MoST needed to collaborate for the national cause of promoting hi-tech venture firms, although they competed for the initiative in the promotion of venture firms. In order to overcome the economic crisis, the economic ministries in the Kim Dae-jung administration competitively developed the 1997 Special Law for the Promotion of Venture Businesses in which, unlike US venture capital in the market, the Korean government selected hi-tech venture firms strategically, mostly focusing on IT-related firms, rather than traditional SMEs. Offering massive support including tax incentives, exemptions from general corporate laws, and R&D support, economic ministries invested their funds in their own strategic industries. For example, MIC used its Informatization Promotion Fund, sponsoring consortia of IT firms to develop software industry, while MoST used its Science and Technology Promotion Fund to develop hi-tech firms. Through this competitive promotion of venture firms, the number of hi-tech venture firms increased to more than 10 thousand, employing one million workers, and successfully built a new industrial base for the next growth engine (Weiss 2003: 257–258; Chang, Jiho 2005: 23–34).

To sum up, unlike many DS demise theorists' accounts, the Korean state could continue its developmentalism through competition within the state. For example, through competition among economic ministries, the venture promotion policy continued across different administrations, at least to the Park Gunhye administration (2013–17) although the brand name changed to *Changjo Kyungjae* (literally 'Creative Economy' in Korean).[16] As seen in the Special Law for Parts and Materials, if their original idea failed to materialize in this administration, economic ministries like MoI get a chance to make its law as a national developmental agenda in the next administration, improving and renewing the rationale and policy. In competition for legitimate authority, the ministries within the Korean state continue their own developmental policy by changing their rationale, strategy, and methods of developmentalism.

---

[16] Personal interview with Chief of the R&D Strategy Planning Bureau in the MoI on June 18, 2018.

8

Continuation of Developmentalism across Administrations

In the 2010s, Korea continued its state-led developmentalism, in part through strategic targeting, using R&D incentives as a main policy instrument. Many industrial policies in Korea, including the Special Law for Parts and Materials and the New Growth Engine Promotion policy, continue across ideologically different governments. For example, the Special Law for Parts and Materials, a key developmental policy to promote innovation-oriented interfirm ecosystems, began in 2001 as a ten-year special law in the left-wing government of Kim Dae-jung. But considering its effects on developmentalism, the right-wing government of Lee Myung-bak extended this law another 10 years, to 2021, although changing its name to the Special Law for Materials and Parts, with an emphasis on materials. In addition, the Moon Jae-in administration (May 2017–present) extended the Special Law for Materials and Parts into the Special Act for the Promotion of Material, Parts, and Equipment Industries as a constant law in December 2019, considering Japan's export control of core material which aroused national sentiments in Korea. Many important national R&D programs, including the World Premium Merchandise (WPM) have lasted for more than five years.[1] In particular, the Korean developmental policy to promote next growth-engine industries began in the left-wing Roh Moo-hyun administration (2003–07), and continues across the right-wing governments of Lee Myung-bak (2008–12) and Park Geun-hye (2013–17), to the current left-wing administration of Moon Jae-in. Administrations, though, change the brand names, such as the Next Generation of Growth Engine project, the Green Economy, and Innovation Economy.

Korea's state-led developmentalism was mainly realized through competitive politics within as well as outside the state, rather than by simple repetition of a developmental mindset or old institutional legacy. By exploring the industrial politics of three administrations—Roh Moo-hyun (2003–07), Lee Myung-bak (2008–12), and Park Geun-hye (2013–17), as well as the Moon administration (2017–present)—this chapter examines how the Korean government continued its developmentalism across ideologically different administrations. This chapter

---

[1] Personal interview with Chief of R&D Strategy Planning Bureau in the MoI on June 18, 2018.

Changes by Competition: The Evolution of the South Korean Developmental State. Hyeong-ki Kwon, Oxford University Press (2021). © Hyeong-ki Kwon. DOI: 10.1093/oso/9780198866060.003.0008

first studies why the Roh Moo-hyun administration continued with state-led developmentalism, rather than pursue the economic democratization proposed by the original supporters of Roh Moo-hyun. Then, it examines how Korean state-led developmentalism continues across ideologically different governments by focusing on competition and conflicts within the state.

Economic Democracy versus State Developmentalism

Unlike the Kim Dae-jung administration (1998–2002) which seized power through alliance with the traditional pro-business party United Liberal Democrats (ULD) led by Kim Jongpil, Roh Moo-hyun independently won the presidential election mainly through the support of progressives in the civil society. After gaining power, the Roh Moo-hyun administration actively proclaimed "economic democratization" as an alternative to traditional developmentalism, arguing for a power balance between workers and employers and workers' active participation in business decision-making. For example, Roh Moo-hyun as a president-elect visited the Federation of Korean Trade Unions (FKTU) and the Korean Confederation of Trade Unions (KCTU), saying that "we will correct the power imbalance between different value proponents for the coming five years, because business is now much stronger" and "if the balance of power is realized, the conflicts will be resolved voluntarily without the president's intervention" (Lim and Lee 2018: 8).

Paradoxically, despite the attempted chaebol reforms, their wealth concentration grew. And despite the opposition of its original supporters, including trade unionists and progressive civil associations, the Roh Moo-hyun government pursued trade liberalization, such as the FTAs with the United States. The Roh administration abandoned its initial economic democracy and developed new industrial policies like the Promotion Project of the Next Generation Growth Engine. What triggered this turnaround? The Roh Moo-hyun administration's failure in economic democracy reveals how state-led developmentalism continues in Korea through competition with other alternatives, and why Korea has difficulty in establishing social democratic corporatism.

Economic democracy had been proposed as an alternative to state-led developmentalism which relied mainly on the alliance between state and large corporations. Traditionally, the Korean government selected and exclusively funneled preferential credits to large corporations in strategic industries, while suppressing labor to secure the international competitiveness of strategic industries, although small and medium-sized enterprises (SMEs) were included in the alliance later in the 1990s. As progressive social forces such as trade unions and civil associations grew following democratization in 1987, economic democracy has been proposed as an alternative to correct the imbalance in political power and wealth distribution.

Table 8.1. Economic Wealth Concentration of 50 Largest Corporations

50 Largest Corporation Index	1987	1992	1997	2002	2007	2012
50 Firms' Assets/GDP (%)	52.17	52.64	70.71	57.80	63.06	84.44
50's Gross Sales/GDP (%)	45.77	41.51	50.86	49.42	52.97	73.78

Source: We (2014) Table 1, 2, 7; Park, H.S. (2017: 220).

For example, the Citizens' Coalition for Economic Justice, established in 1989, actively proposed economic democracy, criticizing chaebols' speculation in real estate and playing an active role to introduce the real-name financial transaction system. In addition, the People's Solidarity for Participatory Democracy (PSPD), established in 1994, constituted the Committee for Economic Democracy in 1996 to point out the problems of chaebols' wealth concentration and unfair insider transactions among chaebols' affiliates. PSPD also inaugurated the campaign for small-sum stockholders while accusing chaebol family members' illegal and private use of company property (Park, H.S. 2017: 203).

Due to social pressure, The Roh Tae-woo (1988–92) and Kim Young-sam (1993–7) administrations made reform attempts early on in their administrations, but failed to reform the chaebol-dominant industrial structure. After the Asian financial crisis of 1997, the debate on economic democracy was rekindled, yet state-led developmentalism and chaebol dominance continued, although they changed the strategy from input-oriented to knowledge-intensive specialization (Park, H.S. 2017: 197, 204).

During the presidential election of 2002, issues of economic democracy, including chaebol reform, expansion of welfare, raising taxes on the rich, and reducing income polarization, were raised in earnest. Roh Moo-hyun made serious attempts to establish economic democracy in the initial stage of his presidency. Yet despite these attempts, wealth concentration increased. In the pro-business governments of Lee Myung-bak (2008–12) and Park Geun-hye (2013–17), economic power became further concentrated among chaebols, as seen in Table 8.1.

The Roh Moo-hyun administration turned its initial policy of economic democracy toward a more pro-business policy, prioritizing economic growth, as criticism grew over the decline of Korea's economic growth potential. An executive director of FKI, the large corporations' association, says about changes in the Roh Moo-hyun administration's attitude toward chaebols:

The Roh Moo-hyun government was very critical of large corporations until three years of his presidency, but thereafter, our relations turned very good, because three years later after he seized power, the economy seriously worsened. They supported us so much. In the late term of his presidency, his government implemented pro-business policy intensively. For instance, with FTA, the relaxation of the equity investment limit on large conglomerates, and so on.... Actually, the Roh government was supposed to oppose the FTA.[2]

The reason that the Roh Moo-hyun administration turned toward pro-business developmentalism and abandoned the economic democracy agenda may be the relative weakness of the progressive forces. For example, the trade union movement had apparently grown since the democratization of 1987, but trade unions became conservative as their unions gained legal status because their unions were mostly organized as company units rather than industrywide. Experiencing corporate restructuring after the Asian financial crisis of 1997, Korean labor movements suffered from internal division of insider-outsider, not integrating part-time and irregular workers. The unionists focused on their narrow interests rather than on issues affecting the working class as a whole. As Korean workers divided into insiders and outsiders in the labor market and trade unions of the large corporations supported their insiders, the expectation of economic democracy waned (Yang, J. 2017: 154–166, 170–183; Chang, K. 2019: 97–99).

However, absent from the progressives' vision for economic democracy as an alternative to developmentalism was a persuasive strategy for economic growth. As the economy deteriorated, the Roh Moo-hyun administration could not but focus on boosting the economy and employment in order to maintain power in the next presidential election. But the progressives put forth no alternative growth strategy beyond wealth redistribution or criticism against the chaebols (Lim and Lee 2018:12). Due to chaebols' large share in the Korean economy, as seen in Table 8.1, their collaboration was crucial to improving economic competitiveness. Hence the economic democracy of the Roh Moo-hyun administration, as well as the former administrations of Roh Tae-woo, Kim Young-sam, and Kim Dae-jung, was discarded for a turn toward new developmentalism based on collaboration with large corporations.

New Developmentalism in the 2000s

Turning from confrontation toward more collaborative relations with large corporations, the Roh Moo-hyun administration developed an industrial policy to promote new growth engine industries, like the Next Generation Growth Engine Project and the Establishment of Science & Technology-centered Society. This new developmentalism initiated in the 1990s to promote knowledge-intensive, hi-tech industries, has been continuously developed by Korean economic bureaucrats across the administrations of Lee Myung-bak (2008–12) and Park Geun-hye

---

[2] Personal interview with a director of FKI on May 17, 2018.

(2013–17), up to the present day, although each administration brands this new developmentalism differently—Green Growth Model, Creative Economy, and Innovative Economy.

Facing the economic crisis and declining growth potential of Koran industries, the Roh Moo-hyun administration (2003–07) proposed the New Korean Growth Model rather than economic democracy. The New Korean Growth Model emphasized establishment of a knowledge-based, innovation-led economy and mutual growth of large corporations and SMEs, as an alternative to the traditional input-oriented developmentalism and unbalanced growth strategy which exclusively focused on large corporations (Chamyeo Jungboo Special Briefing Team of State Affairs 2008: 13; Lee, Y.S. 2009: 358). The earlier administrations of Kim Young-sam (1993–7) and Kim Dae-jung (1998–2002) formed their developmental visions to emphasize the transformation of Korean developmentalism from "government-led, input-oriented growth" to an "innovation-led, knowledge-based economy" in their government reports, including "21st Century Korea" of 1994, "National Tasks for Open Market Economy" of 1997, "DJ-nomics: Opening Tomorrow with People" of 1998, and "2011 Vision and Task: Open World and Flexible Economy" of 2002. However, in criticizing former administrations' vision reports for not developing detailed practical plans, the Roh Moo-hyun administration attempted to develop detailed plans with a financial strategy, while proposing the new conception of "mutual growth of large and small firms" in the reports of "Korea of Dynamics and Opportunity" and "Vision 2030" (Chamyeo Jungboo Special Briefing Team of State Affairs 2008: 339–340).

For detailed strategy to realize the new developmentalism in the New Korean Growth Model, the Roh Moo-hyun administration emphasized further development of export-led growth. Particularly, even though the Roh administration's own supporters, including trade unions and progressive civil associations, opposed it, the administration aggressively carried forward the Free Trade Agreements (FTAs) to expand export markets, forming alliances with large corporations. For example, in order to carry out the FTAs effectively, the Roh Moo-hyun administration established the Council of Foreign Economic Advisors (CFEA) to deliberate collectively on how to carry out the FTAs and report directly to the President. The Council was a collective meeting in which economic ministers and business representatives took part, including the President of FKI, Chief of the Korea Chamber of Commerce and Industry (KCCI), the President of the Korea Foreign Trade Association (KFTA), and chiefs of other state research institutes (Kim, H.J. 2010: 20–21, 42–43, 50).

Like other Korean governments, the Roh Moo-hyun administration emphasized exports as a key method for economic growth. Depending on exports for 70.3% of GDP in 2004, in contrast to 20.0% in the United States and 21.8% in Japan, Korean economic bureaucrats believed that the Korean economy could not grow if export markets were closed (Chamyeo Jungboo Special Briefing Team of State Affairs 2008: 305). Korean economic bureaucrats along with businessmen thought that if other countries, such as Mexico, restricted applicants for their national business projects to the FTA partners, Korean corporations would lose their export markets; or that if Korea were late in FTAs, Korean corporations would suffer from higher duties than their competitors. Despite the opposition of its civil supporters, the Roh Moo-hyun administration aggressively carried forward the FTAs with large economies, including the United States and European Union, simultaneously in May 2004, while changing its existing plan to make a FTA with Japan and Singapore subsequently after the Korea-Chile FTA (Chamyeo Jungboo Special Briefing Team of State Affairs 2008: 306).

In contrast to Latin American countries, including Mexico and Argentina, whose governments abandoned industrial policies to promote endogenous industries while emphasizing liberalization and exports, Korea emphasized developmental policy to promote the international competitiveness of national industries. Expanding export markets through FTAs was one alternative to Korean firms' overseas relocation under globalization. By expanding export markets through FTAs, Korean bureaucrats thought that Korean firms were more likely to invest and to create more jobs at home, rather than move overseas (Kim, H.J. 2010: 32). The Korean government expanded export markets through FTAs while emphasizing industrial policy to upgrade the competitiveness of national industries.[3] For example, in the third meeting of the Council of Foreign Economic Advisors in December 2004, after hearing the report on the Korea-US FTA, President Roh Moo-hyun emphasized the need to search for the best ways to improve Korea's parts and materials industries and overcome dependence on Japanese parts industries by analyzing the European parts industries (Kim, H.J. 2010: 52).

While expanding export markets through FTAs, Korean governments had emphasized industrial policies to promote international competitiveness of national industries, which mainly focused on promotion of new growth engine industries and building an industrial ecosystem for innovation-oriented interfirm collaboration. Before exploring the building of industrial ecosystems, this section examines the new growth engine projects which began in the Roh Moo-hyun administration.

In order to improve international competitiveness of national industries, the Roh Moo-hyun administration proposed the New Growth Engine project to promote the future growth engine industries, such as next-generation mobile communications, digital content software solutions, and intelligent home

---

[3] The Korean government tried to maintain the policy loan even in the negotiation process of Korea- United States FTA, although the US team requested the Korean government not to intervene in financial market with policy loan (Han, K. 2008).

networks. The New Growth Engine project actually began in the Kim Dae-jung administration which in 1999 drafted the "Long-term Vision 2025 for Improvement of Science and Technology Competitiveness." However, the Kim administration emphasized IT industry as a new growth engine, whereas the Roh administration selected multiple industries as future growth engine industries. The Roh administration selected ten industries, while the Lee Myung-bak administration (2008–12) promoted "17 New Growth Engine Industries," and the Park Geun-hye administration (2013–17) carried out the "13 Future Growth Engine Industries" project. Although each government had different brand names and slightly different priorities, they often overlap in the selected industries, including intelligent robotics, biopharmaceuticals, and future automobiles. For example, the name "future automobiles" in the Roh administration changed into "smart automobiles" in the Park administration's Future Growth Engine project (Lee, Taekyu 2015: 24–25).

For the new growth engine project, Korean governments have made significant investments in R&D consortia. For example, for the Next Generation Growth Engine project, the Roh Moo-hyun administration invested 2.9 trillion Korean won (2 trillion Korean won by the government and 9000 billion Korean won by private firms) in the new growth engine project in 2004–08. This Next Generation Growth Engine project was not government support for the pure and basic sciences but a strategic industrial policy to promote future industries in Korea. The Roh administration emphasized knowledge-based and innovation-oriented growth strategies, criticizing the traditional input-oriented developmentalism.

Economic bureaucrats in Korea thought that the public R&D resources to promote new growth engine industries was limited and used efficiently and strategically. Kim Taewoo, Presidential Secretary for Science and Technology, who designed the New Growth Engine project, says about the strategic industrial policy:

> Our R&D size is one seventh of Japan and one twentieth of the United States. We need an efficient strategy like the Dschinghis Khan strategy which was "selection and concentration." In addition, Japan and Germany as latecomers carried out their economic development by state-led developmentalism. We thought, Korea also needed the government's active role in development as a latecomer. Regarding this, we exchanged our views with the President ever so often. We planned to carry out our Next Generation Growth Engine Project by selecting the competitive technology and industries, and concentrating our efforts on promoting them. And we planned to reinvest our accumulated wealth.
>
> (Policy Briefing, February 10, 2008)

Although the Lee Myung-bak administration (2008–12) had ideological conflicts with the Roh Moo-hyun administration, it continued the Roh administration's

New Growth Engine Promotion Project under a new brand name of Green Growth Strategy. Emphasizing new challenges, including the energy crisis, high-pressure international competition, and problems of an aging society, the Lee Myung-bak administration proposed a Green Growth Strategy to solve the energy problem and also to open opportunities for new growth engine industries (Kim, S.Y. 2019). In particular, the Lee administration used industrial policy to strategically target new green growth engine industries, as the Roh administration had done.

The Lee administration poured about 19% of the government's budget into the new green growth engine industries in 2009–13, while Korean financial institutions were induced to increase policy loans from 20% to 25% of total banking sector loans (Thurbon 2016: 125, 130). In 2008 when the financial crisis broke out, the Korean Development Bank (KDB) immediately increased its policy loans to Korean manufacturers, from 10.3 trillion Korean won in 2005 to 16.5 trillion won in 2008, a growth of 160%. More than 60% of the policy loans were earmarked for investment in new growth engine industries including green energy industries. Establishing the Green Industry Development Fund, the KDB provided firms investing in the ten green industries, including green IT and green cars, and renewable energy, which the Ministry of Industry (MoI) strategically selected, with approximately US$ 4 billion at preferential interest rates (KDB 2011: 79; Thurbon 2016: 132). In addition to the KDB, the Korea Finance Corporation (KOFC) and Korea Export Import Bank (KEXIM) played an active developmental role, providing special funds for Korean firms in new growth engine industries (Thurbon 2016: 133–134, 193 endnote 21).

The Park Geun-hye administration (2013–17) also continued the new developmentalism to promote new growth engine industries and to nurture the industrial ecosystem for an innovation-oriented economy. When a new administration raised a new national priority agenda for economic development, such as Park Geun-hye's "Creative Economy," economic bureaucrats competitively rebranded the former administration's policy initiative, such as Lee Myung-bak's "Green Growth Strategy," to render their ministries' strategic programs compatible with the new president's catchphrase. In the Park Geun-hye administration, almost all ministries removed the phrase "green growth" from their programs, while adding "creative." However, the Park Geun-hye administration continued the developmental policy to promote new growth engine industries as well as an innovation-oriented industrial ecosystem through interfirm collaboration. New growth engine industries by the Creative Economy of the Park administration include renewable energy, smart-grids, electric vehicles, and energy storage devices which the former Lee administration strategically selected under the Green Growth Strategy. The Park administration continued those developmental plans and financial support allocated to these industries in the Lee administration (Shin Dong-A, May 2015; Sept. 2016; Thurbon 2016: 139).

In order to support developmentalism, the Park administration also continued with financial activism. The plan to privatize the KDB was abandoned in 2014, and the KDB increased its policy loan to support SMEs with the KOFC. In addition, Korean financial institutions still tended to use financial activism to target strategic industries. For example, KOFC's Frontier Champion program provided low-interest, long-term loans to strategically selected firms with a viable technology and a marketable product. Financial institutions in the Park Geun-hye administration, like the KEXIM, expanded the Hidden Champion Program, which began in the Lee administration, to promote world-leading SMEs (Oh, D.K. 2012; Thurbon 2016: 135–136, 140).

In the process of developing new growth engine industries, Thurbon succinctly notes that Korean governments played "the roles of producer, procurer, promoter, and financier—just as it had under IT-839" (Thurbon 2016: 129). In order to create new technologies and products, Korean governments provided massive R&D funds while they increased demand for the products through government purchasing programs. State-owned financial institutions and venture funds financially assisted Korean firms to expand their markets at home as well as overseas, increasing their policy loans up to 25% of all loans in the Korean financial system (Fitch 2013: 4).

Meanwhile, following the Roh Moo-hyun administration (2003–07), Korean governments began to emphasize the industrial ecosystem for new developmentalism, putting forth a new conception of mutual growth between large corporations and SMEs. In contrast to the Korean traditional developmentalism in which, in order to improve the competitiveness of Korean exports, the governments provided strategic favor exclusively to large corporations, the Roh Moo-hyun administration further developed Kim Dae-jung administration's developmentalism to promote parts and material industries, and emphasized interfirm collaboration for an innovation-oriented economy. Reflecting upon the problems of the traditional developmental strategy which exclusively favored large assemblers and caused underdevelopment of parts and materials industries, Korean economic bureaucrats began to emphasize collaborative interfirm relations to promote parts and materials SMEs, starting with the Kim Dae-jung administration, as seen in the Special Law for Promotion of Parts and Materials in 2001. The Roh Moo-hyun administration further developed the interfirm collaboration for an innovation-oriented economy with new concepts, including mutual growth of large and small corporations, and development of regional innovation clusters.

Following the Roh Moo-hyun administration, Korean governments began to emphasize the industrial ecosystem by constructing regional innovation systems and smart microgrids, rather than targeting individual firms (Kim, S.Y. 2019). For example, MoI (then MoCIE) in the Roh Moo-hyun administration initiated its own developmental plan for building "Regional Innovation Clusters" in order to competitively find its new role and to enlarge its influence. It utilized the presidential catchphrases, including the "Mutual Growth" of large and small corporations, as well as "Regional Balanced Growth." Further developing its own conception of an industrial ecosystem, MoI began to construct regional innovation clusters by establishing and financing local institutions, technical centers, and public-private R&D consortia to grow hi-tech industries like the Liquid Crystal Display (LCD) industry (Lee, Heo and Kim 2014: 120–121). MoI in the Roh Moo-hyun administration established the Regional R&D Center Business Leaders' Council in 2005 to carry out the program of regional R&D centers. This policy continued into the Lee Myung-bak administration, building nine regional R&D centers.

Like the Roh Moo-hyun administration's regional R&D cluster, the Lee administration (2008–2012) made efforts to increase local technology levels and promote local equipment, parts, and materials industries. For example, MoI (then the Ministry of Knowledge Economy, MoKE) developed a plan to increase the growth of new growth engine equipment by four times. In order to promote parts and equipment in the new hi-tech industries, the Lee administration increased its R&D investment and built a host of public-private consortia. For example, MoI established an R&D consortium with Samsung Electronics, LG Electronics, local research institutes, and many small firms in 2008, in order to develop new technologies to locally produce lithographic devices. These lithographic devices were one of five key components in making LCD and organic light emitting diode display screens. Until that time, Korea imported these devices mainly from Japan. The R&D consortium succeeded in developing a Korean-made device in 2013, now used nationwide, increasing the localization rate of display equipment from 60% to 90% (Business Korea, December 18, 2013).

The project to build the innovation-oriented industrial ecosystem, including regional R&D clusters, hidden champion projects, and R&D consortia, was continued in the Park Geun-hye administration (2013–2017) and complemented by the new project called the Creative Economy, in which new Innovation Centers for Creative Economy were established. The key idea of these centers was the government-initiated mating between large corporations and hi-tech SMEs and startups in many regions, in which large corporations were induced to participate and support the SMEs.[4]

Now, we look at the Asan-Tanjung cluster to examine in detail a case of regional R&D clusters for an innovation-oriented ecosystem. Korean governments had constructed regional and local institutions and technology centers, such as the Chungnam Techno Park Display Center and the Display R&D Cluster, beginning with the Roh Moo-hyun administration. These centers provided technical assistance and encouraged interfirm networks among small firms for innovation

---

[4] Personal interview with staff reporter of Business Desk in Dong-A newspaper on September 25, 2014.

and commercialization of R&D outputs (Lee, Heo and Kim 2014: 121). The Korean government provided the Display R&D Center with two billion Korean won every year from 2004 to 2013. The R&D Center aimed to establish regional innovation systems to support local firms, particularly firms producing display parts and equipment, and to strengthen industry-academic cooperation. Through this developmental policy, the Asan-Tanjung R&D Center registered 145 patents related to the display industry in 2004–14. As of 2014, they were working on display-related R&D projects, including complex input devices with touch and tablet functions, low-power and high-efficiency LED backlight component technology, and high-power LED. The total R&D budget from 2004 to 2013 was approximately 26 billion Korean won, 18 billion of which came from MoI (MoCIE in 2004–08 and then MoKE in 2008–14), with 2.25 billion Korean won from the local government and 5.57 billion won from local universities and companies (Lee, Heo and Kim 2014: 121–123).

Due to the Korean state's active role in building the innovation-oriented industrial ecosystem, Korean large corporations pursued a home-based strategy in the course of globalization, in which private firms made efforts to upgrade their home bases while globalizing their production overseas. For example, after investigating Korean lead firms' globalization in the electronics industry, Yeung (2016) points to Korean lead firms' home-based strategy in building global production networks:

> Both lead firms [Samsung and LG] have been reluctant to internationalize their R&D and manufacturing activity and have preferred to keep a large portion of their manufacturing activity in South Korea, particularly within the Seoul Metropolitan Area. The home region benefits from the enormous innovative capability, employment generation, and industrial linkages of both chaebols. In particular, Samsung has pursued a home-based and export-oriented production system that offers several key competitive advantages, such as faster-time-to-market and better control of production cost and technological know-how.
>
> (Yeung 2016: 169)

The home-based strategy of Korean lead firms occurs not only in the electronics industry but also in automobiles, another Korean flagship industry. As seen in Figure 8.1, Korean automakers brought their home suppliers overseas and built global production networks with home suppliers on foreign soil, rather than with global or local suppliers overseas, while simultaneously upgrading their innovation capabilities at home through collaboration with home suppliers (Yeung 2016: 177–178; Kim, S.Y. 2019; Kwon and Kim 2020).

In contrast to the globalization of many advanced economies, including the United States where individual lead firms moving overseas created an industrial hollowing-out leaving many holes in the industrial ecosystem at home, Korean

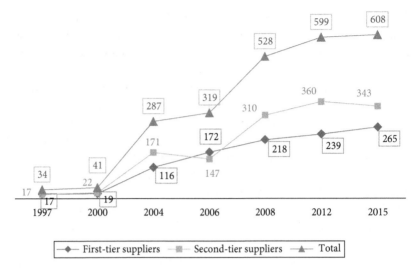

Figure 8.1. The Number of Korean Suppliers who Coglobalized with Hyundai and Kia

Source: Hyundai Motor Group (2015) *Together for a Better Future*.

lead firms' globalization did not cause a hollowing-out at home, but reinforced the connection between home and overseas production (Kwon and Kim 2020).

How could this happen? Traditionally, due to Korea's imbalanced developmentalism favoring large corporations exclusive of SMEs, Korean SME parts suppliers were underdeveloped and Korean interfirm relations were known for their exploitative and adversarial relations. But recently relations between lead firms and core suppliers have grown more trustful and collaborative. For example, Yeung (2016) points to trustful interfirm relations when describing how Korean lead firms like Hyundai could build nationally-oriented supplier networks with home suppliers on foreign soil: "Hyundai's strong coupling process of localizing its global production networks is generally well supported by its key suppliers in South Korea. This strong and trusting relationship with its suppliers represents Hyundai's most significant home-based advantage" (Yeung 2016: 178).

One of the main reasons why Korean lead firms pursued a home-based globalization strategy while upgrading their innovation capability at home comes from the Korean lead firms' own experience on foreign soil, suffering from latecomers' disadvantages in globalization. For example, when Korean lead firms went overseas, global competitors from advanced countries like the United States, Japan, and Germany had already claimed the pool of global suppliers. Samsung faced difficulty in finding reliable global and local suppliers when it entered China later than its main competitors, because suppliers were already taken by its rival Multinational Corporations (MNCs). In response, Samsung Electronics brought home suppliers to China (Lee and He 2009: 288; Hemmert and Jackson 2016:

582). Korean automakers like Hyundai also changed their initial strategy of independent globalization toward co-globalization with home suppliers, given their difficulty in building reliable and competitive parts supply networks with global and local suppliers which the foreign competitors had already taken (Shin Dong-A, May 2014).[5]

In addition, as seen in the regional R&D clusters, the Korean state changed its developmentalism from traditional exclusive promotion of large firms to building an innovation-oriented industrial ecosystem through collaboration of large corporations, SMEs, and research institutes, and Korean governments began to promote innovation-oriented collaboration between large and small parts suppliers. As seen above, from the Kim Dae-jung administration, the Korean government began to consider national competitiveness not in terms of a few large exporters such as Hyundai (vs Toyota) or Samsung (vs Sony), but in terms of the entire ecosystem, including final assemblers and parts suppliers. Now, through the assistance of state-initiated developmentalism, Korean firms could develop a home-based strategy in globalization with close connections between home and overseas production, while upgrading their innovation capabilities at home.

Continuity of Developmentalism through Competition Inside the State

The Roh Moo-hyun administration (2003–07) initially pursued economic democracy as an alternative to existing developmentalism, but soon turned toward a new version of developmentalism to promote the New Growth Engine industries and mutual balanced growth strategy. The administrations of Lee Myung-bak (2008–12), Park Geun-hye (2013–17) and Moon Jae-in (2017–present) continued similar developmentalism, even though they rhetorically and ideologically differed from each other. By focusing on competition among industry-related ministries, including the Ministry of Industry (MoI), the Ministry of Information and Communications (MIC) and the Ministry of Science and Technology (MoST), this section explores how the Korean state could continue its developmentalism even across different administrations.

First, in contest with private firms and social forces, economic bureaucrats in Korea could offer persuasive and detailed developmental visions and practical plans to overcome challenges, particularly from international competition. Although private firms had initiatives in their investments and more detailed information about their own businesses, economic bureaucrats had more

[5] For the Korean firms' globalization and its reverse effects on home economy, this section mainly relies on my own article, Kwon and Kim (2020).

persuasive views from the perspective of an entire national economy. For example, facing tough challenges in international market competition, in which low-wage countries like China rapidly caught up while advanced economies like the United States and Japan were more concerned with protecting their technology, Korea needed to upgrade its economy toward more knowledge-intensive industries. However, private firms were reluctant to invest in new pioneering industries like robotics, because the risk was too high to invest in such new technology-intensive businesses (Thurbon 2016: 104). From the perspective of national development, economic bureaucrats in Korea shared the idea that the government should lead the charge while shouldering the risk. Actually, MIC, MoI, and MoST competitively proposed detailed plans, such as the IT-839 and New Growth Engine projects, to develop new technology-intensive industries.

Competition within the state among economic bureaucrats was a driving force to reproduce and reinforce developmentalism in Korea, although they caused some problems with overlapping national projects. For example, in the Roh Moo-hyun administration, economic bureaucrats shared an idea that in order to improve its competitiveness, Korea needed both to upgrade its technology levels of existing industries and pioneer new technology-intensive industries. And, considering the private firms' reluctance, they thought the government should lead the developmental strategy. However, the economic ministries inside the state competed over who would take the lead in the national priority goal, called *Je2 Kwahak Gisul Ipkook* (the Second Nation-Building by Science and Technology in Korean), because initiatives in national priority projects like the New Growth Engine Project affected both their influence and massive R&D funds and their organizational fate.

In the Roh administration, in competition with MoI and MoST, MIC proposed a new industrial policy called the IT839 project, in response to the presidential catchphrase of *Je2 Kwahak Gisul Ipkook*. The IT839 project planned to promote eight new IT services, including wireless broadband [Wibro], the wire band code division multiple access [W-CDMA], and three new infrastructure services, such as broadband convergence networks. The new services and networks provided the infrastructure or platforms required to support nine new growth engine industries, such as next-generation mobile devices, embedded software, and intelligent robotics (Chung, C.S. 2010: 143; Kim, S.B. 2011: 6). By actively supporting the development of these interrelated new services, networks, and industries, MIC expected that Korea would rapidly secure its techno-industrial competitiveness and advanced economic status (Thurbon 2016: 103).

However, MoST and MoI proposed their own developmental policies for new growth engines as a national agenda of the Roh administration, independent of MIC's IT-839 project. The final Next Generation Growth Engine Project resulted from severe conflicts and eventual coordination inside the government because the actual development points of MIC's IT-839 and new growth engine programs of MoI and MoST significantly overlapped.

This competition for new growth engine industries began as the new Roh administration was established. MoST presented a national task report on national development of post-semiconductor hi-tech industries to President Roh on March 20, 2003, proposing six new growth engine industries including Tera bit semiconductors, next-generation automobiles, and intelligent computers. Then, MoI and MIC competitively gave their similar reports to President Roh on March 25 and 28 respectively. In its plan called the Excavation and Promotion Project of Next Generation Growth Engine, MoI proposed its own new growth engine industries including ultra-low emission automobiles, optical fibers for communication, and mobile digital TVs, while in its report titled Excavation Strategy of IT New Growth Industries, MIC proposed intelligent robots, post-PCs, and digital TVs (Seoul Shinmoon April 29, 2003). As controversy arose over the overlap in national new growth engine projects, MoST attempted an initiative with building the Future Strategy and Planning Committee under its own jurisdiction to carry out the New Growth Engine Project, which MoI and MIC opposed. Once MoST fumbled, it argued that the project should be carried out as an entire national project, not by a specific ministry. Thus, in 2006, MIC's IT839 Project was reformulated into the Next Generation Growth Engine Project (Kim, S.B. 2011: 11, 17–18).

In response to the MoST plan to build the Future Strategy and Planning Committee, MoI proposed a taskforce for the Excavation and Promotion of Next Generation Growth Engines under the Office for Government Policy Coordination. MoI would lead the coordination while relevant ministries would be in charge of each development. MoI thought that mobile devices, computers and digital broadcasting were under its jurisdiction, but MIC encroached. In competition with MIC, MoI proposed many alternatives for developmental policies and negotiated with them (Kim, S.B. 2011: 17). In competition with MoI and MoST, MIC proposed a more detailed alternative plan to carry out R&D projects through commercialization in contrast to other ministries' proposals which focused on technology development. MIC emphasized that because the nine new growth engine industries under its own IT-839 project were so closely related, MIC should coordinate the project, given their hi-tech services and industrial impacts (Kim, S.B. 2011: 13, 16).

Although these conflicts and competition were riddle with overlaps and waste, the competition had positive effects in further expanding and reinforcing the government's developmental policies. For example, through competition for initiative in the New Growth Engine Project, the industry-related ministries developed new rationales for developmentalism and proposed new policies. MoI emphasized that technology should be materialized in commercial products, while MIC emphasized industrial linkages and an IT based ecosystem (Seoul

Shinmoon April 29, 2003). Through this competition, the Roh Moo-hyun administration could materialize a new version of developmentalism, different from the traditional input-oriented growth strategy, while increasing total R&D in Korea from 17 trillion Korean won in 2002 to 27 trillion Korean won in 2006, and raising Korea's technology status from 24th rank in 2003 to 6th rank in the IMD world technology evaluation (Policy Briefing, February 10, 2008; Chamyeo Jungboo Special Briefing Team of State Affairs 2008: 272).

Through competition to lead national developmental projects, the industry-related ministries including MoI, MIC, and MoST reinforced their own developmental visions by further developing new industrial projects across different administrations. For example, since 1995, MIC had established itself as a ministry in charge of IT-related industries. Subsequently MIC made developmental plans, such as the Basic Plan for Promoting Informatization in 1999, the IT-839 Project in 2004, and U-Korea in 2006, further expanding its national priority projects. These projects were established from long-term perspectives to span about 10 years, as MoI did for the Special Law for Promotion of Parts and Materials (Choi and Kim 2013: 179). Although MoI (then MoKE) took over the lion's share of MIC functions by proposing a new development roadmap to build new growth engines by combining IT and non-IT industries, MIC was revived under the new name of Ministry of Future Planning by offering a new developmental vision to materialize the presidential catch phrase, Creative Economy in the Park Geun-hye administration (Money Today October 18, 2012).

Competition among economic ministries in Korea did not result in any extreme case of mutual destruction. Competition over who most contributed to the national growth tended to constrain any mutually destructive attempts. More importantly, in order to reduce the problems of competition among economic ministries, the Korean government developed a new method of horizontal mutual adjustments, different from the traditional method of central and hierarchical coordination, as seen in the Park Chung Hee era. The process of establishing a new governance system was conflict-laden, and a trial-and-error process.

For example, as industry-related ministries including MoI, MoST, and the Ministry of Health and Welfare (MoHW), say, in the biotech industry, competed for R&D resources, it was difficult to decide divisions of labor and to coordinate the allocation of functions and resources. In the 1990s, the Ministry of Planning and Budget (MPB) was in charge of allocation of R&D resources, but MPB was little authority in allocation because it lacked technology expertise. Although MPB consulted the Korean Institute of Science and Technology Evaluation and Planning (KISTEP), MPB was still weak in coordination because KISTEP was closely affiliated with MoST and lacked a neutral and moral authority. In 1999, the National Science and Technology Council (NSTC) was established in the Presidential Office to coordinate interministerial competition and conflicts over national R&D projects, but NSTC also was ineffective in coordination because the Minister of MoST co-chaired NSTC (Wong 2011: 54–55).

However, around the mid-2000s, the Korean government was able to develop a more horizontal rather than top-down coordination system. By learning through the repeated conflicts, Korean economic bureaucrats developed a new horizontal method of implicit coordination and accommodation over time, through which industry-related ministries developed a more discernible division of labor. For example, MoST focused more on upstream science and technology, while MoI intentionally focused on downstream applied technologies that could be assimilated quickly by private firms. Around 2010, MoI focused on collaboration with SMEs in new technology sectors.

Horizontal accommodation happened first through repeated conflicts, as Korean ministries came to recognize that such conflicts could destroy both common goods and their organizational interests. To justify their rationale, economic ministries could not carry out such destructive attempts because to do so would undermine their own legitimate influence. Through repeated competition, they learned that their own policies would need other ministries' collaboration. A former Minister of Industry says in a personal interview:

Yes, we need other ministries' collaboration. If our MoI tried to implement our industrial policy, we would have to borrow our policy instrument [like financial incentives] from the MoF. Our MoI played a role of promotor but we did not have many policy instruments.... In the past, 1960s to 1970s, for example, in the Comprehensive Export Promotion Conference, President Park directly commanded it to other ministers if the MoI requested a policy.... However, now MoI and MoF mutually negotiate.[6]

In the early 2000s, through repeated conflicts, industry-related ministries realized that duplication and overlapping of national projects were beneficial neither to their own ministerial interests nor to the larger goal of national development (Wong 2011: 59). Through repeated competition, Korean economic bureaucrats not only shared their common interests, but also came to recognize that extreme selfish and unexpected attempts were not beneficial to their own interests.

In addition, through organizational changes, now MoST has more neutral and moral authority to coordinate the allocation of R&D resources by establishing an organization independent of real R&D projects. In the early 2000s, MoST reorganized into two distinct sections, each headed by a vice minister. One section continues to plan and execute the ministry's R&D programs, while the other is responsible for R&D planning for all government ministries. The vice

---

[6] Personal interview with former Minister of Industry on June 11, 2018.

minister in charge of this second section heads up the Office of Science Technology Innovation (OSTI) established in 2004. Unlike its predecessors such as NSTC, OSTI enjoys considerable autonomy from, and authority over, other government agencies.

OSTI gained such authority because it has the right to review all annual ministerial R&D budget proposals and the formal power to unilaterally change resources from one ministry to another. More importantly, ministerial stakeholders perceive OSTI as a legitimate and impartial R&D budgeting institution. OSTI overcame the legitimacy problem which its predecessors MPB and NSTC faced. Unlike MPB, OSTI staff included capable and expert consultants who understand science and technological innovation. Furthermore, OSTI is perceived to work independently of MoST, based on changes in MoST's own identity. MoST put a distance between the two sections to ensure the impartiality of OSTI in coordinating all R&D projects across ministries.[7] In order to do this, it turned the focal point of its own R&D activity to upstream basic science, rather than to mid- and down-stream R&D which was its focus in the 1980s and 1990s. In addition, MoST reduced its own share of R&D resources in the first decade of the 2000s to benefit other ministries, including MoI and MIC, which reinforced the perception of OSTI's impartiality in coordinating R&D plans across ministries. Although the OSTI did not create the complementary division of R&D labor, it could play an important role in sustaining such arrangements (Ehm, S.H. 2004; Kim, S.K. 2008: 204; Wong 2011: 59–60).

Now, in Korea, the governing mechanism to adjudicate and coordinate competition among economic ministries has changed from a traditional top-down, hierarchical system to a more horizontal, mutual adjustment system. Many problems resulting from interministerial competition, such as overlapping public R&D investments, have been relatively reduced. However, this does not mean the end of competition among industry-related ministries within the state. On the contrary, ministries even in the current Korean government, including MoI, the Ministry of Future Planning, and the Ministry of SMEs and Startups (MSS), seriously compete for national developmental agenda by suggesting new policies. For example, at the start of the Moon Jae-in administration (2017–present), MoI is struggling to find a new role and developmental policy as the newly established Ministry of SMEs takes over MoI's existing functions to promote the SMEs.[8] As

[7] This change in the MoST organizational identity is based on the President Roh Moo-hyun's argument that players and the umpire should be mutually independent (Ehm, S.H. 2004).

[8] Ministry of SMEs and Startups (MSS) was created as a separate entity from the MoI (currently named as the Ministry of Commerce and Industry)'s SME section in 2017 under the current Moon Jae-in administration. MSS's purpose is to promote business growth, foster startups, and support micro-enterprises through policies and investments. MSS plays a significant role in creating a viable ecosystem that helps startups flourish and succeed. Recently MSS and MoI have competed for initiatives of promoting SME parts and materials suppliers as Japanese government began to prohibit the free export of important parts and materials to Korea in 2019 (Jeon, Jinju 2020).

one MoI high-ranking director describes, "MoI now needs serious brainstorming because it is in a really hard time."[9] However, in July 2019 when Japan launched control over export of core materials for semi-conductors and OLEDs, the Korean government's MoI began to lead the initiative in developmental policy to promote materials, parts, and equipment industries. MoI could respond to Japan's export control immediately with new developmental programs because, in competition with other ministries, MoI had prepared to develop new programs to develop materials and parts one year before Japan's export control aroused a national sentiment in Korea (Koonmin Ilbo, August 19, 2019).[10] In the competition for initiatives in the new developmental agenda, Korean economic bureaucrats continue their state-led developmentalism by renewing their developmental policies and searching for a new rationale, as well as their identity and roles.

[9] Personal interview with former director of MoI on June 19, 2018; personal interview with another former director of MoI on May 29, 2018.

[10] Although political parties in Korea seriously fight each other politically and ideologically, they share a common economic nationalism and the vision of national developmentalism. For example, political parties, whether they are conservative or progressive, commonly criticize the Minister of Science and ICT (MSIT) for being late to respond to Japan's export control and not devising appropriate developmental programs to promote national material industries (Money Today, July 15, 2019; Asia Economy, July 15, 2019).

9

Generalization through Comparison

Considering the Korean experience presented here, the evolution of Korean capitalism reveals tensions with current theoretical approaches, both neoliberalism and institutionalist state developmentalism. Contrary to the neoliberal argument, the state has played an active role in nurturing national industries and reconstituting the national economy in globalization. Yet, contrary to the current developmental state (DS) theorist arguments, some institutional elements of a cohesive and strong Weberian state do not sufficiently account for the Korean economic success over the past 50 years. Korean developmentalism has been sustainable and successful, not because of any DS institutional elements, but because key economic agencies have been capable of long-term change, adaptation, and readjustments, as new challenges emerge in the changing contexts of domestic and international political economy. Even in the course of globalization, the Korean state has adjusted its mode of intervention rather than retreat or simply resist to change, as the problems posed by the global economy have changed. We claim that such adaptability of Korean state-led capitalism can be explained by elite competition within and outside the state regarding policies and how best to boost the national economy.

We also emphasize the politics among elites in order to better account for the endogenous evolution of state-led developmentalism, rather than the institutionalist path dependence or the punctuated equilibrium thesis which accounts for changes only by external shocks. To account for the continuity of state-led developmentalism in Korea, we propose a theoretical alternative, *continuity by changes*. The Korean model is still state-led developmentalism, but its continuity is not due to persistence of the traditional DS, nor the remnants of historical legacy. Continuity is possible only by changes. Unlike the current theoretical approaches, whether neoliberal or institutionalist DS theorist, continuity and changes are not mutually exclusive. In fact, continuity occurs only through changes. If Korea had not changed its traditional developmental institutions and kept using traditional methods such as authoritarian regulation of market entry and price, it would have failed in its state-led developmentalism. This continuity of state-led developmentalism is possible only by changing strategy from input-oriented expansionism toward a knowledge-intensive, innovation-oriented growth model in a changed context.

More importantly, this book emphasizes that these endogenous changes can be better explained through competition among elites. The continuity of Korean

Changes by Competition: The Evolution of the South Korean Developmental State. Hyeong-ki Kwon,
Oxford University Press (2021). © Hyeong-ki Kwon. DOI: 10.1093/oso/9780198866060.003.0009

state-led developmentalism occurred by competition within as well as outside the state. Unlike prevalent accounts of DS theory and state theories in comparative politics, the state is neither unitary nor cohesive, but a locus of competition. Even in the Park Chung Hee era, the heyday of the Korean traditional DS, interministerial competition and conflicts continued. Such contest among economic elites over the visions of economic development is not evidence of the DS demise, but a driving force to the endogenous evolution of the developmental state through flexible adjustments. For example, Korean EPB had initiated liberalization in the late 1970s before globalization shocks began.

Theoretical implications of this book—organizational adaptability and institutional changes through elite competition in the Korean case—extend to analysis of other developing countries. This final chapter examines the generalizability of our findings by considering other East Asian DS countries, including Japan, Taiwan, and China.

Flexible Adaptability Matters for Sustainable Development

To account for economic success in Korea and other East Asian countries, neoclassical economists suggest the free market features of the East Asian economies, including the outward-looking market-oriented policy, limited state intervention, and private entrepreneurship. By contrast, DS theorists point to the state's *dirigisme* based on its Weberian institutional elements, such as meritocracy and the cohesiveness and rationality of bureaucracy. From the Korean experience, we claim that institutional adaptability is vital for sustainable development, as new challenges continuously emerge in the ever-changing contexts of domestic and international political economy.

Unlike the neoliberal arguments, East Asian countries' economic success is due to the state's active role in industrialization. In the Park Chung Hee era, Korean economic development was not a free market system. Unlike the neoliberal and neutral state, the Korean state was strategically involved in its economic development. Although neoliberals emphasize the discontinuity of the liberal 1960s and the DS of the 1970s in Korea, even in the 1960s the Korean state mobilized massive capital and strategically allocated it in order to systematically build national industries. Korea of the 1970s was an extreme case of the DS as a total mobilization system.

With globalization operating in earnest, Korea also has changed significantly since the Asian financial crisis of 1997, abandoning traditional developmental state institutions, including liberalization of financial markets and deregulation of market entry. Yet arguments presented here show that the state has still played an active role in reconstituting a national economy in globalization, rather than retreating and converging to a neoliberal free market system. As national corporations globalize in pursuit of their individual interests, some national economies are more likely to lose their industrial commons, as in the United States. By contrast, as seen in Chapter 2, the Korean state is actively involved in nurturing the industrial commons to improve its national industrial capabilities in the course of corporations' globalization. The Korean case reveals that even in globalization, state-led coordination can be still effective for the national economy.

Many advanced countries, such as Taiwan, Japan, and Ireland, reveal the effectiveness of the state's active role in rebuilding the national economy under globalization. Countering the arguments of neoliberal globalism, the state's active role may be strategic in rebuilding the industrial commons and improving national industrial capabilities, as national corporations move freely across national borders. Korea, Taiwan, and Nordic countries have successfully upgraded their national industrial capabilities by building home-based advantages, such as inter-firm networks, production systems, and industrial clusters. In globalization, concerted policy action is more effective than a free market in building industrial commons and systemic capabilities. However, the state's active role even in globalization does not ensure the relevancy of traditional DS measures, including protection of emerging industry, control over finance and market entry, nor persistent relevance of the traditional DS *dirigisme*. On the contrary, the state's active role in globalization is relevant because of the state's adaptability to new challenges, such as more industrial complexity and changes in global competition.

The Korean economy could sustain its high economic growth even after the 1997 Asian financial crisis precisely because Korea changed toward a new version of state-led developmentalism. A senior official of the R&D Strategy Planning Bureau of the Ministry of Industry (MoI) in Korea observed in a personal interview that the Korean state could not carry out its developmentalism to improve the competitiveness of national industries in globalization if it did not change its traditional methods of developmentalism, including the regulation of market entry and exclusive funneling to a few large corporation to realize the scale of economy. Taiwan, Ireland, and Israel improve their industrial capabilities by the state's new roles in mediating and connecting activities between domestic and global organizations, as national corporations move across national borders, utilizing global production networks.[1]

More importantly, we emphasize that such flexible and effective adaptability for sustainable development is possible through conflicts and competition among elites, rather than a unitary and cohesive state with a single rationality, as the DS literature argues. Korea could overcome new challenges and sustain its successful

---

[1] For the state's active roles in globalization and success stories of advanced economies including Taiwan, Ireland, Israel, and Nordic countries, see Amsden and Chu (2003); Berger and Lester, eds. (2005); Breznitz (2007); Kwon (2014); Ó Riain (2004); and Ornston (2012).

industrialization even in the economic crises of the late 1970s and late 1990s, not through repetition of the same institutional practices, nor because of sticky institutions' resistance to change, but by creating innovative policies through elite competition. For example, in Korea of the late 1970s, the Economic Planning Board (EPB) proposed a persuasive alternative to the crisis in competition with the Ministry of Commerce and Industry's (MCI) existing input-oriented developmentalism, and in contest with chaebols' proposal of a free market. Even after the 1997 financial crisis, Korean economic ministries including the Ministry of Industry, the Ministry of Information and Communications (MIC), and Ministry of Science and Technology (MoST) competitively proposed new developmental strategies to make their policy a national agenda and to gain influence, which resulted in pragmatic and flexible adaptation to the new challenges emerging from a changed context of national and international political economy. Challenges and risks for economic development are not apparent even to the most astute elites, but they are serious, uncertain, and need interpretation. Economic elites both inside and outside the state contest how to understand the challenges and how to solve the problems. Korea could sustain its long-term economic success because key actors have been capable of change, adaptation, and adjustments over the long term through competition, rather than relying on a single standardized formula for economic development.

Empirical Cases of Elite Competition and Deliberative Development

Most DS theorists emphasize the cohesiveness and coherence inside the state as a key condition for the developmental state, in contrast to the failure of state-led developmentalism in Latin American countries and India. DS theorists regard the conflicts inside the state as evidence of demise of the DS. However, unlike prevalent accounts of the DS theory and state theories in comparative politics, the state is neither unitary nor cohesive, but a locus of competition, as seen in the Korean authoritarian DS of Park Chung Hee era and in other East Asian DS countries, including Japan, Taiwan, and China. The following sections examine the generalizability of our theoretical implications to other countries.

Ubiquity of Elite Competition

Unlike the DS thesis of a unitary and cohesive state for state-led developmentalism, elite conflicts are ubiquitous even in successful DS countries, including Japan, Korea, Taiwan, and China. This section explores this ubiquity of elite competition in East Asian countries before examining the effectiveness of elite competition for economic development.

Japan is regarded as an archetype of the East Asian developmental state. Chalmers Johnson's (1982) *MITI and the Japanese Miracle* initiated DS studies by examining the MITI and Economic Planning Agency (EPA)'s active role in Japanese economic development from the 1920s. Since then most DS literature assumes that Japan is a system of cohesive bureaucratic rule (Johnson 1982: 20–21). According to Johnson (1982), the Japanese state as a developmental and plan-rational state uses strategic industrial policy for economic development, unlike the United States which is a regulatory and market-rational state and does not use industrial policy. DS studies including Johnson (1982) and Pempel (1974) claim that for the plan-rational state to succeed in its developmental policies, power within the state is exercised by a unitary and cohesive bureaucracy. DS literature on Japan holds that decision-making in Japan is centralized and dominated by a cohesive state power of the bureaucracy, the Liberal Democratic Party (LDP), and big business, with the bureaucracy generally seen as taking the lead.

However, the DS thesis of bureaucratic dominance, derived mainly from Chalmers Johnson's 1982 study, has been challenged by accumulating evidence of empirical studies on Japanese economic processes. Many 1980s neo-pluralist studies reveal that Japan is not ruled by bureaucracy unilaterally, but Japan has "patterned pluralism" or "compartmentalized competition" where economic policies are constituted through negotiation and consensus among various actors, including LDP, interest groups, and bureaucrats (Inoguchi and Iwai 1987: 277–278; Muramatsu and Krauss 1987: 60; Pempel 1987: 278–279, 281, 293–294; Campbell and Schneider 2008: 93).

Further, unlike the DS thesis of cohesive bureaucracy, Japanese bureaucracy is not a monolith, but has many competing sources among the different ministries in the policy process.[2] Even in the heyday of Japanese DS, Japanese policy-making was quite fragmented. For example, as Campbell's (1976) study on budgetary politics reveals, the Japanese decision-making system of the 1960s was fragmented into conflicts among sub-government units consisting of agencies, specialized LDP politicians, and interest groups, with much internal bureaucratic division. In Japan of the 1960s, conflict was not between bureaucrats and politicians, but among different alliances of politicians and bureaucrats. The ministerial conflicts in the Japanese bureaucracy were frequently paralleled by cross-divisional battle inside the LDP because the bureaucrats and politicians frequently cooperated in

---

[2] For studies on the fragmented structure of Japanese state policy-making, see Fukui (1987); Muramatsu and Krauss (1984; 1987); Muramatsu (1987, 1993); Pempel (1987); Inoguchi and Iwai (1987); Yamaguchi (1989); and Wright (1999). In particular, for the conflicts among government ministries in the 1960s, see Campbell (1976, 1984); McKean (1977); and Muramatsu (1993).

their strategies (McKean 1977: 201–238; Campbell 1984: 302). Campbell and Schneider (2008) succinctly describe inter-minister conflicts in Japan of the 1960s:

> In the 1960s, fewer policy initiatives came from the top.... Most policy change was initiated at lower levels; taking place within subarenas (Type 1), squabbles across subarena boundaries (Types 2), and subgovernments appealing to heavy-weight actors for approval of some large policy change (Type 3).... Admittedly, bitter fights broke out in non-financial areas, such as the running battle between the Ministry of International Trade and Industry (MITI) and the Welfare Ministry over environment policy (Type 2). However, in the more common pattern, duplications of programs in two or more ministries were permitted, and the Finance Ministry approved many enormous subarena budget requests.
>
> (Campbell and Scheiner 2008: 98–99)

Considering accumulated studies of inter-minister conflicts, Campbell and Scheiner (2008: 91) conclude that "Contrary to the conventional view of strong central bureaucratic power, we argue that in the 1960s policy making was quite fragmented." Contrary to the DS thesis of cohesive state, even in the so-called 1955 System of LDP single party dominance (1955–93), Japanese DS was a quite fragmented policy-making process. As many empirical studies show, ministries in the Japanese state fought each other in order to defend their organizational jurisdiction (*nawabari arasoi*) to maintain policy-making authority and to secure for themselves their post-retirement jobs (*amakudari*).

Japan's intrabureaucratic conflicts can historically trace back to the battles over security and technology fought between the local *han* and the decaying shogunate. During the Meiji period, conflicts among government agencies continued over different visions of development, between those who favored small-scale manufacturing and those who favored heavy industrial development. Similarly, in the devastating militarist interlude, the Imperial Navy and Army fought each other, and in the 1950s, MITI fought with the Finance Ministry over leadership of postwar reconstruction (Samuels 1994: 333).

Through this contesting process, the Japanese state changed its policy priority and developmental strategy. For example, conflicts between MITI and Ministry of Finance (MoF) over postwar reconstruction were important for Japan's post-war trajectory of development, as Prime Minister Yoshida shifted from siding with MITI's policy to rebuild the arsenals in 1952 to MoF's policy to build the aircraft industry in 1953 (Samuels 1994: 333). In the 1980s, through inter-ministerial conflicts, Japan moved its policy priority from traditional high-growth national goals to a new policy priority including social welfare and environmental objectives and development of new technology (Muramatsu 1993: 50–71). Unlike the DS thesis of bureaucratic rationality and state cohesiveness, Japan's successful development strategies were formed neither from a coherent strategy nor from a competent bureaucratic smartness, but through contests of visions among state elites.

Politics inside the developmental state prevailed not only in Japan and Korea but also in Taiwan. Many DS scholars emphasize Taiwan's cohesive and strong state.[3] They hold that the Taiwanese state is a coherent organization, effective, and efficient, and unaffected by interministerial disputes, and that the state is strong enough to authoritatively enforce its will into the society (Wade 1990: 27; Kuo 1995: 26–28, 67–74). However, contrary to the DS argument, the Taiwanese state was fragmented.[4] For example, as Arnold (1989) and Wu (2004) reveal, Taiwanese policy-making on the promotion of the automobile industry was not monolithic but fragmented and conflict-laden between the Ministry of Economic Affairs (MOEA) and the Council for Economic Planning and Development (CEPD). The cleavages between MOEA and CEPD concerning the auto industry represent two main groups in the Taiwanese state—"technocrats" whose power is based on managerial and technological expertise rather than on political affiliation, and "administrative bureaucrats" whose power is essentially political (Arnold 1989: 197). Technocrats in the CEPD supported the accelerated liberalization of the auto industry which enabled Taiwan to source the joint venture partnership for technology, whereas MOEA advocated the existing import-substitution industrialization (ISI) policy and protection of domestic auto and parts suppliers.

Similarly with Japanese policy-making conflicts, the inter-ministerial politics in the Taiwanese bureaucracy was related to factions within the Kuomintang (KMT). The KMT rule system was not a coherent but faction-based authoritarian political system. Under the paramount leaders of Chiang Kai-shek and then his son Chiang Ching-kuo, several factions arose such as the CC Clique, the Political Study Clique, the Youth Corps Clique, and the Military Intelligence Clique. Although many factions in the KMT of mainland time became enfeebled after 1949 when it moved to Taiwan, the ruthless power struggle within the KMT did not stop. That power struggle, until the 1970s, was dominated by rivalry between Chiang Ching-kuo and Chen Cheng (Winckler 1988: 150; Wu 2004: 100–101). The KMT factions determined Taiwan's bureaucratic politics. Policy-making in Taiwan was divided into two main factions, the presidential residence faction and the non-presidential residence faction. The presidential residence faction, based on their close relationship with the Chiang family, mainly include the financial and monetary officials who were used to check the industrial technocrats.

The bureaucrats allied themselves with the factions of the KMT. A typical example of bureaucratic conflicts in Taiwan was the reform of the foreign exchange system (Wu 2004: 97, 100). Bureaucrats competed to sell their proposals to top political leaders, such as Chen Cheng and Chiang Ching-kuo. Before the

---

[3] For DS literature on the Taiwanese state, see Johnson (1985); Haggard and Cheng (1987); Ho (1987); and Wade (1985, 1990).

[4] For the fragmented structure in Taiwanese state, see Noble (1987); Arnold (1989); and Wu (2004).

mid-1960s, conflicts within Taiwanese bureaucracy were mainly between the normal ministries, including the Ministry of Economic Affairs (MoEA) and the Ministry of Finance (MoF), and the US aid-financed economic planning agencies, including the Industrial Development Council (IDC, 1953–8), Economic Development Board (EDB, 1953–8), Council for US Aid (CUSA, 1959–63), and Council for International Economic Cooperation and Development (CIECD, 1963–73). Early on, the US aid-financed planning agencies initiated almost all plans for industrial development, while the routine ministries followed or opposed these plans. Thereafter, as seen in the auto development policy, conflicts in the Taiwanese bureaucracy became rife between routine ministries including MOEA and CEPD (Arnold 1989; Wu 2004).

Unlike the DS thesis of cohesive state, China is also a case of a fragmented but developmental state. As many scholars of Chinese politics call it, Chinese economic decision-making in the post-Mao era is "fragmented authoritarianism," where Chinese decision-making is contested among functionally differentiated clusters, and far less coherent than that of Japan.[5] In the post-Mao era, bureaucrats gained significant decision-making power on economic issues through decentralization. In addition, due to the post-Mao reform's decentralization of budgetary authority, many local and bureaucratic units could acquire considerable budgetary power outside of funds allocated through the central budget. With these independent funds they could pursue their own policy preferences (Lieberthal 1992: 8, 20). According to Breznitz and Murphree (2011), the Chinese bureaucracy is vast, complex, and permeated by competing lines of authority. The same policy agenda could fall under the jurisdiction of multiple ministries.

Many scholars of Chinese politics point out this decentralized experimentation in order to account for how the single party state could make institutional and policy innovations for economic reform to flexibly adapt to rapidly changing environments (Heilmann 2008a: 1). Montinola, Qian and Weingast (1995) and Cao, Qian and Weigngast (1999) hold that due to China's extensive administrative decentralization, local officials could launch economic policy innovation on their own. However, such Chinese experimentation is possible not simply because of a decentralized structure but due to factional competition at the national level. As Cai and Treisman (2006) rightly point out, the driving force behind the policy and institutional reform was not pressures from local officials' initiatives, but competition of rival factions at the center which have different ideologies and local connections. Faction leaders in the Chinese Communist party sought supremacy by demonstrating the effectiveness of their own policies across the chessboard of China's territorial administration. Local officials were linked to the factions within the party's center and sometimes appealed to faction leaders with

---

[5] For the studies which regard Chinese polity as fragmented authoritarianism, see Lieberthal and Oksenberg (1986, 1988); Lampton, ed. (1987); Lampton (1987); and Lieberthal (1992).

their suggestions. Faction leaders at the center were often deeply involved in local experiments and helped to speed the expansion of useful discoveries, reducing redundancy, and overcoming resistance to reform (Cai and Treisman 2006: 507, 516).

Thus, Heilmann (2008a) calls the Chinese experimental methods "experimentation under hierarchy" (2008a: 29). Subnational officials in China are subject to detailed performance reviews by their superiors and central authorities. Subnational officials are rewarded or penalized based on their success in achieving specific targets. Promotions, demotions, and job-related benefits all depend on such reviews (Cai and Treisman 2006: 525). Conflicts and competition in Chinese policy making have been between not the center and locals, but between elite factions in the center, although central factions have relied on vertical networks at all subnational levels.

Chinese politics for institutional and policy change was mainly driven by this factional competition. The reason that Chinese economic reform occurred in the 1980s is that Deng Xiaoping's reform faction gained power in party politics based on successful local experiments of non-socialist special economic zones (Heilmann 2008a: 25–26). In the post-Mao era, the general reform camp was divided again into Deng Xiaoping's pro-growth group and Chen Yun's pro-stability group (Dittmer and Wu 1995: 468). Even after the goal of marketization had been accepted by almost all factions since 1992, factional competition in the Chinese state did not stop, and continuously influenced Chinese politics, as illustrated by the greater emphasis on developing inland provinces since the Hu Jintao faction overtook the Shanghai-centered network of Jiang Zemin (Cai and Treisman 2006: 534).

Elite Competition and Deliberative Development

Competition and conflict among elites within the state does not necessarily produce negative effects on economic development. As seen in the successful cases of East Asian DS countries presented earlier, elite competition can contribute to economic development, rather than result in economic failure. Korea succeeded in rapid economic development over nearly 50 years, not because of the free market nor some elements of stringent Weberian state, but because of institutional adaptability through elite competition. As domestic and international contexts have changed over the last 50 years, Korean elites have faced new problems that they have never met. Through elite competition, the Korean state has adjusted its mode of intervention by pragmatically constituting an innovative policy with an array of perspectives on how to approach the problems.

Taiwan's experience of successful technology upgrades in the 1990s, as Hsieh (2016) shows, confirms that a fragmented and decentralized system, rather than a hierarchical and single-minded state, can innovate upon institutions and strategies through flexible adjustments. In contrast to a hierarchical division of labor between state agencies and private actors in development and commercialization, Taiwan built broad and overlapping ties among a variety of lower-ranked state agencies, public technology-supporting agencies, and various SMEs to advance industrial upgrades and innovation. This decentralized system facilitated cross-industry fertilization as a means of innovation and ensured export-diversification growth, particularly in Taiwan's machinery sector, including bicycles, auto parts, machine tools, and fasteners (Hsieh 2016).

China's successful experience of economic development also shows the benefits of decentralized elite competition which enables local experimentation and flexible adjustments.[6] Due to the decentralized and competitive structure of the Chinese state, Deng Xiaoping could defy the conservative political forces at the center and push his reform program through successful experiments in township and village enterprises (Konai 1986; Walder 1996; Chu 2016: 22). When Chinese national policymakers wanted to change existing policy and institutions, they tended to use experimental programs in order to overcome the opposition of rival policymakers who tried to defend the old rules of the game (Heilmann 2008a, 2008b). Chinese policy experiments, the so-called "Chinese point-to-surface" approach, are normally driven by local initiatives, with the formal or informal backing of higher-level policymakers. Through competition in the decentralized structure, various units in the Chinese state are encouraged to marshal new ideas and conduct innovative experiments through bureaucratic entrepreneurship. Bureaucratic units tend to vigorously promote their projects and their own interests in the policy-making process (Lieberthal 1992: 9). In contrast to the failure of many Latin American countries which pursued a rulebook and standard solution of *Washington Consensus*, China could achieve economic success because of its pragmatic combination of heterodox elements, such as partial liberalization, two-track pricing, and limited deregulation, through local experimentation and flexible adaptation (Heilmann 2008b: 374–375). As Mukand and Rodrik (2005) hold, the Chinese economic success may lie in its usual adaptive capabilities to overcome complex challenges by creating innovative policies and institutions.

In contrast to the traditional DS thesis about a single-minded and cohesive state for developmentalism, we hold that the institutional adaptability resulting from elite competition really matters for sustainable development. Most DS

---

[6] For the argument that China has achieved economic success because of decentralized experimentation that enabled institutional and policy innovation, see Rawski (1995); Chung (2000); Roland (2000); Lin, Cai, and Li (2003); and Mukand and Rodrik (2005).

literature assumes a single and apparent rationality for economic development, such as realization of scale economy, and emphasizes the cohesive and strong state to effectively impose its single rationality on private businesses. However, even the smartest bureaucrat who stringently follows the rules cannot figure out all the new challenges emerging from the changing contexts of domestic and international political economy. As Evans (2004) calls it "deliberative development," the complex challenges need deliberative and participatory political institutions which bring a whole array of diverse perspectives, eliciting and aggregating local knowledge and thereby helping to build better policies and institutions. Elite competition, rather than a single-minded and cohesive state, enables such collective problem-solving and strategizing.

By contrast to the benefits of elite competition, the cohesive and centralized state, which DS literature emphasizes for economic development, may produce economic failure due to its institutional rigidity. For example, in contrast to Chinese economic success based on local experimentation, the Soviet Union and Eastern European communist states failed to sustain economic development despite high rates of investment because of the absence of decentralized experimentation and lack of incentives for efficiency (Hason 2007: 1623). In contrast to Chinese decentralized experimentation, the Soviet Union's national policymakers did not adopt local experimentation, while emphasizing the national standard and disregarding local practices as a necessary evil to plug the gaps in the economy (Gregory 2004; Heilmann 2008a: 2, 17–18).

In addition, Pakistan's neo-fascist military state's failure in economic development also confirms that contrary to the argument of DS scholars like Kohli (2005), too much state cohesiveness constrains economic development over time as much as a predatory state using national resources for private purposes. Against the background of security vulnerability, Pakistan established "a strong, centralized, bureaucratic authoritarian state apparatus" (Naseemullah 2017a: 22–23). The Pakistani state carried out state-led industrialization by privatizing the state-owned industrial enterprises. Like Korean chaebols, a Pakistani industrial oligarchy based in the Karachi area was enabled, supported, and regulated by the state that was both autonomous and embedded in the nation's bourgeoisie (Naseemullah 2017a: 215–216). With an overdeveloped and cohesive state, Pakistan constructed a statist development that was initially more successful than that of India. However, unlike Korea and Taiwan, Pakistan failed in upgrading its industries to higher value-added production (Naseemullah and Arnold 2015). One reason why Pakistani DS failed is not because of the absence of a centralized and cohesive state, but because the Pakistani state was too over-centralized and too strong in decision-making to flexibly respond to new demands and challenges emerging in society (Hasan 2007: 1626). Due to the centralized rule by the military group, the Pakistani state failed to flexibly search for and cultivate new developmental strategies; instead of economic development, the Pakistani state focused on relentless growth in defense and related spending between 1965 and 1990 (Hasan 2007: 1625; Naseemullah 2017a: 222–223).

Contrary to the statist emphasis on cohesiveness of the stringent Weberian state, too much cohesiveness constrains flexible adaptability and deters economic development over time as much as the predatory states, including many sub-Saharan African states. The statist DS literature assumes that the single-minded states steered industrialization in terms of national interests, reining in domestic and international market forces while harnessing them for national ends. The DS literature assumes that the Weberian bureaucracy, due to its formal rationality, has such advantages as precision, stability, stringency of discipline and reliability, as well as a high degree of calculability. The DS statists hold that elite bureaucrats are recruited from the top ranks of the best schools in Japan and Korea. This is believed to guarantee the bureaucratic rationality (Johnson 1982: 314–320; Evans 1995: 30; Woo-Cumings 1999: 14).

However, unlike the bureaucratic rationality of the DS literature, even the smartest and stringent Weberian bureaucrats could not figure out all the complex challenges and problems newly emerging, as domestic and international political economies are changing. The formal rationality of the Weberian bureaucracy has difficulty in dealing efficiently with ongoing changes of tasks generated by changing environments. The strategic rationality differs from the formal rationality. The fulfillment of new tasks requires the modification and reform in their institutions and policies. In order to deal with the changing tasks and complex challenges, the state needs flexibility to search for new adequate problem-solving strategies. The strategic rationality is not apparently given, but continuously reformulated through collective deliberation among competing elites. Through this competition of elites, the state improves the flexible adaptability and creates innovation in policy and institutions.

Conflict Resolution and Coordination

In contrast to the DS thesis on the cohesive state, elite conflicts and competition can significantly contribute to sustainable economic development through institutional adaptability and policy innovation, which can effectively address the complex challenges continuously emerging from domestic and international environments. However, elite competition and conflicts do not always produce positive outcomes. As many empirical studies show, failure to coordinate the competition can result in a stalemate or paralysis in policy formation and implementation. In particular, economic success in the interventionist state mainly relies on successful coordination and conflict resolution in competition among diverse factions. Failure in industrial policy mainly results from failure in coordination. Successful coordination, which can solve the coordination problem within the state, may also enable resolution of conflicts between the state and market actors.

Not all elite competition can produce successful adaptations and innovation in policy and institution. In Chibber's (2002, 2003, 2014) account of India's failure in economic development, elite competition can result in disarray and stalemate in policy formulation and implementation. The Indian state tried to establish a pilot agency like Korea's EPB in order to resolve inter-ministerial conflicts and to develop a consistent policy implementation. However, due to the existing ministers' resistance, India failed to build a mechanism to secure the smooth flow of information and a consistent policy implementation. With opposition of the existing economic ministries, such as the Industry Ministry or the Finance Ministry, India failed to build a pilot agency with institutional power to monitor and coordinate various development agencies. India's Planning Commission (PC) did not have such an institutional power to monitor economic ministries as the Korea's EPB, but remained an advisory agency lacking power over other state agencies. The PC's requests for information were routinely ignored by the normal ministries.

Even Taiwan as a typical East Asian DS state can fail in development policy if it cannot solve the coordination problem. Taiwan failed in promoting the automobile industry due to a failure of coordination within the state—failure to coordinate and resolve conflicts between the Council for Economic Planning and Development (CEPD) and the Ministry of Economic Affairs (MOEA), Taiwan's foremost industrial policymaking institutions (Arnold 1989: 202; Y.-H. Chu 1994; Wu 2004: 103–104). Technocrats in the CEPD advocated the accelerated liberalization of the auto industry which enabled Taiwan to source the joint-venture partnership for technology. By contrast, MOEA supported the existing import-substitution industrialization (ISI) and protection of domestic auto and parts suppliers. The CEPD and MOEA competed over auto industry, advocating contradictory policies and frequently clashing over policy issues to the detriment of policy outcomes. Taiwan's auto industry policy lacked a coordinated strategic rationality and moved in vicissitudes through the process of negotiations with foreign automakers (Arnold 1989: 203–204).

Taiwan's failure to develop wireless communications industry also reveals the importance of coordination. Despite the state's interest, Taiwan failed to promote the industry, which lagged behind in its development in the second half of the 1990s, whereas it succeeded in developing a semiconductor industry (Tso 2004: 301; 303). Successful development of hi-tech industries depends on building a state-technologist nexus where overseas experts participate in policy and technical decision-making. In the case of the semiconductor industry, Taiwan could build an integrated nexus governing system, but the governance system for wireless communications remained fragmented due to a failure to coordinate.

In the semiconductor industry, overseas members of the Science and Technology Advisors' Group (STAG) could play a mediating role in facing Ministry of Finance opposition to the VLSI project by supporting the VLSI project and securing the backing of political leadership. By contrast, projects in the wireless communications industry lacked such technologist groups to effectively mediate between the political elite and state bureaucrats. In the wireless communications program, Taiwan failed to build a clear division of labor among its participants. Two key actors, the Wireless Communications Technical Advisor Committee (WCTAC) and the 3C Strategy Review Board (SRB), regarded each other as potential rivals with more or less equal power while their jurisdiction overlapped in many points. WCTAC members were invited to attend the SRB only sporadically. Overseas technical experts were involved in developing wireless communications technology, mostly outside the ITRI and the MOEA's DoIT (Tso 2004: 311–315). Unlike the close collaboration in the semiconductor project, the CCL-sponsored R&D spin-offs projects in wireless communications lacked the central lab to coordinate the R&D alliances (Tso 2004: 318). In contrast to some institutional elements for successful development which the DS literature emphasizes, the Taiwanese case shows that even the same DS institutions can fail in coordination.

A strategic rationality of DS, which is geared toward national economic development, is not apparently given, but is formulated and rearranged through collective deliberation among competing elites, as domestic and international political economies continuously change. Thus, for successful developmentalism, the state's capability to monitor and coordinate competing subunits around developmental tasks matters, rather than formal elements of the developmental state. Many diverse methods exist to successfully monitor and coordinate competing elites, such as building a pilot agency with hierarchical power and developing horizontal coordination.

Hierarchical coordination is prevalent in the successful coordination stories. For example, as seen in the hierarchical coordination in the Park Chung Hee era presented earlier, a pilot agency like EPB normally monitored and coordinated the economic agencies with authoritarian institutional power. Ultimately, the authoritarian president, Park himself, listened and resolved the ministerial conflicts after collective presentation and deliberation. Comparing Korea with India, Chibber (2003) suggests "nodal agencies" to hierarchically coordinate the economic agencies within the state, after he admits the inevitability of inter-ministerial conflicts and the insufficiency of formal bureaucratic rationality in searching for new adequate problem-solving strategies.[7]

---

[7] Chibber's conception of nodal agency refers to pilot agencies like the MITI in Japan, Korea's EPB, Taiwan's Council for Economic Planning and Development (CEPD), and Singapore's Economic Development Board (EDB), which DS scholars pay attention to (Johnson 1982; Amsden 1989; Haggard 1990; Wade 1990).

China also developed a hierarchical authority to coordinate decentralized experiments, or as Heilmann calls it, "experimentation under hierarchy" (Heilmann 2008a: 29). Although local actors in the decentralized structure are important in the process of Chinese reforms, the Chinese policy-making process is not a decentralization of authority. The driving force for decentralized experimentation comes not from subnational officials, but from competition between political factions at the national center. Elite factions at the center built vertical networks at all levels and tried to demonstrate the effectiveness of their policies through local experimentation, while encouraging local initiatives and monitoring and filtering diverse experiments for generalization (Cai and Treisman 2006: 533; Heilmann 2008a: 29).

In addition to a hierarchical coordination, a horizontal coordination method is also relevant for resolution of elite conflicts and cooperation, as seen in Korea of the 2000s. Around the mid-2000s, development-related ministries in Korean government, including MoI, MoST, and MIC, developed a horizontal rather than a top-down coordination system by learning through the repeated conflicts. Around the mid-2000s, through repeated conflicts, Korean ministries developed a new horizontal method of implicit coordination and accommodation over time. Through repeated competition, they learned that they would need other ministries' collaboration in order to implement their own industrial projects. Korean industry-related ministries tried to develop a more discernible division of labor among the ministries while recognizing that they share common interests through repeated competition, and their selfish attempts would not serve their own interests.

In addition to vertical coordination, the Chinese state developed a horizontal coordination system. The decentralized and fragmented structure of Chinese policy-making does not mean that Chinese bureaucrats are unable to cooperate. On the contrary, they collaborate through sharing goals and norms. Although Chinese bureaucratic units compete for major projects, they retain "a real sense of mission and purpose." They developed "policy communities" that formed around particular projects and issues and that cut across formal bureaucratic lines (Lieberthal 1992: 9).

Japanese economic elites also developed shared values and norms to justify resolution and criteria, through repeated conflicts. Despite a fragmented structure of policy-making, the norm under Japan's 1955 System was "cooperation between politicians and bureaucrats" (Campbell and Scheiner 2008: 94). Unlike the Japanese DS literature on "Japan Incorporated," in actuality, conflicts among elites did occur in Japan. However, due to the need to live together, a set of norms were developed to resolve conflicts and prevent social disruption. Johnson (1977) also holds that "Jurisdictional disputes appear to be the very life-blood of the Japanese bureaucracy," criticizing the idea that Japanese economic decision-making occurs through little or no conflict. He holds that "norms of consensus" are not culturally given but "have been developed primarily as a way of overcoming the ever-present dangers of absolute deadlock among Japan's highly competitive groups" (Johnson 1977: 231).

Samuels (1994) also points out that "Elite struggles [in Japan] contribute to a firmer, more inclusive set of protocols and rules, a higher set of beliefs" rather than resulting in disarray and stalemate (1994: 334). He observes that "Through confrontation and political struggle, actors construct ever denser networks of obligation and reciprocity—tacit compacts and protocols of reciprocal consent— that undergird Japanese national security" (1994: 334). Samuels (1994) agrees with Sabel (1994) on how reciprocal norms evolved through discursive institutions which enabled collective deliberation about goal setting and redefining of governance. Admitting Sabel's argument that "Norms evolve not out of deception but out of collective goal-setting and joint participation in the reconstruction of the past and agreement on a common history," Samuels argues that "Japanese tradition is perpetually reinvented" through a collective act of self-redefinition (Samuels 1994: 337). Despite the competition and conflicts among Japan's bureaucratic ministries, the bureaucrats and their allies in the ruling triad of LDP, and the central bureaucracy and big business, largely agreed on goals such as economic growth and technological development, and developed reciprocal norms to resolve their conflicts (Noble 2016: 187).

The reason why East Asian developmental states, including Japan, Korea, Taiwan, and China, could sustain economic development over quite a long period is not due to some fixed institutional elements such as centralized, cohesive and strong states. Unlike the statist DS literature, even East Asian states are fragmented by competition among elites. Contrary to the DS literature, elite competition can be beneficial to economic success through collective deliberation and flexible adaptation. But elite competition is not always positive to economic development. The elite competition and conflicts are beneficial only when they are resolved through coordination and developed into collaboration for shared goals like economic development and national competitiveness. The more the state democratizes and decentralizes, the more the coordination is needed to resolve conflicts and to achieve collaboration. For successful coordination, democracies need more legitimate authority or shared norms to govern the conflicts. Cooperation for development emerges, not spontaneously due to culture or institutional structure, but through collective deliberation of learning and monitoring of goals as well as norms for governance.

Finally, unlike the institutionalist DS literature, this book emphasizes *changes by competition* to better account for endogenous changes. Based on the institutionalist "punctuated equilibrium theory," many DS scholars hold that once some DS institutional elements are established in a critical juncture, they persist until the next critical juncture caused by external shocks, such as war and global disruption. However, the construction of developmental state institutions is not sufficient for sustaining developmentalism. As mentioned above, even successful developmental states continuously face new challenges because their successful practices create new tasks, like upgrading new technological capability, different from old tasks like building national champions to realize an economy of scale. Reproduction of the developmental state is not due to persistence of its original institutions, but because of changes in policies and institutions. As seen in this study, Korea has sustained its state-led developmentalism, not due to persistence of the traditional DS, nor the remnants of historical legacy, but by changing its strategies and methods. If Korea had not changed its traditional developmental institutions and kept using traditional methods such as authoritarian regulation of market entry and price, it would have failed in its state-led developmentalism. Continuity is possible by changes.

More importantly, this book emphasizes that such adaptation and innovation are possible by elite competition within as well as outside the state. Such contest among elites over the visions of economic development is not a simple problem-solving process, but a political process of competition for legitimate authority. The government's economic ministries competitively proposed new developmental strategies to make their policy a national agenda and to gain influence. Due to their vested interests in the competition for authority, bureaucratic elites are willing to invest their time and energy in decision-making. That is why state elites in East Asian DS countries including Japan, Korea, and Taiwan could sustain state-led developmentalism, not only through effective innovation in policies and institutions but also because their alternatives are confirmed by successful outcomes. Thus, we conclude that in order to understand continuity and change in an economic system, politics inside as well as outside the state, particularly discursive politics among elites, must be brought back in.

Bibliography

Ahn, Byung-jik (1993) "Introduction" (Korean). *Review of Economic History*, 17.

Ahn, Byung-jik (1995) "Hankooke Isusui Kyungjaebaljunkwa Gundaesa Yungoo" (Korean) [A Study on the Economic Development and Modern History of Korea]. Presentation Paper at the 38th History Conference of Korea, Seoul, 1995.

Ahn, Byung-jik (2001) *Hankook Kyungjae Sungjangsa* (Korean) [The History of Korean Economic Growth]. Seoul: SNU Press.

Ahn, Gilwon (1989) "Kongupbaljunbup Ipuphwa Kwajunge isuse Kwankyeboocheoganui Jungchaek Kyungjaenge daehan Yungoo" (Korean) [Interministerial Competition in the Process of Enacting the Industrial Development Law]. MA Thesis, Seoul National University.

Amsden, Alice H. (1989) *Asia's Next Giant: South Korea and Late Industrialization*. Oxford: Oxford University Press.

Amsden, Alice H. (1992) "Theory of Government Intervention in Late Industrialization." In Louis G. Putterman and Dietrich Rueschemeyer, eds., *State and Market in Development Synergy or Rivalry?* Boulder, CO: Lynne Rienner. pp. 53–88.

Amsden, Alice H. (1994) "The Spectre of Anglo-Saxonization is Haunting South Korea." In Lee-Jay Cho and Yoon Hyung Kim (eds.), *Korea's Political Economy*. Boulder, CO: Westview. pp. 67–88.

Amsden, Alice H. (2001) *The Rise of "the Rest": Challenges to the West from Late-Industrializing Economies*. Oxford: Oxford University Press.

Amsden, Alice H. (2013) "Securing the Home Market: A New Approach to Korean Development." Research Paper 2013-1, United Nations Research Institute for Social Development (UNRISD), April 2013.

Amsden, Alice H. (2014) "Securing the Home Market: A New Approach to Korean Development." In Ilcheong Yi and Thandika Mkandawire (eds.), *Learning from the South Korean Developmental Success: Effective Developmental Cooperation and Synergistic Institutions and Policies*. Geneva: Palgrave Macmillan. pp. 54–88.

Amsden, Alice H., and Wan-wen Chu (2003) *Beyond Late Development: Taiwan's Upgrading Policies*. Cambridge: MIT Press.

Amsden, Alice H., and Yoon-Dae Euh (1993) "South Korea's 1980s Financial Reform: Good-bye Financial Repression (Maybe), Hello New Institutional Restraints," *World Development*, 12, no. 3: 379–390.

Arnold, Walter (1989) "Bureaucratic Politics, State Capacity, and Taiwan's Automobile Industrial Policy," *Modern China* 5, no. 2: 178–214.

Asian Survey (2007) vol. 47, no. 6.

Babb, Sarah (2001) *Managing Mexico: Economists from Nationalism to Neoliberalism*. Princeton, NJ: Princeton University Press.

Bae, Kwanpyo (2012) "Hankook Sanupdanji joongsim Sanupjungchaekui Hyungsung Kwajunge Kwanhan Yungoo" (Korean) [A Study on the Formation of Industrial Policy Centered on the Industrial Cluster]. Paper presented at Seoul Association for Public Administration (SAPA), February 2012.

Baek, Jongkook (1993) "Hankookui Kookga, Siminsahoe, Grigo Jibaekyegupui Byundong" (Korean) [The Transformation of the State, Civil Society, and Dominant Class Alliance in Korea]. In the Institute for Far Eastern Studies (ed.), *Hankook Jungchi-Sahoeui Saehurum* [A New Trend in Korean Politics and Society]. Seoul: Nanam. pp. 133–176.

Baek, Wanki (2003) "Hangjungaroseui Kim Jae-ik" (Korean) [Kim Jae-ik as a Public Administrator]. In Nam Duck Woo et al. (eds.), *80 Nyundae Kyungjaekaehyukkwa Kim Jae-ik Susuk* [Economic Reform of the 1980s and First Presidential Secretariat Kim Jae-ik]. Seoul: Samsung Economic Research Institute. pp. 171–202.

Balassa, Bella (1981) *The Newly Industrializing Countries in the World Economy*. New York: Pergamon Press.

Balassa, Bella, and John Williams (1987) *Adjusting to Success: Balance of Payments Policy in the East Asian NICs*. Washington DC: Institute for International Economics.

Bello, Walden, and Stephanie Rosenfeld (1990) *Dragons in Distress: Asia's Miracle Economies in Crisis*. San Francisco, CA: Institute for Food and Development Policy.

Berger, Suzanne, with the MIT Task Force on Production in the Innovation Economy, (2013) *Making in America: From Innovation to Market*. Cambridge, MA: MIT Press.

Berger, Suzanne, and Richard K. Lester, eds. (2005) *Global Taiwan: Building Competitive Strengths in a New International Economy*. Armonk, NY: M.E. Sharpe.

Bhagwati, Jagdish (2010) "The Manufacturing Fallacy." *Project Syndicate*, August 27, 2010.

Blyth, Mark (2002) *Great Transformations: Economic Ideas and Institutional Change in the Twentieth Century*. Cambridge: Cambridge University Press.

Breznitz, Dan (2007) *Innovation and the State: Political Choice and Strategies for Growth in Israel, Taiwan and Ireland*. New Haven, CT: Yale University Press.

Breznitz, Dan, and Michael Murphree (2011) *Run of the Red Queen*. Ithaca, NY: Yale University Press.

Business Korea (December 18, 2013) "Korean Research Team Develops Core Technology for Digital Exposure Equipment."

Cai, Hongbin, and Daniel Treisman (2006) "Did Government Decentralization Cause China's Economic Miracle?" *World Politics* 58, no. 4: 505–35.

Calderon, Cuauhtemoc, and Isaac Sanchez (2012) "Economic Growth and Industrial Policy in Mexico." *Problemas del Desarrollo*, 43, no. 170: 125–145.

Campbell, John C. (1976) *Contemporary Japanese Budget Politics*. Berkeley, CA: University of California Press.

Campbell, John C. (1984) "Policy Conflict and its Resolution within the Governmental System." In E. Krauss, T. Rholen, and P. Steinhoff (eds.), *Conflict in Japan*. Honolulu, HI: University of Hawaii Press. pp. 294–334.

Campbell, John C., and Ethan Scheiner (2008) "Fragmentation and Power: Reconceptualizing Policy Making under Japan's 1955 System" *Japanese Journal of Political Science*, 9, no. 1: 89–113.

Canas, Jesus, and Robert W. Gilmer (2009) "The Maquiladora's Changing Geography." *Southwest Economy*, Second quarter 2009: pp. 10–14.

Cao, Yuanzhen, Yingyi Qian, and Barry Weingast (1999) "From Federalism, Chinese Style to Privatization, Chinese Style." *Economics of Transition*, 7, no. 1: 103–131.

Chamyeo Jungboo Special Briefing Team of State Affairs (2008) *Noh Moohyunkwa Chamyeo Jungboo Kyungjae 5 Nyun* (Korean) [President Roh Moohyun and 5 Years Economy of the Participatory Government]. Seoul: Hans Media.

Chang, Ha-Joon (1994) *The Political Economy of Industrial Policy*. Basingstoke, UK: Macmillan.

Chang, Ha-Joon, Hong Jae Park, and Chul Gyue Yoo (1998) "Interpreting the Korean Crisis: Financial Liberalization, Industrial Policy and Corporate Governance." *Cambridge Journal of Economics* 22, no. 6: 735–746.

Chang, Ha-Joon, and Jangsup Shin (2004) *Restructuring Korea, Inc.* (Korean). Seoul: Changbi.

Chang, Ha-Joon, and Peter Evans (2005) "The Role of Institutions in Economic Change." In Gary A. Dymski and Salivan De Paula (eds.), *Reimagining Growth*. London: Zed Press. pp. 99–129.

Chang, Ha-Joon, and Sungil Chung (2005) *Hankook Kyungjae Koedo Nanma* [An Analysis on Korean Economy] (Korean). Seoul: Booki.

Chang, Ha-Joon, Sungil Chung, and Jongtae Lee (2012) *Moousul Suntaek Hal Gusinga* [What Should We Choose] (Korean). Seoul: Booki.

Chang, Jiho (2005) "Venture Business Policy under the Kim Dae Jung Government: Restructuring of Old Industrial Policy or Catalytic Role of Government?" (Korean). *Korean Public Administration Review*, 39, no. 3: 21–41.

Chang, Kyung-Sup (2019) *Developmental Liberalism in South Korea*. New York: Palgrave Macmillan.

Chen, Edward (1979) *Hyper-Growth in Asian Economies*. New York: Holmes & Meier.

Cheng, Tun-jen, and Cia-lung Lin (1999) "Taiwan: A Long Decade of Democratic Transition." In J.W. Morley (ed.), *Driven by Growth: Political Change in the Asia-Pacific Region*. Armonk, NY: M.E. Sharpe. pp. 227–252.

Cherry, Judith (2005) "'Big Deal' or Big Disappointment? The Continuing Evolution of the South Korean Developmental State." *The Pacific Review*, 18, no. 3: 327–354.

Chibber, Vivek (2002) "Bureaucratic Rationality and the Developmental State." *American Journal of Sociology*, 107, no. 4: 951–989.

Chibber, Vivek (2003) *Locked in Place: State-Building and Late Industrialization in India*. Princeton, NJ: Princeton University Press.

Chibber, Vivek (2014) "The Developmental State in Retrospect and Prospect: Lessons from India and South Korea." In Michelle Williams (ed.), *The End of the Developmental State?* New York: Routledge. pp. 56–80.

Cho, Gab-Je (2015) *Park Chung Hee* (Korean). Seoul: chogabje.com

Cho, Soung Ryoul (1996) "Economic Reforms and the Changes of State Strategies under President Roh's Regime" (Korean). *Korean Political Science Review*, 30, no. 2: 187–208.

Cho, Soung Ryoul (1997) "International Competitiveness, Structural Reform, and National Strategy: The Characteristics of Reform Policy in Kim Yeong Sam Regime" (Korean). *Korean Journal of International Studies*, 36, no. 2: 153–178.

Cho, Yoon Je (2003) "The Political Economy of Financial Liberalization in South Korea." In Chung H. Lee (ed.), *Financial Liberalization and the Economic Crisis in Asia*. New York: Routledge. pp. 82–103.

Choi, Byung-Sun (1987) "The Structure of the Economic Policy-Making Institutions in Korea and the Strategic Role of the Economic Planning Board (EPB)." *Korean Journal of Policy Studies*, 2: 1–25.

Choi, Byung-Sun (1990) "Hankookui Kyungjaejungchaekkyuljung Koojowa Tuksung: Kyungjaekihwoekwonui Wesangkwa Junryakjuk Yukhalul Jongsimuro" (Korean) [The Structure and Characteristics of Korean Economic Decision-Making: On the Status and Strategic Role of the Economic Planning Board (EBP)." In Ahn Chungsi (ed.), *Hankook Jungchikyungjaeron* [Korean Political Economy]. Seoul: Bupmoonsa. pp. 239–276.

Choi, Byung-Sun (1991a) *Economic Policymaking in Korea: Institutional Analysis of Economic Policy Changes in the 1970s and 1980s*. Seoul: Chomyung Press.

Choi, Daesung (2014) *Kiupe Daehan jungboo R&D Toojajiwonui Jungchaekhyokwa Boonsukyungoo* (Korean) [Research Analysis on the Policy Effects of Government R&D Investment on Firms]. Research Report 2014–030, KISTEP.

Choi, Dong-kyu (2006) "Joonghwahakkongup Gunsul wehan Naeja Chongdongwon" (Korean) [Dong-kyu Choi's Memoir: Total mobilization of Domestic Capital for Construction of Heavy-Chemical Industries]. *Wulgan Chosun.* September 2006.

Choi, Hong-Gyu, and Sung-Tae Kim (2013) "A Study on Task Overlap of ICT Policy Related to Informatization" (Korean). *Journal of Broadcasting and Telecommunications Research,* 4: 159–190.

Choi, Jang Jip (1989) *Labor and the Authoritarian State: Labor Unions in South Korean Manufacturing Industries, 1961–1980.* Seoul: Korea University Press.

Choi, Jongwon (1991) "1980 Nyundae Jooyosanupjungchaek Kyuljungkwa Kyungjaengjungchael" (Korean) [Industrial Policy Making and Market Competition Policy in the 1980s]. *Hankookgaebal Yungoo* [Korean Development Study], 13, no. 2: 97–127.

Choi, Jungpyo (1999) "Jaebolgaehyuk Koohoman Yoran, Sundankyungyung Haechega Kwangun" (Korean) [Only Slogan of Chaebol Reform Airs Loud, Dissolution of Chaebol Convoy System is the Real Key]. *Shin Dong-A.* December. pp. 158–162.

Chu, Yin-wah (2009) "Eclipse or Reconfigured? South Korea's Developmental State and Challenges of the Global Knowledge Economy." *Economy and Society,* 38, no. 2: 278–303.

Chu, Yin-wah (2016) "The Asian Developmental State: Ideas and Debates." In Yin-wah Chu (ed.), *The Asian Developmental State: Reexaminations and New Departures.* New York: Palgrave Macmillan. pp. 1–25.

Chu, Yun-han (1994) "The State and the Development of the Automobile Industry in South Korea and Taiwan." In Joel D. Aberbach, David Dollar, and Kenneth L. Sokoloff (eds.), *The Role of the State in Taiwan's Development.* Armonk, NY: M.E. Sharpe. pp. 125–169.

Chun, Byungkyu (1988) *Chunma Chowone Nolda: Dongbaek Chunbyungkyu Koheejajun* (Korean) [Chun Byung Kyu Memoir]. Seoul: Chun Publication Committee.

Chung, Choong Sik (2010) "The Reorganization Policy of Government for IT Convergence: Redesigning the Function of Government to Promote IT Industry" (Korean). *Korean Society and Public Administration,* 21, no. 3: 135–161.

Chung, Jae Ho (2000) *Central Control and Local Discretion in China: Leadership and Implementation during Post-Mao Decollectivism.* New York: Oxford University Press.

Chung, Jina (2007) "Syngman Rhee Government's Economic Policies in the First Republic of Korea (1948–1960): The State-led Industrialization Policies and the Economic Development Plans." PhD Dissertation, Yonsei University.

Cole, David, and Princeton Lyman (1971) *Korean Development: The Interplay of Politics and Economics.* Cambridge, MA: Harvard University Press.

Cole, David, and Young-woo Nam (1969) "The Pattern and Significance of Economic Planning in Korea." In Irma Adelman (ed.), *Practical Approaches to Economic Planning: Korea's Second Five Year Plan.* Baltimore, MD: Johns Hopkins Press.

Cumings, Bruce (1987) "The Origins and Development of the Northeast Asian Political Economy." In Frederic C. Deyo (ed.), *The Political Economy of the New Asian Industrialization.* Ithaca, NY: Cornell University Press. pp. 1–40.

Cumings, Bruce (1998) "The Korean Crisis and the End of 'Late' Development." *New Left Review,* 30: pp. 43–72.

Cypher, James M., and Paul Delgado Wise (2010) *Mexico's Economic Dilemma: The Developmental Failure of Neoliberalism.* New York: Rowman & Littlefield Publishers.

Dent, Christopher M. (2003) "Taiwan's Foreign Economic Policy: The 'Liberalization Plus' Approach of an Evolving Developmental State." *Modern Asian Studies*, 37, no. 2: 461–483.

Deyo, Frederic C. (1987) "State and Labor: Modes of Political Exclusion in East Asian Development." In Frederic C. Deyo (ed.), *The Political Economy of the New Asian Industrialism*. Ithaca, NY: Cornell University Press.

DiMaggio, Paul J., and Walter W. Powell (1991) "Introduction." In Paul J. DiMaggio and Walter W. Powell (eds.), *The New Institutionalism in Organizational Analysis*. Chicago, IL: University of Chicago Press. pp. 1–40.

Dittmer, Lowell and Yu-Shan Wu (1995) "The Modernization of Factionalism in Chinese Politics." *World Politics* 47, no. 4: pp. 467–494.

Dong-A Ilbo Special Report Team (1999) *Ileoburin Ohnyun Kalkooksooeseo IMFkaji: YS Moonmil Jungboo 1800il Bihwa* (Korean) [Lost Five Years, From Korean Noodle Kalkoolsoo to IMF Crisis: Secret Story of the YS Civil Government for the 1800 Days], vol. 1 and vol. 2. Seoul: Dong-A Ilbosa.

Dornbusch, Rudi (1998) "On the Edge: Japan Could Topple as Reform Slips, Debt Mounts." *Far Eastern Economic Review*, 161, no. 9: 52–53.

Eckert, Carter J., Lee Ki-baik, Young Ick Lew, Michael Robinson, and Edward W. Wagner (1990) *Korea Old and New: A History*. Cambridge, MA: Harvard University Press.

Ehm, Sang-Hyun (2004) "Yunkwak Derunanun Jungboohyuksinwee Jungbojojik Gaepyunan" (Korean) [An Emerging Shape of IT-related Organization in the Government Reform Committee]. *Shin Dong-A*. June 2004.

EIAK (Electronic Industries Association of Korea) (1989) *Junja Kongup Smasipnyeonsa* (Korean) [Thirty Year History of Korean Electronics Industries]. Seoul: EIAK.

Eichengreen, Barry, and Duck-koo Chung (2004) "Introduction." In Duck-koo Chung and Barry Eichengreen (eds.), *The Korean Economy Beyond the Crisis*. New York: Edward Elgar. pp. 1–25.

EPB (Economic Planning Board) (1981) *Kyungje Paekse* (Korean) [White Paper on Economy]. Seoul: EPB.

Ertman, Thomas (1997) *Birth of the Leviathan: Building States and Regimes in Medieval and Early Modern Europe*. Cambridge: Cambridge University Press.

Esping-Andersen, Gosta (1990) *Three Worlds of Welfare Capitalism*. Princeton, NJ: Princeton University Press.

Eun, Min Su (2011) "Kookgaui Baljunjooui Junryakkwa Koonminyunkumui Kumyoongsijang Dongwonkwajung" (Korean) [The State's Developmental Strategy and the Mobilization of National Pension Fund in the Financial Market]. Presentation Paper in the Conference, the Korean Social Welfare Policy Association, June 2011.

Evans, Peter (1995) *Embedded Autonomy: States and Industrial Transformation*. Princeton, NJ: Princeton University Press.

Evans, Peter (2004) "Development as Institutional Change: The Pitfalls of Monocropping and the Potentials of Deliberation." *Studies in Comparative International Development*, 38, no. 4: 30–52.

Evans, Peter, Dietrich Rueschemeyer, and Theda Skocpol, eds. (1985) *Bring the State Back In*. New York: Cambridge University Press.

Evans, Peter, and James Rauch (1999) "Bureaucracy and Growth: A Cross-National Analysis of the Effects of 'Weberian' State Structures on Economic Growth." *American Sociological Review*, 64, no. 5: 748–765.

Fackler, Martin (2006) "In Korea, Bureaucrats Lead the Technology Charge." *New York Times* March 16, 2006.

Fairbrother, Malcom (2007) "Making Neoliberalism Possible: The State's Organization of Business Support for NAFTA in Mexico." *Politics and Society*, 35, no. 2: 265–300.

Fields, Karl J. (1995) *Enterprise and the State in Korea and Taiwan*. Ithaca, NY: Cornell University Press.

Fields, Karl J. (2014) "Not of a Piece: Developmental States, Industrial Policy, and Evolving Patterns of Capitalism in Japan, Korea, and Taiwan." In Andrew Walter and Xiaoke Zhang (eds.), *East Asian Capitalism: Diversity, Continuity, and Change*. Oxford: Oxford University Press. pp. 46–67.

Fine, Ben (2013) "Beyond the Developmental State." In Ben Fine, Jyoti Sarawati, and Daniela Tavasci (eds.), *Beyond the Developmental State*. London: Pluto Press. pp. 1–32.

Fioretos, Orfeo (2011) *Creative Reconstructions: Multilateralism and European Varieties of Capitalism after 1950*. Ithaca, NY: Cornell University Press.

Fitch (2013) "Korea's Policy Financial Institutions: Policy Functions Set to Increase to Support Economy." *Special Report*. October. Seoul: Fitch Ratings.

FKI (Federation of Korean Industries) (1983) *Junkyungryun 30 Nyunsa* (Korean) [30 Years History of the Federation of Korean Industries]. Seoul: FKI.

FKI (Federation of Korean Industries) (1991) *Junkyungryun Saupbogoseo* 1990 (Korean) [FDI Business Report 1990]. Seoul: FKI.

FKI (Federation of Korean Industries) (1998) *Saupkoojojojung Choojinsang Moonjaejum mit Gaesunbangan* (Korean) [Problems in the Corporate Restructuring and Plans for Revision]. Seoul: FKI.

FKI (Federation of Korean Industries) (2011) *Jungkyungryun 50nyunsa: Kijukui 50nyunul Numeo Heemang 100nyunuro* (Korean) [Fifity Years History of FKI: Beyond the Miracle of 50 Years and Toward a Hope of 100 Years]. Seoul: FKI.

Friedman, Thomas L. (2007) *The World is Flat: A Brief History of the Twenty-First Century*. New York: Farrar, Straus and Giroux.

Fukui, Haruhiro (1987) "The Policy Research Council of Japan's Liberal Democratic Party: Policymaking Role and Practice." *Asian Thought and Society*, 11: 3–30.

Genieys, William, and Marc Smyrl (2008) *Elites, Ideas, and the Evolution of Public Policy*. New York: Palgrave Macmillan.

Granovetter, Mark (1985) "Economic Action and Social Structure: The Problem of Embeddedness." *American Journal of Sociology*, 91, no. 3: 481–510.

Gray, Kevin (2015) *Labour and Development in East Asia: Social Forces and Passive Revolution*. London: Routledge.

Gregory, Paul R. (2004) *The Political Economy of Stalinism: Evidence from the Soviet Secret Archives*. Cambridge: Cambridge University Press.

Ha, Yong-Chool (2006) *Late Industrialization and the Dynamics of the Strong State in South Korea: Debureaucratization and Hollowing out* (Korean). Seoul: SNU Press.

Haggard, Stephan (1990) *Pathways from the Periphery: The Politics of Growth in the Newly Industrializing Countries*. Ithaca, NY: Cornell University Press.

Haggard, Stephan (2015) "The Development State is Dead: Long Live the Developmental State!" In James Mahoney and Kathleen Thelen (eds.), *Advances in Comparative-Historical Analysis*. New York: Cambridge University Press. pp. 39–66.

Haggard, Stephan (2018) *Developmental States*. New York: Cambridge University Press.

Haggard, Stephen, Byung-kook Kim, and Chung-In Moon (1991) "The Transition to Export-led Growth in South Korea: 1954–1966." *The Journal of Asian Studies*, 50, no. 4: 650–873.

Haggard, Stephen, and Tun-jen Cheng (1987) "State strategies, foreign and local capital in the East Asian NICs." In Fred Dey (ed.), *The Political Economy of the New Asian Industrialism*. Ithaca: Cornell University Press.

Hahm, Sung Deuk and L. Christopher Plein (1997) *After Development: The Transformation of the Korean Presidency and Bureaucracy*. Washington DC: Georgetown University Press.

Hall, Peter A. (1986) *Governing the Economy: The Politics of State Intervention in Britain and France*. Cambridge, MA: Polity Press.

Hall, Peter A., and David Soskice (2001) "An Introduction to Varieties of Capitalism." In Peter A. Hall and David Soskice (eds.), *Varieties of Capitalism: The Institutional Foundations of Comparative Advantage*. Oxford: Oxford University Press. pp. 1–68.

Hamilton, Clive (1986) *Capitalist Industrialization in Korea*. Boulder, CO: Westview Press.

Han, Kang-suk (2008) "Ejae Jungchaek Kumyungun Jaegodoeya" (Korean) [Now We Should Reconsider the Policy Finance]. Paper at KERI (Korean Economic Research Institute), May 2, 2008.

Han, Sung-soo (1994) *Kyungjae Jungchaekron* (Korean) [The Theory of Economic Policy]. Seoul: Donga.

Hangyure (Korean Daily) (1998, February 2) "94nyun choojin Kim Youngsam Jungboo Sinsanup JungchaekKim Dansunja Big Deal Todae" (Korean) [The 1994 New Industrial Policy of the Kim Youngsam administration became the Basis of the Kim President Elect's Big Deal Plan].

Hangyure (Korean Daily) (1998, August 21) "Iraetda Juraetda Rukbigong Kim Woojung" (Korean) [Blowing Hot and Cold, Rugby Ball Kim Woojung].

Harris, Jerry. (2009) "Statist Globalization in China, Russia, and the Gulf States." *Science and Society*, 73, no. 1: 6–33.

Hart-Lansberg, Martin, and Paul Burkett (2001) "Economic Crisis and Restructuring in South Korea: Beyond the Free Market-Statist Debate." *Critical Asian Studies*, 33: 403–430.

Hasan, Parvez (2007) "Role of the State in Pakistan's Economy: Assessing the Past and Exploring Future Challenges." *Economic and Political Weekly*, 42, no. 18: 1623–1630.

Hayashi, Shigeko (2010) "The Developmental State in the Era of Globalization: Beyond the Northeast Asian Model of Political Economy." *The Pacific Review*, 23, no. 1: 45–69.

Heidenreich, Martin (2012) "The Social Embeddedness of Multinational Companies: A Literature Review." *Socio-Economic Review*, 10, no. 3: 549–579.

Heilmann, Sebastian (2008a) "From Local Experiments to National Policy: The Origins of China's Distinctive Policy Process." *The China Journal*, no. 59: 1–30.

Heilmann, Sebastian (2008b) "Policy Experimentation in China's Economic Rise." *Studies in Comparative International Development (SCID)*, 43, no. 1: 1–26.

Hemmert, Martin, and Keith Jackson (2016) "Is There an East Asian Model of MNC Internationalization? A Comparative Analysis of Japanese and Korean Firms." *Asia Pacific Business Review*, 22, no. 4: 567–594.

Heredia, Blanca (1996) "Contested State: The Politics of Trade Liberalization in Mexico." PhD Dissertation, Columbia University.

Ho, Samuel P. S. (1987) "Economics, Economic Bureaucracy, and Taiwan's Economic Development." *Pacific Affairs* 60, no. 2: 226–247.

Hoff, Karla, and Joseph Stiglitz (2001) "Modern Economic Theory and Development." In Gerald M. Meier and Joseph Stiglitz (eds.), *Frontiers of Development Economics*. New York: Oxford University Press. pp. 389–459.

Hong, Sung Gul (1995) "Policies, Institutions, and Development: The Korean Semiconductor Industry." *Pacific Focus*, 10, no. 1: 39–61.

Hong, Sung Gul (1997) *The Political Economy of Industrial Policy in East Asia*. Cheltenham, UK: Edward Elgar.

Hong, Sung Gul (2004) "Kwahak Kisool Boonya Jungboojojikgaepyun" (Korean) [Government Organizational Reform in the Area of Science and Technology]. Paper at the Conference of the Korean Association of Public Administration (KAPA), May 2004.

Horikane, Yumi (2005) "The Political Economy of Heavy Industrialization: The Heavy and Chemical Industry (HCI) Push in South Korea in the 1970s." *Modern Asian Studies* 39, no. 2: 369–397.

Hourihan, Matt, and David Parkes (2018) *Guide to the President's Budget Research & Development FY 2018*. Washington DC: American Association for the Advancement of Science.

Hsieh, Michelle F. (2016) "Embedding the Economy: The State and Export-led Development in Taiwan." In Yin-wah Chu (ed.), *The Asian Developmental State: Reexaminations and New Departures*. New York: Palgrave Macmillan. pp. 73–95.

Hughes, Helen (1980) "Achievements and Objectives of Industrialization." In John Cody, Helen Hughes, and David Wall (eds.), *Policies for Industrial Progress in Developing Countries*. New York: Oxford University Press. pp. 11–37.

Hundt, David (2005) "A Legitimate Paradox: Neo-liberal Reform and the Return of the State in Korea." *Journal of Development Studies*, 41, no. 2: 242–260.

Hundt, David (2009) *Korea's Developmental Alliance: State, Capital and the Politics of Rapid Development*. New York: Routledge.

Hundt, David (2014) "Economic Crisis in Korea and the Degraded Developmental State." *Australian Journal of International Affairs*, 68, no. 5: 1–16.

Hwang, Byungtae (2011) *Parkjunghee Paradigm: Kyungjaekihoekwon Kwajangee Bon Parkjunghee Daetongryung* (Korean) [Park Chung Hee Paradigm: President Park Chung Hee from the Perspective of a Section Director of the Economic Planning Board (EPB)]. Seoul: Chosun News Press.

Inoguchi, Takashi, and Tomoaki Iwai (1987) *Zoku giin no kenkyu*. Tokyo: Nihon Keizai Shinbunsha.

ITU (International Telecommunications Union) (2010) *Measuring the Information Society 2010*. Geneva: ITU.

Jayasuriya, Kanishka (2005) "Beyond Institutional Fetishism: From the Developmental to the Regulatory State." *New Political Economy*, 10, no. 3: 381–387.

Jeon, Jinju (2020) "Supporting Korean Startups: Ministry of SMEs & Startups (MSS) to encourage and strengthen innovation." Korea Tech Desk, April 6th 2020 from online https://www.koreatechdesk.com/supporting-korean-startups-ministry-of-smes-startups-mss-to-encourage-and-strengthen-innovation/

Jeong, Kuk-Hwan, and John L. King (1996) "National Information Infrastructure Initiatives in Korea." *Information Infrastructure and Policy*, 5, no. 2: 119–134.

Jeong, Seongjin (1997) "The Social Structure of Accumulation in South Korea: Upgrading or Crumbling?" *Review of Radical Political Economics*, 29, no. 4: 92–112.

Ji, Joohyung (2011) *Hankook Sinjayujoouiui Kiwonkwa Hyungsung* [The Origin and Formation of Korean Neoliberalism] (Korean). Seoul: Chaeksesang.

Jo, Chulhwan (1999) "Jaebolgaehyuk Moolgunegan gut ahnya" (Korean) [Isn't the Chaebol Reform Gone]. *Weekly Korea*. August 5, 1999.

Jo, Hyung Jae (2016) *The Agile Production System of Hyundai Motor Company* (Korean). Seoul: Hanul Academy.

Jo, Youngho (2000) "Lee Kungeeui Samsung, Gu Daebyunsinui Bimil" (Korean) [Lee Kunhee's Samsung, Secret Story on its Great Transformation]. *Wulgan Chosun*. July 2000, pp. 189–239.

Johnson, Chalmers (1977) "MITI and Japanese International Economic Policy." In Robert A. Scalapino (ed.) *The Foreign Policy of Modern Japan*. Berkeley: University of California Press.

Johnson, Chalmers (1982) *MITI and the Japanese Miracle: The Growth of Industrial Policy, 1925–1975*. Stanford, CA: Stanford University Press.

Johnson, Chalmers (1985) "Political institutions and economic performance: the government-business relationship in Japan, South Korea, and Taiwan." In Robert A. Scalapino, S. Sato, and J. Wanandi (eds.) *Asian Economic Development-Present and Future*. Research Papers and Policy Studies no. 14. Berkeley: Institute of East Asian Studies.

Johnson, Chalmers (1998) "Economic Crisis in East Asia: The Clash of Capitalisms," *Cambridge Journal of Economics*, 22, no. 6: 653–661.

Joo, Eun-sun (2009) "1998 nyunbootu 2007nyunkaji Hankook Yunkum Jungchaekui Jungaebanghyang" (Korean) [The Evolution of Korean Pension Fund Policy from 1998 to 2007]. Korean Social Policy, 15, no. 2: 144–180.

Jun, Byung-Yoo (2008) "Sungjang Junryakui Boojaewa Misookhan Boonbaejunryak" (Korean) [Absence of Economic Growth Strategy and Premature Distribution Strategy]. In Hanbando Sahoekyungjae Yungoohoe [Socio-Economic Studies in Korean Peninsula], ed., *Noh Moohyun Sidaeui Jwajul* [Frustration in the Roh Moohyun Era]. Seoul: Changbi. pp. 89–107.

Jun, Changwan (2004) "1980yundae Baljunkookgaui Jaepyun, Kujojojyung, grigo Kyumyungjayuhwa" (Korean) [Transformation of the Developmental State in the 1980s, Corporate Restructuring, and Financial Liberalization]. In Yu Chulkyu (ed.), *Park Chunghee Model kwa Sinjayujuui Saieseo* (Korean) [Between Park Chung Hee Model and Neoliberalism]. Seoul: CoBook. pp. 85–134.

Jung, Duck-Goo (2006) *Kiumkwa Nanumul Numesu* (Korean) [Beyond Cultivating and Sharing]. Seoul: 21st Century Books.

Jung, Hong-Sik (2003) "Kim Jae-ik Susukkwa Jungbohwa Jungchaek" (Korean) [Presidential Secretariat Kim Jae-ik and Informatization Policy]. In Nam Duck Woo et al., eds. *80 Nyundae Kyungjaekaehyukkwa Kim Jae-ik Susuk* [Economic Reform of the 1980s and First Presidential Secretariat Kim Jae-ik]. Seoul: Samsung Economic Research Institute. pp. 117–142.

Jung, Joo Young (1991) *Naui Sam Naui Yisang: Siryunun isudo Silpaenun Upda* (Korean) [Jung Joo Young Memoir: There Might be Challenges, But No Failure]. Seoul: Hyundai Moonhwa.

Jung, Seyoung (2000) *Miraenun Mandenun Gusida* (Korean) [Future is What We Make]. Seoul: Haengrim.

Jun-Hong, Kihye (2009) "IMFnun Utuke Daejungkyungjaeui Kumul Hoesonsikyutna" (Korean) [How Has the IMF Crisis Destroyed the Dream of Daejung Economics]. *Presian*. August 19, 2009.

KAICA (Korea Auto Industries Cooperative Association) (2011) *Jadongcha Sanup Pyunram* [2011 Korean Auto Industry Annual Review]. Seoul: KAICA.

Kalinowski, Thomas (2008) "Korea's Recovery since the 1997/1998 Financial Crisis: The Last Stage of the Developmental State." *New Political Economy* 13, no. 4: 447–462.

KAMA (Korea Automobile Manufacturers Association) (2005) *Hankookjadongchasanup 50nyunsa* (Korean) [The 50 Years History of Korean Automobile Industry]. Seoul: KAMA.

Kang, C. S. Eliot (2000) "Segyehwa Reform of the South Korean Developmental State." In Samuel S. Kim (ed.) *Korea's Globalization*. Cambridge: Cambridge University Press. pp. 76–101.

Kang, Kwangha, Younghoon Lee, and Sangoh Choi (2008) *Hankook Godosungjangkiui Jungchaekkyuljungchaegae* (Korean) [Policy Decision-Making System in Korean High-Growth Period: EPB and Policy Pilot Agency]. Seoul: Korean Development Institute (KDI).

Kang, Kyungsik (1987) *Beyond Economic Stability* (Korean). Seoul: Korean Economic Daily News Press.

Kang, Kyungsik (2003) "Kumyungsilmyungjaewa Anjunghwa Sichaek" (Korean) [Real Financial Transaction System and Stabilization Policy." In Nam Duck Woo et al., eds., *80 Nyundae Kyungjaekaehyukkwa Kim Jae-ik Susuk* [Economic Reform of the 1980s and First Presidential Secretariat Kim Jae-ik]. Seoul: Samsung Economic Research Institute. pp. 83–116.

Kang, Seojin (2014) "Chungsokiup Jungchaekgumyung Koojowa Yihae" (Korean) [Policy Financing Structure of SMEs and Its Understanding]. *KB Knowledge Vitamin*. No. 14–31, Management Research Institute, KB Finance.

Kang, Woojin (2015) "Why Korean Citizens Support Economic Growth over Democracy: An Empirical Analysis about the Determinants of Developmentalism" (Korean). *Hankookkwa Kookjejungchi* [Korea and International Politics], 31, no. 3: 25–55.

Katz, Richard (2003) *Japanese Phoenix: The Long Road to Economic Revival*. New York: M.E. Sharpe.

Katzenstein, Peter J. (1987) *Policy and Politics in West Germany*. Ithaca, NY: Cornell University Press.

Katznelson, Ira. (2003) "Periodization and Preferences: Reflections on Purposive Action in Comparative Historical Social Science." In James Mahoney and Dietrich Rueschemeyer (eds.), *Comparative Historical Analysis in the Social Sciences*. New York: Cambridge University Press. pp. 270–301.

KDB (Korea Development Bank) (2011) *Annual Report*. Seoul: KDB.

KDI (Korea Development Institute) (1981) *Collection of Documents and Study Reports Related to Economic Stability Policies* (Korean), vols. 1 and 2. Seoul: KDI.

KDI (Korea Development Institute) (1982) *Sanup Chungshak-ui Kibon Kwaje-wa Chiwaon Sichak-ui Kaepyeon Panghyang* (Korean) [Basic Tasks of Industrial Policy and New Directions for Promotional Measures]. Seoul: KDI.

KEI 50 HCC (Korean Electronics Industry 50 Years History Compilation Committee) (2009) *Daehanminkook Junjasanup 50 Nyunsa: Kijukui Sigan 50* (Korean) [Korean Electronics Industry 50 Years History: The Miraculous Time 50 Years]. Seoul: Junja Sinmoonsa.

Kelly, Tim, Vanessa Grayand and Michael Minges (2003) *Broadband Korea: Internet Case Study*. International Telecommunications Union, March.

KEMHCC (Korean Economic Miracle History Compilation Committee) (2013) *Korean Miracle 1: Yuksunguro Dutnun Kyungjaekijuk* (Korean) [Korean Miracle 1: The Korean Economic Miracle Listening through National Voice]. Seoul: Nanam.

KEMHCC (Korean Economic Miracle History Compilation Committee) (2014) *Korean Miracle 2: Dojunkwa Bisang* (Korean) [Korean Miracle 2: Challenges and Taking Off]. Seoul: Nanam.

KEMHCC (Korean Economic Miracle History Compilation Committee) (2015) *Korean Miracle 3: Soomun Kijukdul* (Korean) [Korean Miracle 3: Hidden Miracles]. Seoul: Nanam.

KEMHCC (Korean Economic Miracle History Compilation Committee) (2016) *Korean Miracle 4: Oehwan Wekiui Pagorul Nume* (Korean) [Korean Miracle 4: Beyond the Challenges of the 1997 Financial Crisis]. Seoul: Nanam.

Kienzle, Rene, and Mark Shadur (1997) "Developments in Business Networks in East Asia," *Management and Decision*, 35, no. 1: 23–32.

KIET (Korea Institute for Industrial Economics and Trade) (1983) *Chumdan Kisoolsanupui Donghyangkwa Wooriui Daeung* (Korean) [The Trend of Cutting-Edge Technology Industries and Our Tasks]. Seoul: KIET.

KIET (Korea Institute for Industrial Economics and Trade) (1996) *Jadongcha Sijange daehan Insik Josa* (Korean) [Perception survey on Automobile Market]. Seoul: KIET.

KIET (Korea Institute for Industrial Economics and Trade) (2008). "Hankook Sanupjungchaekui Gwaguwha Hyungjae Grigo Mirae" (Korean) [The Past, Present and the Future of Korean Industrial Policy]. *e-KIET Sanup Kyungjaejungbo*, no. 379.

KIET (Korea Institute for Industrial Economics and Trade) (2012) *Boopoom Sojae Mirae Bijun Soorip Yungoo* (Korean) [A Study of the Establishment of Future Vision in Parts and Materials]. Seoul: KIET.

Kim, Bohyun (2006) *Parkjunghee Jungkwonki Kyungjaegaebal: Minjokjoouiwa Baljun* (Korean) [Economic Development in Park Chung Hee Era: Nationalism and Development]. Seoul: Galmoori.

Kim, Byung-Kook (2011a) "Introduction: The Case for Political History." In Byung-Kook Kim and Ezra F. Vogel (eds.), *The Park Chung Hee Era: The Transformation of South Korea*. Cambridge, MA: Harvard University Press. pp. 1–34.

Kim, Byung-Kook (2011b) "The Leviathan: Economic Bureaucracy under Park." In Byung-Kook Kim and Ezra F. Vogel (eds.), *The Park Chung Hee Era: The Transformation of South Korea*. Cambridge, MA: Harvard University Press. pp. 200–234.

Kim, Byung-Kook (2003) "The Politics of Chaebol Reform, 1980–1997." In S. Haggard, W. Lim, and E. Kim (eds.), *Economic Crisis and Corporate Restructuring in Korea*. Cambridge: Cambridge University Press. pp. 53–78.

Kim, Chung-Soo (1998) "How the Chaebol Can Survive." *Korea Focus* 6, no. 1: 41–54.

Kim, Chung-yum (2006) *Hankook Kyungjaejungchaek 30 nyunsa: Choibinkookeseo Sunjinkook Montukkaji* (Korean) [The 30 years of Korean Economic Policy: From the Poorest right to the Door of the Advanced Economy]. Seoul: Random House.

Kim, Dohoon (2014) "Hankook Sanupbaljunkwa Hyanghoo Kwajae" (Korean) [Korean Industrial Development and Future Tasks]. *Korean Economic Forum* 6, no. 4: 15–35.

Kim, Dong-One and Johngseok Bae (2005) "Workplace Innovation, Employment Relations and HRM: Two electronics companies in South Korea." *International Journal of Human Resource Management* 16, no. 7: 1277–1302.

Kim, Eun Mee (1997) *Big Business, Strong State: Collusion and Conflict in South Korean Development, 1960–1990*. Albany, NY: State University of New York Press.

Kim, Eun Mee (2014) "The South Korean Developmental Alliance between Business, Labor and Government." In Ilcheong Yi and Thandika Mkandawire (eds.), *Learning from the South Korean Developmental Success: Effective Developmental Cooperation and Synergistic Institutions and Policies*. New York: Palgrave. pp. 235–255.

Kim, Eun Mee, and Gil-Sung Park (2011) "The Chaebol." In Byung-Kook Kim and Ezra F. Vogel (eds.), *The Park Chung Hee Era: The Transformation of South Korea*. Cambridge, MA: Harvard University Press. pp. 265–294.

Kim, Hongki (1998) "Suhgoosikul Taraya Sanda" (Korean) [We Should Follow the Western Style to Survive]. *Wulgan Chosun*. August, pp. 173–176.

Kim, Hungki (1999) *Youngyokui Hankook Kyungjae: Bisa Kyungjaekihoekwon 33 Nyun* (Korean) [Glory and Shame in Korean Economy: Secret Story of the Economic Planning Board for 33 Years]. Seoul: Maeilkyungjae

Kim, Hyung-A (2004) *Korea's Development under Park Chung Hee: Rapid Industrialization, 1961–1979*. New York: Routledge Curzon.

Kim, Hyung-Kook (1991) "Bandoche Sanupkoojojojung Jungchaekkwa Jungboo, Mingan Kiup Kwangaeui Jungrip" (Korean) [Industrial Structural Adjustments in the

Semiconductor Industry and the Reestablishment of the Relationship between Government and Private Firms]. In Kang Min et al. (eds.), *Kookgawa Gonggong Jungchaek* [State and Public Policy]. Seoul: Bupmoonsa.

Kim, Hyun-Jong (2010) *Kim Hyunjong, Hanmi FTArul Malhada* (Korean) [Hyun-Jong Kim Speaks about Korea-US FTA]. Seoul: Hongsungsa.

Kim, Jaemyung (1988) "The Godfather of the TK Corps." *Monthly Chosun* (Korean). November 1988.

Kim, Jinhyun (1964) "Boojungchookjaecheri Junmalsu" (Korean) [The Whole Story of Dealing with Illegal Wealth Amassers]. *Shin-Dong-A*. December, 1964.

Kim, Jongil (2007) "Chungsokiup Jungchaekui Yukhal Jaejungrip" (Korean) [Reestablishment of SME Policy Roles]. In KDI (ed.), *Woorikyungjae Sunjinhwarul wehan Jungbooyukhalui Jaejungrip* (Korean) [Readjustments of Government Roles for Advancement of Korean Economy]. Seoul: KDI.

Kim, Jungjoo (2005) "1950–1960 Yundae Hankookui Jabonchookjukkwa Kookgagigooui Junmyunhwa Kwajung" (Korean) [Capital Accumulation and Strengthening the State in Korea of the 1950s and 1960s]. In Jaewook Kong and Sukgon Jo (eds.), *The Prototype Formation and its Transformation of the Korean Development Model in the 1950s–1960s*. Seoul: Hanwool Academy.

Kim, Kiwan (2007) "Jungboo Yungugaebaltujaui Hyunwhangjindankwa Hyokwajukin Tujabanghyang Mosaek" (Korean) [The Assessment of Current Government's Investment of R&D and Exploration of Effective Investment Direction]. In Korea Development Institute (KDI), ed., Woorikyungjaeui Sunjinhwarul wuihan Jungboo Yukhalui Jaejungrip [Readjustments of Government Role for Our Economic Advancement]. Seoul: KDI. pp. 263–320.

Kim, Kwanghee (1998) *Hanil Jadongcha Boopoom Sanup* [Korean and Japanese Auto Parts Industries]. Ulsan, Korea: University of Ulsan Press.

Kim, Kyeong-Won (2001) *Three Years after the IMF Bailout: A Review of the Korean Economy's Transformation since 1998*. Seoul Samsung Economic Research Institute.

Kim, Kyung Mi (2020) *The Korean Developmental State*. London: Palgrave Macmillan.

Kim, Kyung Mi, and Hyeong-ki Kwon (2017) "The State's Role in Globalization: Korea's Experience from a Comparative Perspective." *Politics & Society* 45, no. 4: 505–531.

Kim, Linsu (1993) "National System of Industrial Innovation: Dynamics of Capability Building in Korea." In Richard R. Nelson (ed.), *National Innovation System: A Comparative Analysis*. New York: Oxford University Press. pp. 357–383.

Kim, Linsu (1997) *Imitation to Innovation*. Cambridge, MA: Harvard Business Press.

Kim, Sang-Bong (2011) "Kookga R&D Saup Jungchaek Kyuljungkwajunge isuse Jungboo Boocheogan Galdung Jojung: Chamyeo Jungboo Shinsungjangdongryuk Saup Sonjungul Joongsimuro" (Korean) [Government Interministerial Conflicts Resolution in the Decision-Making of State R&D Projects: A Study on Chamyeo Government's New Growth Engine Project]. Paper at the Conference held by the Korean Association of Public Administration, December 2011.

Kim, Sangjo (1993) "Sulbijagumui Dongwon mit Baeboonchaegaee Kwanhan Yungoo" (Korean) [A Study on the Mobilization of Facility Capital and Allocation System]. PhD Dissertation, Seoul National University.

Kim, Seung Hee (1970) *Foreign Capital for Economic Development: A Korean Case Study*. New York: Praeger.

Kim, Sookil, Jungjae Lee, Kyungmin Jung, and Sangyul Lee (2003) *Kumgoga Biutsupdida: DJ Jungkwon 5 nyunui Kyungjaesilrok* (Korean) [The Vault was Empty: Economic History Record of the Five Years DJ Regime]. Seoul: Choongang M&B.

Kim, Suk-Hyun (2008) "Kwahakgisooljungchaek, Sungjangrone Pohoekdoen Kookgahyuksinchaeje" (Korean) [Science and Technology Policy, State Innovation System captured by Growth-First-ism]. In Hanbando Sahoekyungjae Yungoohoe [Socio-Economic Studies in Korean Peninsula] (ed.), *Noh Moohyun Sidaeui Jwajul* [Frustration in the Roh Moohyun Era]. Seoul: Changbi. pp. 201–216.

Kim, Sung-Young (2012) "Transition from Fast-follower to Innovator: The Institutional Foundations of the Korean Telecommunications Sector." *Review of International Political Economy* 19, no. 1: 140–168.

Kim, Sung-Young (2019) "Hybridized Industrial Ecosystems and the Makings of a New Developmental Infrastructure in East Asia's Green Energy Sector." *Review of International Political Economy*, published online DOI:10.1080/09692290.2018.1554540.

Kim, Sung-Young (2020) "East Asia's Developmental States in Evolution: The challenge of sustaining national competitiveness at the technological frontier." In Ernesto Vivares (ed.), The Routledge Handbook to Global Political Economy. London: Routledge. pp. 551–527.

Kim, Sunhyuk and Do Chul Shin (2004) *Economic Crisis and Dual Transition: A Case Study in Comparative Perspective*. Seoul: Seoul National University Press.

Kim, Yang-Hwa (2017) "A Critique of Developmental Dictatorship Theory: Based on the Institutional Forms and an Analysis of the Profit Rate in the Korean Cotton Textile Industry, 1960–1976" (Korean). *Journal of Koreanology* 62: 405–432.

Kim, Yeonchul (1993) "Hankookui Kookga Nungryukui Byunhwawa Kyungjae Baljun" (Korean) [Transformation of State Capability and Economic Development in Korea]. PhD Dissertation, Korea University.

Kim, Yong-bok (1996) "Kyungjaejayuhwa Sidaee isus Sanupjojungui Jungchi" (Korean) [Politics of Industrial Adjustments in Economic Liberalization: A Comparative Analysis of Korean and Japanese Industrial Policy Making]. PhD Dissertation, Department of Political Science, Seoul National University.

Kim, Yong-bok (2005) "1980 Nyundae Hankook Sanupjungchaek Kwajungui Tukjing" (Korean) [The Characteristics of the Korean Industrial Policy Decision Making Process in the 1980s]. *Kukjejungchiyungoo* [International Politics Review], 8, no. 1: 237–255.

Kim, Yonghwan (2002) *Yimja, Janega Saryungkwan Aninga* (Korean) [You Are an Economic Commander]. Seoul: Maeilkyungjaesinmoonsa.

Kim, Yongki (2004) "Kumyungui Gongongsungkwa Kumyung Kyujae" (Korean) [The Publicness of Finance and Financial Regulation]. In Lee, Changun et al. (eds.), *Hankook Kyungjaega Sarajinda* [Korean Economy Is Disappearing]. Seoul: 21st Century Books. pp. 143–165.

Kim, Youngbum (2003) "Kookjaekyungjaeng Jibaedamron Boonsuk: Park Jung Hee Jungkwonesu Kim Daejung Jungkwonkaji" (Korean) [An Analysis on the Dominant Discourse, "International Competition": From Park Chung Hee to Kim Daejung Regime]. In Heeyun Jo (ed.), *Hankookui Jungchisahoejuk Jibaedamronkwa Mijoojooui Donghak* [The Political-Social Dominant Discourse in Korea and Dynamics of Democracy]. Seoul: Hamkeilnun Chaek. pp. 397–428.

Kim, Yun-myung and Eun-sun Joo (2010) *Kookmin Yunkumkikume Daehan Jinbojuk Damron mit Toojajungchaek Yungoo* (Korean) [Progressive Discourse on the Use of National Pension Fund and A Study on the Investment Policy]. Department of Social Welfare, Choong Ang University.

Kim, Yun Tae (2000) *Jaebolkwa Kwonryuk* (Korean) [Chaebols and Power]. Seoul: Saeroun Saramdul.

Kim, Yun Tae (2005) "DJnomics and the Transformation of a Developmental State." *Journal of Contemporary Asia* 35, no. 4: 471–484.

Kim, Yung Bong (1977) "The Growth and Structural Change of Korean Textile Industry." KDI Working Paper No. 7710, Korea Development Institute (KDI), Seoul.

Kirk, Donald M. (2000) *Korean Crisis: Unraveling of the Miracle in the IMF Era*. London: Macmillan.

KISTEP (Korea Institute of S&T Evaluation and Planning) (2015) "Woorinara Mingankiup Yungoogaebalhwaldong Hyunhwang" (Korean) [The Current Situation of Our Private Companies' R&D Activity]. *KISTEP Statistics Brief*, no. 22.

Ko, Kyungmin (2000) "Hankookui Sanupjungchaek Byunhwa Kwajung: Jungbo Tongsin Sanupui Jayuhwa Sarye" (Korean) [Transformation of Korean Industrial Policy: A Case Study on the Liberalization of Information and Communications Industry]. PhD Dissertation, Kukkook University, Korea.

Ko, Sungchul, and Wanbae Lee (2013) *Kim Jae-ik Pyungjun* (Korean) [Critical Biography on Kim Jae-ik]. Seoul: Miraerul Soyohan Saramdul.

Ko, Youngsun (2007) "Kyungjae Saehoeyukunui Byunhwawa Jungbooyukhalui Byunhwa" (Korean) [The Changes of Socio-Economic Conditions and the Changes in Government Role]. In Korea Development Institute (KDI) (ed.), *Woorikyungjaeui Sunjinhwarul wehan Jungboohyukhalui Jaejungrip* (Korean) [The Readjustments of the Government Roles for Advancement of Korean Economy]. Seoul: KDI. pp. 15–96.

Kochan, Thomas A. (2012) "A Jobs Compact for America's Future." *Harvard Business Review*, Special Report: Reinventing America 90, no. 3: 64–73.

Kohli, Atul (2005) *State-Directed Development: Political Power and Industrialization in the Global Periphery*. New York: Cambridge University Press.

Kohli, Atul (1999) "Where Do High-Growth Political Economies Come From? The Japanese Lineage of Korea's 'Developmental State.'" In Meredith Woo-Cumings (ed.), *The Developmental State*. Ithaca, NY: Cornell University Press. pp. 93–136.

Konai, Janos (1986) "The Hungarian Reform Process: Visons, Hopes, and Reality." *Journal of Economic Literature* XXIV (December), pp. 1687–1737.

Kong, Tat Yan (2000) *The Politics of Economic Reform in South Korea: A Fragile Miracle*. London: Routledge.

Kong, Tat Yan (2002) *Politics of Economic Reform in South Korea*. New York: Routledge.

Kong, Tat Yan (2012) "Cooperation in Unlikely Settings: The Rise of Cooperative Labor Relations among Leading South Korean Firms." *Politics and Society* 40, no. 3: 425–452.

Koo, Hagen and Eun Mee Kim (1992) "The Developmental State and Capital Accumulation in South Korea." In Richard P. Appelbaum and Jeffrey William Henderson (eds.), *States and Development in the Asian Pacific Rim*. Newbury Park, CA: Sage Publication. pp. 121–149.

Korea Exchange Bank (1980) *Monthly Review*, 14, no. 11.

Korea Herald (August 27, 2009) "Equipment Industry is Crucial to Growth."

Korea Institute of Social Research (1995) "Shinkyungjae 2 Nyunui Pyunga: Shinkyungjaeseo Segyehwakaji" (Korean) [Evaluation of 2 years New Economy]. *Donghyangkwa Junmoon*, no. 26. Summer.

Korean Times (2001, Nov. 6) "Broadband Consolidation Enters Final Stage."

Krasner, Stephen (1984) "Approaches to the State: Alternative Conceptions and Historical Dynamics." *Comparative Politics* 16, no. 2: 223–246.

Krasner, Stephen (1988) "Sovereignty: an institutional approach." *Comparative Political Studies*, 21: 66–94.

Krause, Lawrence B. (2003) "Kisooljinborul Hyanghayu" (Korean) [For the Improvement of Technology]. In Nam Duck Woo et al. (eds.), *80 Nyundae Kyungjaekaehyukkwa Kim Jae-ik Susuk* [Economic Reform of the 1980s and First Presidential Secretariat Kim Jae-ik]. Seoul: Samsung Economic Research Institute. pp. 59–82.

Krueger, Anne O. (1980) "Trade Policy as an Input to Development." *American Economic Review* 70, no. 2: 228–292.

Krueger, Anne O., and Jungho Yoo (2002) "Falling Profitability, Higher Borrowing Costs and Chaebol Finance during the Korean Crisis." In David T. Coe and Se-Jik Kim, *Korean Crisis and Recovery*. Washington, DC: International Monetary Fund. pp. 157–196.

Krugman, Paul (1994) "Competitiveness: A Dangerous Obsession." *Foreign Affairs*, 73: 28–44.

Krugman, Paul (1998) *"What happened to Asia?" Mimeo.* Cambridge, MA: Department of Economics, Massachusetts Institute of Technology.

Kuk, Minho (2011) "From State-Led to Chaebol-Led: Changing Relationship between the State and Chaebols after the IMF Foreign Exchange Crisis" (Korean). *Hyunsangkwa Insik* [Phenomena and Perception], 35, no. 3: 129–158.

Kuo, Cheng-Tian (1995) *Global Competitiveness and Industrial Growth in Taiwan and the Philippines*. Pittsburgh: University of Pittsburgh Press.

Kwon, Hyeong-ki (2012) "Politics of Globalization and National Economy: The German Experience Compared with the U.S." *Politics & Society*, 40, no. 4: 581–607.

Kwon, Hyeong-ki (2013) "Politics of Institutional Change: Evolution of the Irish Social Concertation Model," *Comparative European Politics* 11, no. 4: 481–510.

Kwon, Hyeong-ki (2014) *Segyehwa Sidaeui Yukhaeng? Jayoojoouiesu Sahoehyupyakui Jungchiro* (Korean) [A Reverse Steam against Globalization? From Liberalism to Social Partnership Politics: Evolution of the Irish Social Partnership Model]. Seoul: Humanitas.

Kwon, Hyeong-ki, and Kyung Mi Kim (2020) "Varieties of Globalization and National Economy: Korea's Experience from a Comparative Perspective." *Journal of International Relations and Development,* 23: 728–754.

Kwon, O. Yul (2010) *The Korean Economy in Transition: An Institutional Perspective.* Cheltenham, UK: Edward Elgar.

Kwon, Youngki (2000) "Frontispice Interview: Kang Bong Kyun, Minister of Finance and Economy" (Korean). *Wulgan Chosun.* January 2000, pp. 64–77.

Lall, Sanjaya (2004) "Reinventing Industrial Strategy: the Role of Government Policy in Building Industrial Competitiveness." G-24 Discussion Paper No. 28, United Nations Conference of Trade and Development, New York and Geneva, United Nations, April 2004.

Lampton, David M., ed. (1987) *Policy Implementation in Post-Mao China.* Berkeley, CA: University of California Press.

Lampton, David M. (1987) "Chinese Politics: The Bargaining Treadmill." *Issues and Studies*, 23, no. 3: 11–41.

Larson, James F., and Jaemin Park (2014) "From Developmental to Network State: Government Restructuring and ICT-led Innovation in Korea." *Telecommunications Policy*, 38, no. 4: 344–359.

Lee, Byungchun (1999) "Parkjunghee Jungkwonkwa Baljunkookga Mohyungui Hyungsung" (Korean) [Park Chung Hee Regime and the Formation of Developmental State Model." *Kyungjaebaljun Yungoo* [Journal of Korean Development Economics], 5, no. 2: 141–187.

Lee, Byungchun (2001) "Junhwankiui Hankook Kyungjaewa Kim Daejung Jungbooui Koojojojung Silhum: Gulrobul Standardwa Goochejaeui Akjohap" (Korean) [Korean Economy in Transformation and Kim Dae-jung Government's Corporate Restructuring Experimentation: A Bad Combination of Global Standards and Old Practices]. In Byung-Chun Lee and Won-Hee Cho, eds. *Hankook Kyungjae Jaesaengui Kilun Inunga* [Is There a Recovery Way for Korean Economy]. Seoul: Dangdae. pp. 11–68.

Lee, Choongok, and Silvia M. Chan-Olmsted (2004) "Competitive Advantage of Broadband Internet: A Comparative Study between South Korea and the United States." *Telecommunications Policy*, 28, no. 9–10: 649–677.

Lee, Dae Kun (1987) *Hankook Kyungjaeui Goojowa Kasun* (Korean) [The Korean Economic Structure and Reform]. Seoul: Changjaksa.

Lee, Dae Kun (1997) "Historical Conditions of the East Asian Economic Development" (Korean). *Review of Economic History*, 23, no. 3: 3–17.

Lee, Hyun-Duck (2012) *Daetongryungkwa Jungbotongsinboo: Moonmin Jungboo Jungbo Tongsin Bisa* (Korean) [President and MIC: Secret Story on the ICT Industry in the Civil Government]. Seoul: Book Concert.

Lee, Jangkyu (2008) *Kyungjaenun Dangsinee Daetongryngeeya* (Korean) [You are the President of Economy: Secret Story in Chun Doohwan Era]. Seoul: Olim.

Lee, Jong-hwa (1994) "Chaebol Kiupui Upjongjunmoonhwa Yudo Jungchaeke kwanhan Yungoo" (Korean) [A Study on the Core Business Specialization Policy about Chaebols]. MA Thesis, Seoul National University.

Lee, Kang-Kook (2005) *Davos, Porto Alegre gurigo Seoul: Seykyehwaui Doo Kyungjaehak* (Korean) [Davos, Porto Alegre, and Seoul: Two Economics in Globalization]. Seoul: Humanitas.

Lee, Keun, and Chaisung Lim (2001) "Technological Regimes, Catch-up and Leapfrogging: Findings from the Korean Industries," *Research Policy* 30, no. 3: 459–483.

Lee, Keun, and Xiyou He (2009) "The Capability of the Samsung Group in Project Execution and Vertical Integration: Created in Korea, Replicated in China," *Asian Business and Management*, 8, no. 3: 277–299.

Lee, Kiyul (1995) *Soriupnun Hyukmyung: 80nyundae Jungbo Tongsin Bisa* (Korean) [Silent Revolution: Secret Story on the Information and Communication Industry in the 1980s]. Seoul: Junja Shinmoonsa.

Lee, Kunmi (1996) "Hankook Hyundaesaui Kyuljungjuk Soongan 9" (Korean) [The Decisive Moment in Korean Modern History 9: Export-Oriented or Import Substitution?" Wolgan Chosun, no. 192 (March 1996): pp. 536–551.

Lee, Kwang-Suk (2009) "A Final Flowering of the Developmental State: The IT Policy Experiment of the Korean Information Infrastructure, 1995–2005," *Government Information Quarterly*, 26, no. 4: 567–576.

Lee, Man-Hee (1993) *EPBnun Kijukul Nautnunga: Hankook Sanupjungchaekui Yisangkwa Hunsil* (Korean) [Did the EPB Create a Miracle: The Vision and Reality of Korean Industrial Policy]. Seoul: Hadoji

Lee, Man-Hee (1996) *Kookjekyungjangryuk Jungchaekron: Hankook Sanuphwaui Jungchikyungjae* (Korean) [Policy Theory on International Competitiveness: Political Economy of Korean Industries]. Seoul: Daekwangsa.

Lee, Man-Hee (2010) "The Dynamics between the President and The Economic Planning Board in Korea's Industrialization Policy, 1961–1979" (Korean), *The 21st Century Political Science Review*, 20, no. 3: 79–99.

Lee, Sangchul (2002) "1960–1970 Nyundae Hankook Sanupjungchaekui Jungae" (Korean) [The Evolution of Korean Industrial Policy in the 1960s–1970s: A Study on the Formation of the Hierarchical Resource Allocation Mechanism]. *Economy and Society*, 56: 110–137.

Lee, Sangchul (2003) "1960–1970 Nyundae Sanupjungchaekui Hyungsungkwa Junhwan: HwahakSumyusanupul Joongsimuro" (Korean) [Formation and Transformation of the Industrial Policy in the 1960s–1970s: A Study on the Chemical Textile Industry]. In Chulkyu Yu (ed.), *Economic Development in Korea II: Developmentalism and Beyond*. Seoul: CoBook. pp. 315–354.

Lee, Sangchul (2004a) "1979–80nyun Kyungjaewekiwa Sanupjungchaekui Byunmo" (Korean) [Economic Crisis and Changes of Industrial Policy in 1979–1980]. In Yu

Chulkyu (ed.), *Between Park Chung Hee Model and Neoliberalism* (Korean). Seoul: CoBook. pp. 167–220.

Lee, Sangchul, Chulkyu Yu, and Jinwook Bang (2005) "Hyuksinjoodohyung Kyungjaewa Shinsanupjungchaek" (Korean) [Innovation-led Economy and New Industrial Policy]. *Jungchaek Yungoo* [Policy Research]. No. 12.

Lee, Sangwoo (1985) *Parkjunghee Sidae* I (Korean) [Park Chung Hee Era I]. Seoul: Chungwonmuhwasa.

Lee, Soo Hee, and Taeyoung Yoo (2007) "Government Policy in Trajectories of Radical Innovation in Dirigiste States: A Comparative Analysis of National Innovation Systems in France and Korea." *Technology and Analysis & Strategic Management*, 19, no. 4: 451–470.

Lee, Suk-Chae (1991) "The Heavy and Chemical Industries Promotion Plan (1973–79)." In Lee-Jay Cho and Yoon Hyung Kim (eds.), *Economic Development in the Republic of Korea: A Policy Perspective*. Honolulu, HI: East-West Center. pp. 431–472.

Lee, Sungtae, Sidong Kim, and Sungho Han (1989) *Hankookui Sanup Jungchaek: Sanup Koojojojung Jungchaek Jaryujip* (Korean) [Korean Industrial Policy: Materials for the Industrial Restructuring Policy]. Seoul: KIET.

Lee, Taekyu (2015) "Sungjang Dongryuk Jungchaekui Hyunhwangkwa Jungchaekjuk Sisajum" (Korean) [The Current Situation of Growth Engine Policy and its Policy Implication]. *Jungchaek Yungoo* [Policy Studies] 2015–14, Korean Economic Research Institute.

Lee, Wanbum (2006) *Park Chung Heewa Hankangui Kijuk* (Korean) [Park Chung Hee and Korean Economic Miracle]. Seoul: Sunin.

Lee, Yeonho, and Hak-Ryul Kim (2018) "Economic Crises and Augmenting Financial Bureaucratic Power in South Korea." *Pacific Review*, 31, no. 3: 352–372.

Lee, Yeonho, Yoo Jin Lim, and Suk Kyu Chung (2002) "The Rise of the Regulatory State and Government-Business Relations in South Korea" (Korean). *Korean Political Science Review*, 36, no. 3: 199–222.

Lee, Yong-Sook (2009) "Balanced Development in Globalizing Regional Development? Unpacking the New Regional Policy in South Korea." *Regional Studies*, 43, no. 3: 353–368.

Lee, Yong-Sook, Inhey Heo, and Hyungjoo Kim (2014) "The Role of the State as an Interscalar Mediator in Globalizing Liquid Crystal Display Industry Development in South Korea." *Review of International Political Economy*, 21, no. 1: 109–129.

Lee, Yoonkyung (2009) "Divergent Outcomes of Labor Reform Politics in Democratized Korea and Taiwan." *Studies in Comparative International Development*, 44, no. 1: 47–70.

Lee, Young-Ryul (1999) *Big Deal Game: DJ vs Jaebol, Milsil Hyupsang, Gu Soomgapatdun 1 nyun 6gaewol Choojukbogoseo* (Korean) [Big Deal Game: DJ versus Chaebols, Report on the Hectic Time1 of the 1 Year 6 Months]. Seoul: Choong-Ang Ilbo J&P.

Levi, Margaret (2009) "Reconsiderations of Rational Choice in Comparative and Historical Analysis." In Mark Irving Lichbach and Alan S. Zuckerman (eds.), *Comparative Politics* (2nd edition). New York: Cambridge University Press. pp. 117–133.

Levy, Jonah D. (2015) "The Transformations of the Statist Model." In Stephan Leibfried et al. (eds.), *the Oxford Handbook of Transformation of the State*. Oxford: Oxford University Press. pp. 393–409.

Lew, Seok Choon, and Hye Suk Wang (2007) "Did the Financial Crisis Transform the Developmental State: Focused on the Public Fund in Korea" (Korean). *Korean Journal of Sociology*, 41, no. 5: 64–97.

Lieberthal, Kenneth G. (1992) "Introduction: The 'Fragmented Authoritarianism' Model and Its Limitations." In Kenneth G. Lieberthal and David M. Lampton (eds.),

Bureaucracy, Politics, and Decision Making in Post-Mao China. Berkeley, CA: University of California Press. pp. 1–30.

Lieberthal, Kenneth G., and Michel Oksenberg (1986) "Understanding China's Bureaucracy: The First Step to a Better Corporate Strategy." *China Business Review*, 13, no. 6: 24–31.

Lieberthal, Kenneth G., and Michel Oksenberg (1988) *Policy Making in China*. Princeton, NJ: Princeton University Press.

Lim, Haeran (1998) *Korea's Growth and Industrial Transformation*. London: Macmillan Press.

Lim, Haeran (2009) "Democratization ad the Transformation Process in East Asian Developmental States: Financial Reform in Korea and Taiwan." *Asian Perspective*, 33, no. 1: 75–110.

Lim, Haeran (2010a) "The Transformation of the Developmental State and Economic Reform in Korea." *Journal of Contemporary Asia*, 40, no. 2: 188–210.

Lim, Haeran (2010b) "Hankook Dae/Joongso Keeup Yanggukwha Hyunsangû Jungchikyungjae" (Korean) [Political Economy of the Polarization of LMEs-SMEs Structure in Korea]. *21st Century Political Science*, 20, no. 1: 145–170.

Lim, Hyun-chin (1985) *Dependent Development in Korea: 1963–1979*. Seoul: Seoul National University Press.

Lim, Hyun-chin, and Jin-ho Jang (2006) "Between Neo-liberalism and Democracy: The Transformation of the Developmental State in South Korea." *Development and Society*, 35, no. 1: 1–28.

Lim, Youjin, and Yeonho Lee (2018) "Hankook Kyungjae Minjoohwaui Sungkwawa Hankye" (Korean) [The Success and Limits of the Korean Economic Democratization]. Paper presented at Conference held by the Institute of Yun Bosun Democracy Studies, May 2, 2018.

Lim, Youngil (1981) *Government Policy and Private Enterprise: Korean Experience in Industrialization*. Korea Research Monograph, Institute of East-Asian Studies, University of California at Berkley.

Lim, Youngil (1999) *Technology and Productivity: The Korean Way of Learning and Catching Up*. Cambridge, MA: MIT Press.

Lin, Justin Yifu, Fang Cai, and Zhou Li (2003) *The China Miracle: Development Strategy and Economic Reform*. Hong Kong: Chinese University Press.

Lindsey, Brink and Aaron Lukas (1998) "Revisiting the Revisionists: The Rise and Fall of the Japanese Economic Model." *Trade Policy Analysis*, no. 3, Cato Institute.

Little, Ian, Tibor Scitovsky, and Maurice Scott (1970) *Industry and Trade in Some Developing Countries*. Oxford: Oxford University Press.

Mahoney, James (2000) "Path Dependence in Historical Sociology." *Theory and Society*, 29, no. 4: 507–548.

Mahoney, James, and Kathleen Thelen (2010) "A Theory of Gradual Institutional Change." In James Mahoney and Kathleen Thelen (eds.), *Explaining Institutional Change: Ambiguity, Agency, and Power*. Cambridge: Cambridge University Press. pp. 1–37.

March, James, and Johan Olsen (1989) *Rediscovering Institutions: The Organizational Basis of Politics*. New York: Free Press.

Mathews, John A. (1998) "Fashioning a New Korean Model out of the Crisis: The Rebuilding of Institutional Capabilities." *Cambridge Journal of Economics*, 22: 747–759.

Mathews, John A., and Dong-Sung Cho (2000) *Tiger Technology: The Creation of a Semiconductor Industry in East Asia*. Cambridge: Cambridge University Press.

MCI (Ministry of Commerce and Industry) (1969) *Sangkong Jungchaek Sipnyunsa, 1960–1969* (Korean) [10 Years History of Commercial-Industrial Policy, 1960–1969]. Seoul: MCI.

MCI (Ministry of Commerce and Industry) (1985) *Bandoche Sanuphyunhwangkwa Jonghap Yuksung Daechaek* (Korean) [The Current Situation of Semiconductor Industry and Comprehensive Developmental Policy]. Seoul: MCI.

MCI (Ministry of Commerce and Industry) (1988) *Joongso Kiup Yooksung 40 Nyun* (Korean) [40 Years History of Promotion of the Small and Medium-sized Enterprises (SMEs)]. Seoul: MCI.

McKean, Margaret A. (1977) "Pollution and Policy-making." In T. John Pempel (ed.), *Policymaking in Contemporary Japan*. Ithaca, NY: Cornell University Press. pp. 201–238.

McKinsey & Company (2003) *Offshoring: Is It a Win-Win Game?* San Francisco, CA: McKinsey Global Institute.

Mo, Jongryn (2009) "The Korean Economic System Ten Years after the Crisis." In John Ravenhill, T. John Pempel, and Andrew MacIntyre (eds.), *Crisis as Catalyst: Asia's Dynamic Political Economy*. Ithaca, NY: Cornell University Press. pp. 251–270.

Mo, Jongryn, and Chung-In Moon (2003) "Business-Government Relations under Kim Dae-jung." In Stephan Haggard, Wonhyuk Lim, and Euysung Kim (eds.), *Economic Crisis and Corporate Restructuring in Korea: Reforming the Chaebol*. New York: Cambridge University Press. pp. 127–149.

Mo, Jongryn, and Daniel I. Okimoto, eds. (2006) *From Crisis to Opportunity*. Stanford, CA: Walter H. Shorenstein Asia-Pacific Research Centre.

MoF (Ministry of Finance) (1991) *Je 156 hoe Jungki Kookhoe Jaemoowewon Yogoojaryo*, III and IV (Korean) [the Materials requested by Congressmen of Finance in 156 Regular Meeting of National Assembly]. October.

MoFE (Ministry of Finance and Economy) (2006) *3 Mangae Hyuksinhyung Joongsokiup Yooksungul wehan Jungchaek Kwajaewa Daeung Junryak* (Korean) [Policy Task and Strategy for Promotion of 30 Thousand Innovation-oriented SMEs]. Seoul: MoFE.

Money Today (October 18, 2012) "ICT Control Tower Boohwal Choilgee" (Korean) [The Countdown of the Revival of the ICT Control Tower].

Montinola, Gabriella, Yingyi Qian, and Barry Weingast (1995) "Federalism, Chinese Style: The Political Basis for Economic Success in China." *World Politics* 48, no. 1: 50–81.

Moon, Chung-in (1994) "Changing Patterns of Business-Government Relations in South Korea." In Andrew MacIntyre (ed.), *Business and Government in Industrializing Asia*. Ithaca, NY: Cornell University Press. pp. 142–166.

Moon, Chung-in, and Byung-joon Jun (2011) "Modernization Strategy: Ideas and Influences." In Byung-Kook Kim and Ezra F. Vogel (eds.), *The Park Chung Hee Era: The Transformation of South Korea*. Cambridge, MA: Harvard University Press. pp. 115–139.

Moon, Chung-in, and Yongchul Kim (1996) "A Cycle of Paradox." In Adrian Leftwich (ed.), *Democracy and Development: Theory and Practice*. Cambridge: Polity Press. pp. 139–167.

Moon, Hwy-Chang (2016) *The Strategy for Korea's Economic Success*. Oxford: Oxford University Press.

Moreno-Brid, Juan Carlos (2013) "Industrial Policy: A Missing Link in Mexico's Quest for Export-led Growth." *Latin American Policy*, 4, no. 2: 216–237.

Morgan, Glenn, and Izumi Kubo (2016) "Institutions, Dominant Coalitions, and Firms: Comparing How Japan and Korea Responded to Deregulation, Globalization, and Competition in the Telecommunications Industry." In Richard Whitely and Xiaoke Zhang (eds.), *Changing Asian Business Systems: Globalization, Socio-Political Change, and Economic Organization*. Oxford: Oxford University Press. pp. 65–88.

Mukand, Sharun W., and Dani Rodrik (2005) "In Search of the Holy Grail: Policy Convergence, Experimentation, and Economic Performance." *American Economic Review*, 95, no. 1: 374–393.

Muramatsu, Micho (1987) "In Search of National Identity: The Politics and Policy of the Nakasone Administration." *Journal of Japanese Studies*, 13, no. 2: 307–342.

Muramatsu, Micho (1993) "Patterned Pluralism under Challenge." In Gary D. Allison and Yasunori Sone (eds.), *Political Dynamics in Contemporary Japan*. Ithaca, NY: Cornell University Press. pp. 50–71.

Muramatsu, Micho, and Ellis S. Krauss (1984) "Bureaucrats and Politicians in Policymaking: The Case of Japan." *American Political Science Review*, 78, no. 1: 126–146.

Muramatsu, Micho, and Ellis S. Krauss (1987) "The Conservative Policy Line and the Development of Patterned Pluralism." In Kozo Yamamura and Yasukichi Yasuba (eds.), *The Political Economy of Japan, vol. 1: The Domestic Transformation*. Stanford, CA: Stanford University Press. pp. 224–266.

Mytelka, Lynn, and Dieter Ernst (1998) "Catching Up, Keeping Up and Getting Ahead: The Korean Model under Pressure." In Dieter Ernst, Tom Ganiatsos, and Lynn Mytelka (eds.), *Technological Capabilities and Export Success in Asia*. London: Routledge. pp. 103–172.

Nam, Duck Woo (1994) "Korea's Economic Takeoff in Retrospect." In Kwack, Sung Yeung (ed.), *The Korean Economy at a Crossroad*. Westport: Praeger. pp. 1–19.

Nam, Duck Woo (2009) *Kyungjae Gaebalui Kilmokeseo: Jiam Nam Duck Woo Hoegorok* (Korean) [Nam Duck Woo Memoir: In the Process of Economic Development]. Seoul: Samsung Economic Research Institute.

Naseemullah, Adnan (2017a) *Development after Statism*. Cambridge: Cambridge University Press.

Naseemullah, Adnan (2017b) "The Political Economy of Economic Conservatism in India: From Moral Economy to Pro-business Nationalism." *Studies in Indian Politics*, 5, no. 2: 233–247.

Naseemullah, Adnan, and Caroline E. Arnold (2015) "The Politics of Developmental State Persistence: Institutional Origins, Industrialization, and Provincial Challenge." *Studies of Comparative International Development*, 50, no. 1: 121–142.

Noble, Gregory (1987) "Contending Forces in Taiwan's Economic Policymaking: The Case of Hua Tung Heavy Trucks." *Asian Survey*, 27, no. 6: 683–704.

Noble, Gregory (2000) "Conspicuous Failures and Hidden Strengths of the ITRI Model: Taiwan's Technology Policy toward Hard Disk Drivers and CD ROMs." UCSD/ISIC Research Report 2000–2. San Diego, CA: University of California, San Diego.

Noble, Gregory (2016) "Who—If Anyone—Is in Charge? Evolving Discourses of Political Power and Bureaucratic Delegation in Postwar Japanese Policymaking." In Gill Steel (ed.), *Power in Contemporary Japan*. New York: Palgrave Macmillan. pp. 185–200.

Noble, Gregory W. (2011) "Industrial Policy in Key Developmental Sectors: South Korea versus Japan and Taiwan." In Byung-Kook Kim and Ezra F. Vogel (eds.), *The Park Chung Hee Era: The Transformation of South Korea*. Cambridge, MA: Harvard University Press. pp. 603–628.

Noh, Yujin (1991) "Sanup Koojojojung Jungchaek Younghyang Pyunggae kwanhan Yungoo: Choonghwahakkongup Toojajajojungkwa Upjongjunmoonhwajochi Sarye Joogsim" (Korean) [A Study about the Evaluation of Industrial Policy on Corporate Restructuring: Focusing on Heavy-Chemical Industry and Core Business Policy]. MA Thesis, Policy Science Graduate School, Korea University.

Noland, Marcus (2002) "Economic Reform in South Korea: An Unfinished Legacy." Paper prepared for the conference Korea as a 21st Century Power, University of Cambridge, April 3–6.

Nordlinger, Eric (1981) *On the Autonomy of the Democratic State*. Cambridge, MA: Harvard University Press.

Odell, John S. (1985) "The Outcomes of International Trade Conflicts: The US and South Korea." *International Studies Quarterly*, 29, no. 3: 263–286.

OECD (1996) *Reviews of National Science and Technology Policy, Republic of Korea*. Paris: OECD.

OECD (2000) "OECD Economic Surveys 1999–2000: Korea." Paris: OECD.

OECD (2006) *Main Science and Technology Indicators* 2006/2, 2006.

OECD (2007) "Making the Most of Globalization," ECO/CPE (2007) no. 5.

OECD (2009) *OECD Reviews of Innovation Policy: Korea 2009*. OECD.

Oh, Duck-kyo (2012) "Hidden Championui Yuksung Bangan" (Korean) [Policy to Promote Hidden Champions]. *Corporate Governance Service* Report No. 1, 2012.

Oh, Myung, and James F. Larson (2011) *Digital Development in Korea: Building an Information Society*. New York: Routledge.

Oh, Wonchul (1995) *Hankookhyung Kyungjaekunsul* (Korean) [Korean Pattern of Economic Development: Engineering Approach], vol. 1. Seoul: Kia Economic Research Institute.

Oh, Wonchul (1996) *Hankookhyung Kyungjaekunsul* (Korean) [Korean Pattern of Economic Development: Engineering Approach], vols. 3 and 4. Seoul: Kia Economic Research Institute.

Oh, Wonchul (1999) *Hankookhyung Kyungjaekunsul* (Korean) [Korean Pattern of Economic Development: Engineering Approach], vol. 7. Seoul: Kia Economic Research Institute.

Ó Riain, Seán (2004) *The Politics of High-Tech Growth: Developmental Network States in the Global Economy*. Cambridge: Cambridge University Press.

Ornston, Darius (2012) *When Small States Make Big Leaps: Institutional Innovation and High-Tech Competition in Western Europe*. Ithaca, NY: Cornell University Press.

Pack, Howard, and Kamal Saggi (2006) "Is There a Case for Industrial Policy? A Critical Survey." *World Bank Research Observer*, 21, no. 2: 267–297.

Pang, Eul-Soo (2000) "The Financial Crisis of 1997–98 and the End of the Asian Developmental State." *Contemporary South East Asia*, 22, no. 3: 570–593.

Park, Byung-yoon (1980) "Joonghwahakkongupkyeui Naemak" (Korean) [Inside Story of Heavy-Chemical Industry Sector]. *Shin-DongA*. May 1980.

Park, Choong-hoon (1988) *Yidang Hoegorok* [Park Choonghoon Memoir]. Seoul: Parkyungsa.

Park, Dongchul (1993) "Hankookesu Kookgajudojuk Jabonjooui Baljunbangsilui Hyungsung Kwajung" (Korean) [The Formation of State-led Capitalism in Korea]. PhD Dissertation, Seoul National University.

Park, Heebum (1962a) "Kyungjaejaripul wehan Oejadoip" (Korean) [Introduction of Foreign Capital for Economic Independence]. *Chogohoeuibo* [News of Supreme Council], no. 4.

Park, Heebum (1962b) "Hoojinkooke Isusui Jabonui Chodalkwa Sanupbyul Baeboon" (Korean) [Capital Mobilization and its Allocation on Industries]. *Kyungjaenonjip Byulchaek* [Economics, Special Report], 1, no. 1: 9–26.

Park, Heebum (1968) *Hankook Kyungjaesungjangron* (Korean) [Theory of Korean Economic Growth]. Seoul: Asia Research Institute.

Park, Hyeon-Seok (2017) "Hankookui Jungchijuk Minjoohwawa Kyungjae Minjoojooui" (Korean) [Political Democratization and Economic Democracy in Korea]. In Kang, Wontaek, ed., *Daehanminkook Mijoohwa 30Nyun Pyungga* [Evaluation of 30 Years Democratization in Korea]. Seoul: National Museum of Korean Contemporary History. pp. 195–238.

Park, Jaehung, and Sootaek Kang (2012) Hankookui Sedae Byunhwawa Talmooljiljooui" (Korean) [Generation Changes in Korea and Dematerialization]. *Hankook Sahoehkak* [Korean Sociology], 46, no. 4: 69–95.

Park, Jihoon (2007) "Hankook Shinjayujoouiui Kiwon, 1979.4–1998.2" (Korean) [The Origin of Neoliberalism in Korea, April 1979–February 1998]. MA Thesis, Seokang University.

Park, Joongoo, and Hongsuk Kim (1997) *Hankook Jadongcha Sanup ui Sekyewha Julyak* [Korean auto industry's globalization strategy]. Seoul: KIET.

Park, Jung-Taek (2003) "Study on Inter-Ministerial Policy Conflict and Coordination: With the Science and Technology Basic Law Making Process in Korea" (Korean). *Kwahak Gisoolhak Yungoo* [Science and Technology Studies], 3, no. 3: 105–156.

Park, Sangsoo (2001) "Oehwanweeki ehoo Daegiupjipdanui 10gaji Kyungyung Haengtae Byunhwa" (Korean) [Ten Changes in Chaebols' Management Behaviors after the 1997 Financial Crisis]. *LG Weekly Economy*, no. 623, May 16, 2001. pp. 4–11.

Park, Taegyeon (1997) *Gwanryomangkookronkwa Chaebolsinhwaui Boongkoe* (Korean) [The Collapse of a Nation By Bureaucrats and the Demise of Chaebol Miracle]. Seoul: Salim.

Park, Tae-gyun (2000a) "1956–1964 nyun Hankook Kyungjaegaebalgyehoekui Sungripkwajung" (Korean) [The Formation Process of Korean Economic Development Plans, 1956–1964]. PhD Dissertation, Seoul National University.

Park, Tae-gyun (2000b) "1961–1964 nyun Goonsajungbooui Kyungjaebaljungyehoek Soojung" (Korean) [The Military Government's Revision of Economic Development Plan, 1961–1964]. *Society and History*, 57: 113–148.

Park, Tae-gyun (2004) "1970, 80 Nyundae Kyungjaejungchaek Jucheui Byunhwawa Saeroun Kyungjaedamron" (Korean) [Changes in the Economic Policymakers and New Economic Discourse in the 1970s–1980s]. In Chulkyu Yu (ed.), *Parkjunghee Modelkwa Sinjayujooui Saieseo* [Between Park Chung Hee Model and Neoliberalism]. Seoul: CoBook. pp. 25–62.

Park, Tae-gyun (2007) *Wonhyungkwa Byunyong* (Korean) [Original Form and Changed Application: The Origin of Korean Economic Development Plans]. Seoul: SNU Press.

Park, Younggoo (2008) "Process and Character of 4 Core Plants Plan, 1969.11–1971.11" (Korean). *Review of Economic History*, 44: 81–107.

Pempel, T. John (1974) "The Bureaucratization of Policymaking in Postwar Japan." *American Journal of Political Science* 18, no. 1: 647–664.

Pempel, T. John (1977) *Policymaking in Contemporary Japan*. Ithaca, NY: Cornell University Press.

Pempel, T. John (1987) "The Unbundling of 'Japan Inc.': the Changing Dynamics of Japanese Policy Formation." In Kenneth B. Pyle (ed.), *The Trade Crisis: How Will Japan Respond?* Seattle, WA: University of Washington Press. pp. 117–152.

Pempel, T. John (1999) "The Developmental Regime in a Changing World Economy." In Meredith Woo-Cumings (ed.), *The Developmental State*. Ithaca, NY: Cornell University Press. pp. 137–181.

Pempel, T. John (1999) *Regime Shift: Comparative Dynamics of the Japanese Political Economy*. Ithaca, NY: Cornell University Press.

Pierson, Paul (2000) "Increasing Returns, Path Dependence and the Study of Politics." *American Political Science Review*, 94, no. 2: 251–267.

Pierson, Paul (2015) "Power and Path Dependence." In James Mahoney and Kathleen Thelen (eds.), *Advances in Comparative Historical Analysis*. Cambridge: Cambridge University Press. pp. 123–146.

Pierson, Paul, and Theda Skocpol (2002) "Historical Institutionalism in Contemporary Political Science." In Ira Katznelson and Helen V. Milner (eds.), *Political Science: State of the Discipline*. New York: Norton. pp. 693–721.

Pirie, Iain (2005) "The New Korean State." *New Political Economy*, 10, no. 1: 25–42.

Pirie, Iain (2008) *The Korean Developmental State: From Dirigisme to Neoliberalism*. London: Routledge.

Pirie, Iain (2016) "South Korea after the Developmental State." In Yin-wah Chu (ed.), *The Asian Developmental State: Reexaminations and New Departures*. New York: Palgrave Macmillan. pp. 139–158.

Pisano, Gary P., and Willy C. Shih (2012) *Producing Prosperity: Why America Needs a Manufacturing Renaissance*. Boston, MA: Harvard Business Review Press.

Pisano, Gary P., and Willy C. Shih (2012b) "Does America Really Need Manufacturing?" *Harvard Business Review*, Special Report: Reinventing America, vol. 90, no. 3: 94–102.

Polanyi, Karl (1944) *The Great Transformation*. New York: Holt, Reinhart.

Policy Briefing (February 10, 2008) "Silrok Kyungjae Jungchaeksa: Kwaki Sanja Jungtong Chiyulhan 3Pajun...Mirae 10Dae Sungjang Engine Sidonggulda" (Korean) [Real History: Severe Competition among the MoST, the MoI, and the MIC, Igniting the 10 Growth Engines].

Porter, Michael E., and Jan W. Rivkin (2012) "The Looming Challenge to U.S. Competitiveness." *Harvard Business Review*, Special Report: Reinventing America, vol. 90, no. 3: 54–62.

Ramaswamy, Ramana, and Robert Rowthorn (2000) "Does Manufacturing Matters?" *Harvard Business Review*. November-December 2000 issue.

Ravenhill, John (2001) *From national champions to global partnerships: the Korean auto industry, financial crisis and globalisation*. Boston, MA: Center for International Studies, Massachusetts Institute of Technology.

Rawski, Thomas G. (1995) "Implications of China's Reform Experience." *The China Quarterly*, 144: 1150–1173.

Rhee, Jong-Chan (1994) *The State and Industry in South Korea: The Limits of the Authoritarian State*. London: Routledge.

Rhee, Jong-Chan (1994b) "6Gong Kyungjaekaehyukui Jungchikyungjae: Sijangjoodo Sanupjojungui Hwansangkwa Siltae" (Korean) [Political Economy in the Economic Reform of the 6th Republic: Illusion and Reality of the Market-led Industrial Adjustments." *Sahoebipyung* [Social Critics], 12: 252–275.

Rhyu, Sang-young, and Seok-jin Lew (2011) "Pohang Iron & Steel Company. In Byung-Kook Kim and Ezra F. Vogel (eds.), *The Park Chung Hee Era: The Transformation of South Korea*. Cambridge, MA: Harvard University Press. pp. 322–344.

Robinson, Williamson (2004) *A Theory of Global Capitalism*. Baltimore, MD: Johns Hopkins University Press.

Robinson, Williamson (2014) *Global Capitalism and the Crisis of Humanity*. New York: Cambridge University Press.

Roland, Gerard (2000) *Transition and Economics: Politics, Markets, and Firms*. Cambridge, MA: MIT Press.

Routley, Laura (2012) "Developmental States: A Review of the Literature." Effective States and Inclusive Development Working Paper, no. 3. Manchester: ESID.

Ryu, Jaehun, and Sangchul Lee (1993) "Sanup Koojojojungui Jungae" (Korean) [The Process of Industrial Structural Reform]. In Korean Industrial Society Study Association (ed.), *Hankook Kyungjaeui Sanupkoojo Jojungkwa Nodongjakyegup* [Industrial Structural Reform in Korean Economy and Working Class]. Seoul: Nokdoo. pp. 33–80.

Sabel, Charles F. (1994) "Learning by Monitoring: The Institutions of Economic Development." In Neil Smelser and Richard Sedberg (eds.), *Handbook of Economic Sociology*. Princeton, NJ: Princeton University Press. pp. 137–165.

Sakong, Il (2003) "Daetongryung Kyungjaesusukuroui Yukhal" (Korean) [Role as a First Presidential Secretariat]. In Nam Duck Woo et al. (eds.) *80 Nyundae Kyungjaekaehyukkwa*

Kim Jae-ik Susuk [Economic Reform of the 1980s and First Presidential Secretariat Kim Jae-ik]. Seoul: Samsung Economic Research Institute. pp. 229–238.

Samuels, Richard J. (1994) *Rich Nation, Strong Army: National Security and the Technological Transformation of Japan*. Ithaca, NY: Cornell University Press.

Schmidt, Vivien (2003) "French Capitalism Transformed, yet Still a Third Variety of Capitalism." *Economy and Society*, 32, no. 4: 526–554.

Seoul Shinmoon (April 29, 2003) "Chasedae Sungjangsanup Sunjunghagido June Golbyung"(Korean) [The Next Generation Growth Engine, its Revealing Problems even before its real launching].

Shim, Jae Hoon, and Charles S. Lee (1998) "Reality Check." *Far Eastern Economic Review*. March 12, 1998, pp. 18–19.

Shin Dong-A (March 1997) "Gumyoong Jayoolhwa Heoulsseugo Jungchi Silsega Gumyoong Jibae" (Korean) [Political forces dominate finance under its fake-mask of financial autonomy].

Shin Dong-A (July 2001) "Jungtongboo Sanjabooui IT Sanup Daehyultoo" (Korean) [The Bloody Fight over IT Industry between the Ministry of Information and Communications and the Ministry of Industry and Energy].

Shin Dong-A (May 2014) "Global Kiupero Wootuk sun Hyundaicha Grup Hyupryuksadul" (Korean) [Hyundai Parts Suppliers which Established Themselves as Global Companies].

Shin Dong-A (May 2015) "People Interview: Choi Yanghee Minister of Science, ICT and Future Planning" (Korean).

Shin Dong-A (Sept. 2016) "Joongso Benche Matchoom Jiwon Dowajoogo Nappoombatgo" (Korean) [Supporting SMEs and Venture Firms, Helping and Receiving Parts].

Shin, Dong-Hee (2008) "Next Generation of Information Infrastructure: A Comparative Case Study of Korea versus the United States of America." *Journal of the American Society for Information Science and Technology*, 59, no. 11: 1785–1800.

Shin, Dong-Hee, and Sang Hee Kweon (2011) "Evaluation of Korean Information Infrastructure Policy 2000–2010: Focusing on Broadband Ecosystem Change." *Government Information Quarterly*, 28, no. 3: 374–387.

Shin, Heekwon (1994) "Jungboowa Chaebolganui Junrakjuk Sanghojakyonge Kwanhan Yungoo" (Korean) [An Analysis on the Strategic Interaction between Government and Chaebols]. PhD Dissertation, Seoul National University.

Shin, Kookhwan (1994) *Sunjinsanupkookul Hyanghan Hankook Kyungjaeui Suntaekkwa Dojun* (Korean) [Korean Economy's Challenges and Choices for Advanced Industrialized Country]. Seoul: Wooshinsa.

Shonfield (1965) *Modern Capitalism: The Changing Balance of Public and Private Power*. Oxford: Oxford University Press.

Sirkin, Harold L., Michael Zinser, and Douglas Hohner (2011) "Made in America, Again: Why Manufacturing will Return to the U.S." Boston Consulting Group, August 2011 from http://www.bcg.com/documents/file84471.pdf.

Sohn, Sangho, and Donghwan Kim (2013) "Chungsokiup Kumyoongui Baljunkwajae" (Korean) [Tasks for the Development of SME Finances]. Report of the Korean Institute of Finance Research (KIF), June 2013.

Song, Byung-Nak (1990) *The Rise of the Korean Economy*. Oxford: Oxford University Press.

Song, Insang (1994) *Hoenam Song Insang Memoir Hoegorok* (Korean) [Song Insang Memoir]. Seoul: 21st Century Books.

Song, Jiyeoun (2014) *Inequality in the Workplace: Labor Market Reform in Japan and Korea*. Ithaca, NY: Cornell University Press.

Stern, Joseph J., Jihong Kim, Dwight H. Perkins, and Jung-ho Yoo (1995) *Industrialization and the State: The Korean Heavy and Chemical Industry Divide*. Cambridge, MA: Harvard University Press.

Story, Louise (2012) "As Companies Seek Tax Deals, Governments Pay High Price." *New York Times*, December 1, 2012.

Streeck, Wolfgang, and Kathleen Thelen (2005) "Introduction: Institutional Change in Advanced Political Economies." In Wolfgang Streeck and Kathleen Thelen (eds.), *Beyond Continuity: Institutional Change in Advanced Political Economies*. Oxford: Oxford University Press. pp. 1–39.

Stubbs, Richard (2009) "Whatever Happened to the East Asian Developmental State? The Unfolding Debate." *The Pacific Review*, 22, no. 1: 1–22.

Stubbs, Richard (2011) "The East Asian Developmental State and the Great Recession: Evolving Contesting Coalitions." *Contemporary Politics*, 17, no. 2: 151–166.

Suh, Jaejin (1991) *Hankookui Jabonga Kyegup* (Korean) [Capitalist Class in Korea]. Seoul: Nanam.

Suh, Joonghae, and Derek H. C. Chen (2007) *Korea as a Knowledge Economy: Evolutionary Processes and Lessons Learned*. Washington DC: The World Bank.

Suh, Junghwan (2007) "Hankook Kyunjae Kwanryo, Sungjangjooui Kyungjaejungchaekui Sasaengadul" (Korean) [Korean Economic Bureaucrats, Illegitimate Children of Growth-First Economic Policy]. *Monthly Mal*. June 2007.

Suh, Junghwan (2010) "Jungkwoni Bakyiedo Jookjianun Kwonryukchae" (Korean) [Die-Hard Power Body even in the Changes of Governments]. *Economy Insight*. August 1, 2010.

Sunwoo, Sukho, and Wonkun Yang (1991) *Daekiup Jipdan Upjongjunmoonhwa Yudobangan* (Korean) [Industrial Policy for Inducement of Large Corporations' Specialization in Core Business]. Seoul: KIET.

Tassey, Gregory (2010) "Rationales and Mechanisms for Revitalizing US Manufacturing R&D Strategies." *Journal of Technology Transfer*, 35, no. 3: 283–333.

Thelen, Kathleen (2004) *How Institutions Evolve*. New York: Cambridge University Press.

Thelen, Kathleen (2006) "Institutions and Social Change: The Evolution of Vocational Training in Germany." In Ian Shapiro, Stephen Skowroneck, and Daniel Galvin (eds.), *Rethinking Political Institutions: The Art of the State*. New York: New York University Press. pp. 135–170.

Thelen, Kathleen, and James Mahoney (2015) "Comparative-historical Analysis in Contemporary Political Science." In James Mahoney and Kathleen Thelen (eds.), *Advances in Comparative Historical Analysis*. Cambridge: Cambridge University Press. pp. 3–36.

Thurbon, Elizabeth (2001) "Two Paths to Financial Liberalization: South Korea and Taiwan." *Pacific Review*, 14, no. 2: 241–267.

Thurbon, Elizabeth (2003) "Ideational Inconsistency and Institutional Incapacity: Why Financial Liberalization in South Korea Went Horribly Wrong." *New Political Economy* 8, no. 3: 341–361.

Thurbon, Elizabeth (2007) "The Developmental Logic of Financial Liberalization in Taiwan." In William Garside (ed.), *Institutions and Market Economies: The Political Economy of Growth and Development*. London: Palgrave Macmillan. pp. 87–106.

Thurbon, Elizabeth (2016) *Developmental Mindset: The Revival of Financial Activism in South Korea*. Ithaca, NY: Cornell University Press.

Thurbon, Elizabeth, and Linda Weiss (2019) Economic statecraft at the frontier: Korea's drive for intelligent robotics." *Review of International Political Economy*, online published from https://doi.org/10.1080/09692290.2019.1655084.

Toledo, Enrique de la Garza (2007) "The Crisis of the Maquiladora Model in Mexico." *Work and Occupations*, 34, no. 4: 399–429.

Tsebelis, George (1990) *Nested Games: Rational Choice in Comparative Politics*. Berkeley, CA: University of California Press.

Tso, Chen-Dong (2004) "State-Technologist Nexus in Taiwan's High-Tech Policymaking: Semiconductor and Wireless Communications Industries." *Journal of East Asian Studies*, 4, no. 2: 301–328.

Vogel, Steven K. (2006) *Japan Remodeled: How Government and Industry Are Reforming Japanese Capitalism*. Ithaca, NY: Cornell University Press.

Wade, Robert (1985) "State Intervention in 'Outward-looking' Development: Neoclassical Theory and Taiwanese Practice." In Gordon White and Robert Wade (eds.), *Developmental States in East Asia*. Brighton: Institute for Development Studies Research Report 16.

Wade, Robert (1988) "State Intervention in 'Outward-looking' Development: Neoclassical Theory and Taiwanese Practice." In Gordon White (ed.), *Developmental States in East Asia*. New York: St. Martin's Press. pp. 30–67.

Wade, Robert (1990) *Governing the Market: Economic Theory and the Role of Government in East Asian Industrialization*. Princeton, NJ: Princeton University Press.

Wade, Robert (2010) "After the Crisis: Industrial Policy and the Developmental State in Low-income Countries." *Global Policy*, 1, no. 2: 150–161.

Wade, Robert, and Frank Veneroso (1998) "The Asian Crisis: the High Debt Model versus the Wall-Street-Treasury-IMF Complex." *New Left Review*, 228: 3–23.

Walder, Andrew G. (1996) *China's Transitional Economy: Interpreting its Significance*. Oxford: Oxford University Press.

Wallerstein, Immanuel (1979) *The Capitalist World-Economy*. New York: Cambridge University Press.

Walter, Andrew, and Xiaoke Zhang (2014a) "Debating East Asian Capitalism: Issues and Themes." In Andrew Walter and Xiaoke Zhang (eds.), *East Asian Capitalism*. Oxford: Oxford University Press. pp. 3–25.

Walter, Andrew, and Xiaoke Zhang (2014b) "Understanding Variations and Changes in East Asian Capitalism." In Andrew Walter and Xiaoke Zhanng (eds.), *East Asian Capitalism*. Oxford: Oxford University Press. pp. 247–280.

We, Pyungryang (2011) "Daegiupkwa Chungso Giup Ganui Kyungyoung Kyukcha Boonsukkwa Sisajum" (Korean) [An analysis of business differences of large corporations and SMEs]. *Economic Reform Report* no. 2011–25. Seoul: ERRI.

We, Pyungryang (2014) "Jaebol mit Daekiupuroui Kyungjaeryuk Jipjoonkwa Dongtaejuk Byunhwaboonsuk, 1987–2012" (Korean) [A Dynamic Analysis on the Economic Wealth Concentration on the Chaebols and Large Corporations]. *Kiupjibaekoojo Yunkoo* [Corporate Governance Studies], 48: 22–43.

Weingast, Barry R. (2002) "Rational-Choice Institutionalism." In Ira Katznelson and Helen V. Milner (eds.), *Political Science: The State of the Discipline*. New York: Norton. pp. 660–692.

Weiss, Linda (2003) "Guiding Globalization in East Asia: New Roles for Old Developmental States." In Linda Weiss (ed.), *States in the Global Economy: Bringing Domestic Institutions Back In*. Cambridge: Cambridge University Press. pp. 245–270.

Weiss, Linda, and Elizabeth Thurbon (2020) "Developmental State or Economic Statecraft? Where, Why and How the Difference Matters." *New Political Economy*, online published in May 2020 from https://doi.org/10.1080/13563467.2020.1766431.

Whitley, Richard (1992) *Business Systems in East Asia*. London: Sage.

Whitley, Richard (2016) "Changing Business Systems in East Asia: Continued Diversity Between, and Varied Change Within, Japan, South Korea and Taiwan." In Richard Whitley and Xiaoke Zhang (eds.), *Changing Asian Business Systems: Globalization, Socio-Political Change, and Economic Organization*. Oxford: Oxford University Press. pp. 35–64.

Winckler, Edwin (1988) "Elite Political Struggle: 1945–1985." In E. Winckler and S. Greenhalgh (eds.), *Contending Approaches to the Political Economy of Taiwan*. New York: M.E. Sharpe. pp. 151–172.

Witt, Michael A. (2014a) "Japan: Coordinated Capitalism between Institutional Change and Structural Inertia." In Michael A. Witt and Gordon Redding (eds.), *The Oxford Handbook of Asian Business Systems*. Oxford: Oxford University Press. pp. 100–122.

Witt, Michael A. (2014b) "South Korea: Plutocratic State-led Capitalism Reconfiguring." In Michael A. Witt and Gordon Redding (eds.), *The Oxford Handbook of Asian Business Systems*. Oxford: Oxford University Press. pp. 216–237.

Wong, Joseph (2004) "The Adaptive Developmental State in East Asia." *Journal of Asian Studies*, 4, no. 3: 345–363.

Wong, Joseph (2011) *Betting on Biotech: Innovation and the Limits of Asia's Developmental State*. Ithaca, NY: Cornell University Press.

Woo, Jung-en (1991) *Race to the Swift: State and Finance in Korean Industrialization*. New York: Columbia University Press.

Woo-Cumings, Meredith, ed. (1999) *The Developmental State*. Ithaca, NY: Cornell University Press.

World Bank (1993) *The East Asian Miracle: Economic Growth and Public Policy*. Policy Research Report. Washington DC: World Bank.

World Value Survey (1981–2008) Official Aggregate. World Value Survey Association (from www.worldvaluesurvey.org). Madrid.

Wright, Maurice (1999) "Who Governs Japan? Politicians and Bureaucrats in the Policy-making Processes." *Political Studies*, 47, no. 5: 939–954.

Wu, Yongping (2004) "Rethinking the Taiwanese Developmental State." *The China Quarterly*, 117: 91–114.

Wulgan Chosun (Sept. 1999) "Japanese Economist Ohmae Kenichi Criticism against Kim Daejung Economic Policy" (Korean).

Yamaguchi, Jiro (1989) *Itto Shinhai Taisei no Hokai*. Tokyo: Iwanami Shoten.

Yang, Jae-jin (2017) *The Political Economy of the Small Welfare State in South Korea*. Cambridge: Cambridge University Press.

Yeung, Henry Wai-chung (2016) *Strategic Coupling: East Asian Industrial Transformation in the New Global Economy*. Ithaca, NY: Cornell University Press.

Yeung, Henry Wai-chung (2017) "State-led Development Reconsidered: The Political Economy of State Transformation in East Asia since the 1990s." *Cambridge Journal of Regions, Economy and Society*, 10, no. 1: 83–98.

Yoon, Dae-yeob (2011) "Crisis of Export-led Development and the Politics of Industrial Policy, 1980–2007 Idea, Institution and Developmental Governance" (Korean). PhD Dissertation, Department of Political Science, Yonsei University.

Yoon, Jinhyo (2006) *Hankook Gisooljungchaekron: Hankook Gisoolnungryuk Baljun 40nyunsa* (Korean) [Korean Technology Policy Theory: 40 Years History of the Development of Korean Technology Capability]. Seoul: Kyungmoonsa.

Yoon, Sang-Woo (2016) "The Historical Emergence and Reproduction of Growthism as Dominant bet in Korea" (Korean). *Korean Society*, 17, no. 1: 3–38.

Yoon, Youngho (1999) "Moonujin Daewoo Sinhwa, Haebupun Mongdang Palgi?" (Korean) [Collapsed Deawoo, Is It Solution to Sell Everything?]. *Shin Dong-A*. June 1999. pp. 264–277.

Yoon, Youngho (1999b) "Kang Kyungsik Ttugo Byun Hyungyoon Jigo" (Korean) [Kang Kyungsik is Rising while Byun Hyungyoon Declining]. *News Plus*. June 10, 1999.

You, Hee-yul (1996) "Between the Developmental State and Pluralist Tinkering: Institution, Politics, and Science and Technology Policy-Making in South Korea." PhD Dissertation, Korea University.

Yu, Chulkyu (2004) "1980 Nyundae Hooban Kyungjaekoojo Byunhwawa Oeyunjuk Sanuphwaui Jonggyul" (Korean) [Transformation of Economic Structure of the late 1980s and the End of Expansion-oriented Industrialization]. In Yu Chulkyu (ed.), *Between Park Chung Hee Model and Neoliberalism* (Korean). Seoul: CoBook. pp. 63–84.

Yu, Ho-yul (1996) "Kunsajungbooui Kyungjejungchaek: 1961–1963" (Korean) [The Economic Policy of the Military Government, 1961–1963]. In Yongwon Han and Baeho Han (eds.), *Modern Korean Politics: The Formation, Political Process, and Policy of the Third Republic*. Seoul: Orum. pp. 77–105.

Yu, Wonsik (1987) *Hyukmyungun Eodero Gatna* (Korean) [Where Is the Revolution Gone? The Secret Record of 5.16]. Seoul: Inmoolyungusa.

Zhang, Xiaoke (2014) "Dominant Coalitions and Capital Market Changes in Northeast Asia." In Andrew Walter and Xiaoke Zhang (eds.), *East Asian Capitalism: Diversity, Continuity, and Change*. Oxford: Oxford University Press. pp. 223–243.

Zysman, John (1983) *Governments, Markets, and Growth: Financial Systems and the Politics of Industrial Change*. Oxford: Cornell University Press.

Index